Everyday Artfulness

New Disciplinary Perspectives on Education

Series Editors:

Stephen Cowden and Jones Irwin

Volume 7

PETER LANG
Oxford - Berlin - Bruxelles - Chennai - Lausanne - New York

Everyday Artfulness

A posthuman perspective on young children's play with materials

Lucy Hill

PETER LANG
Oxford - Berlin - Bruxelles - Chennai - Lausanne - New York

Bibliographic information published by the Deutsche Nationalbibliothek. The German National Library lists this publication in the German National Bibliography; detailed bibliographic data is available on the Internet at http://dnb.d-nb.de.

A catalogue record for this book is available from the British Library.

Library of Congress Cataloging-in-Publication Data

Names: Hill, Lucy, 1968- author.
Title: Everyday artfulness : a posthuman perspective on young children's play with materials / Lucy Hill.
Description: New York : Peter Lang, 2024. | Series: New disciplinary perspectives on education, 2297-6531 ; Volume 7 | Includes bibliographical references and index.
Identifiers: LCCN 2023056299 (print) | LCCN 2023056300 (ebook) | ISBN 9781800797840 (paperback) | ISBN 9781800797857 (ebook) | ISBN 9781800797864 (epub)
Subjects: LCSH: Art—Study and teaching (Early childhood) | Creative activities and seat work. | Art in education.
Classification: LCC LB1139.5.A78 H55 2024 (print) | LCC LB1139.5.A78 (ebook) | DDC 372.5--dc23/eng/20231218
LC record available at https://lccn.loc.gov/2023056299
LC ebook record available at https://lccn.loc.gov/2023056300

The original PhD research for this book was generously funded by an Irish Research Council Postgraduate Scholarship, a Thomas Dammann Junior Memorial Award, and an Exploring and Thinking Bursary award from the four Dublin Local Authority Arts Offices. This publication has been generously supported by Dublin City University Institute of Education Staff Research Funding Scheme.

Cover image: © Lucy Hill.
Cover design by Peter Lang Group AG

ISSN 2297-6531
ISBN 978-1-80079-784-0 (print)
ISBN 978-1-80079-785-7 (ePDF)
ISBN 978-1-80079-786-4 (ePub)
DOI 10.3726/b19472

Published by Peter Lang Ltd, Oxford, United Kingdom
info@peterlang.com – www.peterlang.com

This publication has been peer reviewed.

This work is dedicated to my children Sadhbh, Cathal and Aenea

Contents

Figures

Tables

Preface

As part of the Peter Lang New Disciplinary Perspectives on Education Series, this book explores the possibilities of one such perspective: Posthumanism. Admittedly, for many the term itself is off-putting. However, I have found that the particular form of posthumanism (there are many) that I adopt here is wholeheartedly inspiring, open, and democratic.

Meaning coming 'after' Humanism, posthumanism disrupts the insistent prior centrality and exclusionary tendencies of the (adult) human and further, upends the notion of the 'fully human' as aspirational and conditional and so only available to the select few. Informed by Spinoza's monist philosophy, it offers openings for new understanding of Nature/Culture and sees children as complexly and intimately co-existing with everything both human and non-human, natural and technological, living and non-living. This demands a radical inclusivity in relation to what and who contributes and matters in the analysis and understanding of phenomena, which in turn has important implications for how children are perceived. The posthuman perspective is particularly exciting and useful for education because it disrupts adults' tendencies toward simplification in relation to understanding children, and instead offers new ways to think about young children's everyday learning and play.

Posthuman theory also offers art education a theoretical framework within which it both naturally fits and is affectively empowered to fulfil its potential. Through the lens of Spinozist posthuman theory, this book develops a position for art in education as having much more to offer than diverting activities grounded by ideas of human exceptionalism. Rather, 'sticky' moments (MacRae et al., 2017) which constantly bubble to the surface in education contexts are revealed through a posthuman lens as the moments of intensity, possibility, and everyday artfulness upon which all learning and growth relies.

Introduction

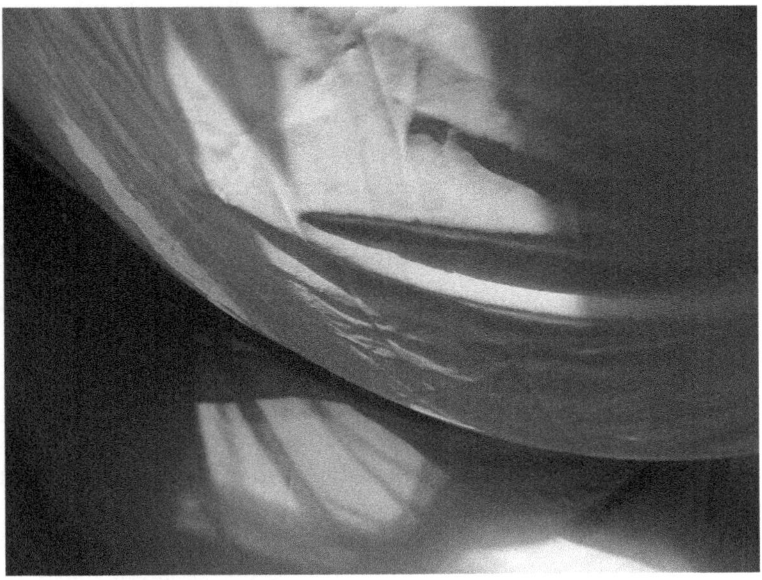

Figure 1: Education as an Artform

> Can we think of education so that it comes closer to an art form, where ambiguities are part and parcel of the work it does in provoking thought and stimulating interest and action instead of aiming for the unachievable and imperfectible goals of instilling the 'right' values, and the 'right' kind of knowledge that we think will lead to change? If education has a role to play at all in questions of environment and sustainability, should it not start with the messiness of education itself, that is, with what it is, and not only what we want it to be? (Todd, 2016, p. 844)

As a free-lance artist my art education practice began with a community employment scheme at my local education centre where I provided afterschool art classes for children. Although I had a master's degree in fine art the only prerequisites for teaching the class were unemployment and a willingness to work with children. I had no idea what to teach. I used the local library as a resource, and we made projects drawn directly from art and craft books for children. Success was measured through the likeness of our outcomes to the pictures in the books. Although we enjoyed a highly convivial time together, after the classes I would return to my painting studio conflicted. The contradictions between the material and conceptual intricacies I was grappling with there and what I was presenting to the children as 'art' worried me greatly. What might the children actually be learning?

As an abstract painter my work is experimental involving 'play' with non-representational forms where the resulting images are never planned in advance. There is a requirement to hover for extended periods within uncertainty, to grapple with multiple possibilities before solutions can begin to emerge. Failure and its risk are inevitable but enlivening companions. Offsetting the conceptual intensity and difficulty of the visual problematizing, I take immense pleasure in making my own paint. Grinding dry pigments using both ancient and new recipes with various oils and resins, stone-dusts, and waxes, affords a necessary and refined attention to the material qualities of the paint.

> Early in this century, a gelatinous extract from the swim bladders of sturgeons was used as an ingredient in oil paint; and before the introduction of collapsible paint tubes in the mid-nineteenth century, artists bought their colours in packets made from pigs' bladders. In the Renaissance, fish glues were sold in rancid wafers; the artists would pop them in their mouths to rehydrate them. (Elkins, 1999, p. 18)

An abstract visual language offers an almost alchemical understanding of the nuances and endless possibilities and unknowns of materials. When viewed artistically it seems, materials can never be fully known. There are constantly new influences be they environmental, chemical, or perceptual that affect their qualities, leading to infinitely new and highly specific problems and resolutions that are rarely verbalised. This understanding is shared amongst many artists, as described lyrically by writer/artist Alice Lyons:

> The brush is akin with a divining stick – it quivers and falls, when twisted, it can jump and scribble, be unpredictable, which is a friendly brush quality, an animated

> and kindly presence. A wide brush is like a digger: it can clear the field in a minute, levelling all earlier brushings. Then a palette knife scrapes the remaining paint, and the field is ready. Re-think. Re-see. Re-feel. Enter the painting-jungle deeper, every preliminary brush mark a signal that leads in the painting's drift. It's a maze. It's a map that leads me astray infinitely. It's an infinitely fluid medium. (Lyons, 2020, p. 228)

At the time of delivering the afterschool art classes no elements of my studio practice seeped into my education practice. The classes I delivered felt based on 'tricks' but much worse I was convinced that my teaching was actively denying and distorting the children's understanding of art and was wholly insufficient in transmitting the inherent struggle and ensuing adventure of an art practice. I had no idea how to reverse this troubling situation.

At the same time, I was noticing my then 2-year-old daughter's interest in the range of materials available to her to play with including clay and paint. She also liked to use irregular materials such as blackberries and sticks for creating with. The materials themselves seemed to spark her playful responses. Her messy explorations bore a much closer resemblance to my own studio practice than my classes did. Watching her, 'doing' art did not just require us setting up materials to explore, but the foundations of her artistic activity seemed to seep into or emerge out of ordinary everyday ways of experiencing her environment. Running a finger through jam on a food tray, touching a spiderweb, pulling a toe through a cooled coffee spill, smearing butter on a window, curling up a leaf or scrunching paper, tearing tiny pieces of packaging, wrapping a finger with wool. These moments seemed to me to rely on what Jane Bennet has described as 'an aesthetic-affective openness to material vitality' (Bennett, 2010, p. x) or an availability to be 'enchanted' by materials.

Bennett states that 'to be enchanted is to be struck by the extraordinary that lives amid the familiar and the everyday' (Bennett, 2001, p. 4). It was this for me which was recognisable as closely related to my own art practice. Quotidian qualities and movements in the everyday material environment caught and held my daughter's attention and invited her to participate with the world. As put by Stewart Lester 'mo(ve)ments of playing are constituted through and with the 'live surface': the sensations, textures, rhythms, and intensities of everyday life' (Lester, 2020, p. 174). It occurred to me that such opportunities and space for experimental 'enchantment' were what my classes were not only sorely missing, but ought to be aiming for. However, these tiniest of moments are utterly and authentically spontaneous and tricky (even, out of bounds) for adults to orchestrate in an education context. They are also pedagogically difficult to defend as they are frequently dismissed as a kind of meaningless messing with stuff.

My research practice has found that theory can rescue and reposition small moments of material contact, not only as the basis of artistic activity and enchantment but by rendering them interesting, complex, and valuable to education. Most importantly, aesthetic activity and theory can also ignite an alternative view of young children that deviates from the modernist concepts embedded in developmental pedagogy. As Jayne Osgood has stated,

> For too long a developmentalist logic has provided the dominant lens through which early childhood art is understood, with profound implications for the ways in which children's artful practices are routinely devalued and often dismissed when they disrupt linear trajectories that demand some form of mastery toward adulthood. The ages and stages notion of child development characterized by predictable milestones provides the basis for most arts curricula and pedagogical approaches to art-making in neo-liberal contexts, with devastating effects when children fall outside normative expectations. (Osgood J., 2022, p. 176)

Through my work I hope to contribute to the discussion surrounding the lenses and theories that we as adults choose to use to develop our understanding and ways of being with children. I am interested in the contribution that an aesthetic lens can make to this discussion and how that in turn, can inform the understanding of the purpose of art in education, particularly in Ireland where such great momentum has been building in this regard in recent years.

This discussion matters not only because as adults we have so much to learn from young children, and we owe them the best education possible but also because theory and perspectives matter. Differing perspectives and theories can radically alter perceptions of children and their experiences of living and learning over which, particularly in education contexts, adults have control. We have a responsibility to never assume that we have already found definitive or sufficient ways of seeing and understanding children. Rather we must continue not only to challenge our ways of paying attention, but also to continuously reassess the lenses and assumptions through which we look and come to form our understandings.

Understanding the significance of attunement with the material environment is enabled by artistic practices and sensibilities. Using an artistic lens is helpful to think differently about learning with the material world, emphasising what some theorists have called 'the "littleness" of meaning making' (Hackett, Pahl, & Pool, 2017, p. 58). The necessity to find new ways of thinking and seeing in education in particular is urgent (Braidotti, 2013), because to acknowledge and respond to challenging environmental, political, and social circumstances for children, education requires paradigms which can embrace complexity, messiness, and difference. As noted by Lodge and Lynch (2004) 'even though Ireland has never been homogenous culturally or politically (…) daring to name differences was seen as a challenge to authority, a deviant act, rather than a statement of fact' (Lodge & Lynch, 2004, p. 3). In light of the desire of Irish ECEC to be open to, and accepting of difference, this book explores how an arts-based, Posthuman, ethico-aesthetic approach can contribute to this imperative.

In addition, arts-based research practice has slowly been making its way into the research domain, but primarily as a tangible activity or method. I am interested to see what happens when, in education in particular where research has been dominated by social science oriented theories and practices, an aesthetically oriented theoretical lens is put to work with and alongside artistic practices and methods in education research. This responds directly to Sharon Todds' quote at the beginning of this chapter and her call to envisage education itself as an artform. It also seems to me to be a logical, ethical, and justified claim to space whereby artistically oriented theories may be fully entrusted to understand and theorise artful practices.

Mapping the Discussion

In Chapter 1, I present a discussion of the historical context of ECEC in Ireland, including Aistear, the Irish ECEC curricular framework and its relatively recent development and underpinnings. This is followed by an exploration of the recent and rapid development of arts in education provision for young children in Ireland. I point out some of the exclusions of the ECEC sector in these important national developments in arts education. I also discuss some examples of arts-based ECEC research in Ireland in relation to the new paradigmatic developments that my project presents. Concluding this chapter I discuss the global context of the Anthropocene and its implications for education.

Chapter 2 introduces my theoretical framework and comprises a detailed discussion of the foundation of a posthuman ethico-aesthetic paradigm. To begin, a broad outline of the many different forms of posthuman theory is provided. Then, an introduction to Spinozist posthuman theory which underpins an ethico-aesthetic paradigm. The implications of Spinozist posthuman theory are explored in relation to ECEC, particularly ethics, approaches to learning, movement, play, and constructions of the child.

Chapter 3 considers materials and the ways in which they connect to ECEC theory through the literature. This approach to the literature exposes how materials have been at the heart of ECEC theory and practice since its inception. It also reveals the underlying perspectives that various materialist approaches have offered to ECEC research and practice throughout history and clarifies how the most relevant of these for the current educational context are open, inclusive, and profoundly democratic.

In Chapter 4 I discuss postqualitative research methodology as appropriate to the posthuman theoretical position. This chapter begins with a review of postqualitative studies which have emerged over the past decade. I also examine a range of postqualitative research methodologies including arts-based approaches. Chapter 5 introduces my research fieldwork site (a single ECEC setting in the West of Ireland) and I discuss the specific postqualitative arts-based research approaches I employed in the empirical part of my study. A clarification of the process of organisation and analysis of the data is also provided through the ideas of mapping the data as a 'bloom space' and working with 'sticky data' (MacRae et al., 2017) in analysis processes.

Chapters 6, 7 and 8 present the heart of the project through the analysis or storying of 'small' moments, through a Posthuman perspective. These chapters each focus on the concepts of Agency, Affect and Care respectively. Through this presentation I explicate these key concepts as they emerged during the research creation process as anchors for the distinct research stories. Finally, I conclude by presenting my final thoughts on the research creation journey and the development of the idea of everyday artfulness.

I will begin this research story with a broad overview of the art in education landscape in Ireland, from its relatively recent beginnings up to the present day.

CHAPTER 1

Digging Deeper: The Irish ECEC Context

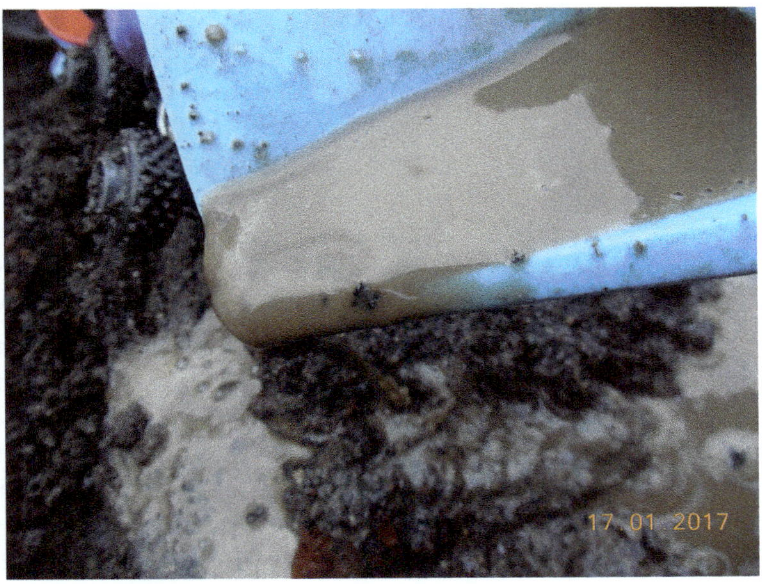

Figure 2: Digging Deeper

The Historical Context in Ireland

> There is a three-letter word which I cherish in the education process, but is rarely expressed, and that is 'joy'. I consider that education is a joyous, fulfilling activity, and this dimension of joyous engagement should be more emphasised. At its heart, learning is a mode of exploration and should be cherished. (Coolahan, 2017 p. vii, in Benson, 2019).

The Irish education system has been on a steep learning curve toward a more joyful experience of learning for children which has been greatly enhanced by its emphasis on the arts in recent years. This particular aspect of Ireland's education journey could be said to have begun in 1979 when, marking the International Year of the Child, the Arts Council of Ireland published a report entitled 'The Place of the Arts in Irish Education' (Benson, 1979). Known as the Benson report it was commissioned to gain a detailed overview of arts education provision in the state at the time, so as to inform and assist with the development of an education policy for the Arts Council which up to that point in time it had lacked. The report referred to previous work which had highlighted the impoverished state of the arts in education in Ireland, from the Bodkin report of 1949 (which later led to the setting up of the Arts Council in 1951) to the Arts Councils 1976 'Provision for the Arts' report (Richards, 1976).

The Benson report notes in its introduction that there was a paucity of cohesive data particularly on arts education provision in schools for the time, and so the ambition of the working group committee therefore, through their consultative work with multiple interest groups was to gather, compile and analyse this important information. Their motivation for the efficient accrual and analysis of the substantial quantity of data, was also so as to influence an impending government White Paper on educational development which was published in 1980 (Benson, 2019). The foundational emphasis throughout the report is on what Benson describes as 'cultural democratic ideals' (Benson 2019, p. 14). It recognised schools as democratic access points for the provision of arts experiences for children and young people. It noted that children's access to making and experiencing art was at that time unfairly arbitrary and largely dependent on individual teachers personal and pedagogical interests. In addition, funding for basic materials was prohibitive as was class size which at the time could average at forty-five children per teacher (Benson, 1979, section 2.13). The Benson report also brought to light the existing hierarchies of perception of different art forms within the Irish cultural sector which had implications in terms of funding, visibility, and accessibility, where 'high' art forms such as painting and music overwhelmed other popular cultural forms such as film (Benson, 2019, p. 13).

Despite its deeply democratic motivation and intention in relation to access to art education however, nowhere within this important and still celebrated report is there reference made to early childhood or to very young citizen's right to artistic experiences. This exclusion reveals the under-valued position that the education and care of young children in the state held at the time, which lacked a sense of cohesion or even of regulation. Shortly after the deep recession of the 1980s significant societal changes began to see the situation of arts provision in both primary schools and the early childhood sector improve. Of course, these political, social and fiscal changes including increases in population and economic growth had important implications for children and their families (McGinnity, Murray & McNally, 2013). In the space of ten years from 1995 to 2004 there was an increase of 60 per cent more women participating in the labour force (NESF, 2005, p. 11), and the need for care of young children became further bound up within the economic argument as the provision of a necessary service for workers. As noted by Rogers and colleagues,

> The establishment of the New Opportunities for Women (NOW) programme created an impetus to enable higher levels of participation by women in the labour market, with childcare being seen as an 'ancillary and technical' measure required to give effect to this ambition. This gave rise to the Equal Opportunities Childcare Programme (EOCP), a programme of capital investment in childcare development. (Rogers, French & EarlyArts UK, 2013, p. 6)

In 2005 the National Economic and Social Forum (NESF) report on Early Childhood Education and Care (No. 31) pointed out further links between economic circumstances and equity in the provision of ECEC which found that,

> Poverty has major effects on children and their educational life chances. High rates of poverty among women are often associated with their caring responsibilities and consequent inability to participate not only in the labour market but in all aspects of society. ECCE has been a priority concern for many of the intervention strategies for disadvantaged areas. It is recognised that early intervention is of crucial importance if children are to move from a disadvantaged status. It is also seen as a response to a multitude of family and community needs to counteract the impacts of poverty. (NESF, 2005, part 2.8)

However, the renewed focus on early childhood also developed out of a series of landmark events and reports not least of which occurred in 1992 when Ireland ratified the United Nations Convention on the Rights of the Child (UNCRC). In addition, The Childcare Act of 1991 'placed a statutory duty on health boards to identify and promote the welfare of children who were not receiving adequate care and to provide a range of childcare and family support services' (Coolahan, 2017, p. 187). The subsequent publication of the Childcare (Preschool Services) Regulations (1996) provided the first formal regulatory document pertaining to Irish ECEC. In 1999 The White Paper on Early Childhood Education: Ready to Learn (1999) was initiated by the National Forum on Early Childhood Education convened by the minister for education and science at Dublin Castle in March 1998. Representatives from twenty two of the main interested agencies were given the opportunity 'to engage in multilateral discussion on key issues involved in the education of young children' (Coolahan, 2017, p. 192). Subsequently, The National Childcare Strategy (1999) was published as well as The National Children's Strategy (2000). This ambitious ten-year plan for the practical activation of obligations pursuant to ratification of the UNCRC (1992) includes commitments to ECEC.

Concurrent with a growing momentum toward equitable, quality education provision for young children, the legacy of the previous hundred years of Ireland's Industrial Schools began to surface and a succession of deeply shocking scandals related to the historical abuse of children were brought to light at this time. It was known that the introduction of compulsory primary education had impacted the relationship between the family, state, and church historically in Ireland (Fahey, 1992). Enforcement occurred through court prosecutions and committals to industrial schools, largely of children from families mired by poverty. Industrial schools were known to have been places of violence for children and were run by various religious orders with the support of the state. In 1970 'The Kennedy Report' published recommendations for the need for improvements across many aspects of the industrial school system and of children in need of care however, only a small percentage of the recommendations were implemented 'for example, the names 'industrial' and 'reformatory' were changed to residential homes and special schools and many reforms were introduced in the operation of these institutions. However many other suggested reforms were not' (Coolahan, 2017, p. 134).

In May 1999, the Taoiseach apologised to survivors on behalf of the state and announced the Commission to Inquire into Child Abuse, established in 2000. Its findings known as The Ryan Report were published in May 2009. An indication of the extent of the abuse is evidenced by the resulting costs of the inquiry and subsequent redress scheme estimated at €1.5 billion (McCarthy, 2016, p. 9). Further, The Ferns Report (2005) and The Murphy Report (2009) each investigated clerical abuse of children in Wexford and Dublin respectively (Independent Editors, 2018). As late as 2015, the government established 'The Commission of Investigation into Mother and Baby Homes', however the campaign for full access to the final published report escalated in 2020 due to the legal threat of sealing access to the report's data archive which, when published in early 2021 warranted another public apology from the Taoiseach.

One outcome of these investigations, reports, and findings is widespread consensus on the need for the regulation of the ECEC system in Ireland. In 2004, the government invited the OECD to undertake a 'Thematic Review of Early Childhood Education and Care Policy in Ireland' (2004) which was critical of provision at the time, concluding that 'funding for early childhood services in Ireland has been low by international standards' (OECD, 2004 cited in Coolahan, 2017, p. 195). Since this criticism however there has been advances within the ECEC sector. The recommendation for standardisation of quality in Irish ECEC brought about the establishment of the Centre for Early Childhood Development and Education (CECDE) in 2002 which developed Síolta as the National Quality Framework for Early Childhood Education (CECDE, 2006). Síolta provides a process through which ECEC settings can volunteer to reach specified quality standards. It is a substantial undertaking for ECEC educators to complete the required processes and documentation within its twelve guiding principles, sixteen standards and seventy-five components. The sixteen quality standards for example encompass the Rights of the Child, Environments, Parents and Families, Consultations, Interactions, Play, Curriculum, Planning and Evaluation, Health and Welfare, Organisation, Professional Practice, Communications, Transitions, Identity and Belonging, Legislation and

Regulation and finally, Community Involvement. Síolta accreditation is achieved through a graded system from 1 to 4 (this research fieldwork setting for example achieved level 4 on the Síolta quality assessment scale, the highest possible attainable). However, despite the desire and need for improvements in ECEC quality and provision, it is important to bear in mind, as pointed out by Rogers and colleagues (2013) that the key political impetus for advancing ECEC in Ireland, was initially at least,

> not operating from a children's rights, wellbeing, or even developmental frame. Rather an equality agenda, focusing on women's participation in the labour market, an emphasis on 'smart economies', and a growing body of evidence that early childhood investment paid dividends in terms of prevention of higher social and economic costs through the life course were, and to a large extent remain, the underpinning rationales. (Rogers et al., 2013, p. 3)

The National Curriculum Framework for ECEC, Aistear, was subsequently published in 2009 and will be discussed in more detail in the following section as a foundational document for the development of ECEC in Ireland.

Aistear – An Emergent Curriculum

'Aistear' (2009) the ECEC National Curriculum Framework is described as an 'emergent' curriculum (Dalke et al., 2007; French, 2007; Brennan, 2015) which emphasises play-based learning within a holistic approach. Aistear is underpinned by four foundational pillars: Well-being, Identity and Belonging, Communicating, and Exploring and Thinking. These pillars are in turn based on twelve principles of early learning and development which are divided amongst three groups; children and their lives in early childhood, children's connections with others, and how children learn and develop. Aistear is grounded in a democratic ethos where it states,

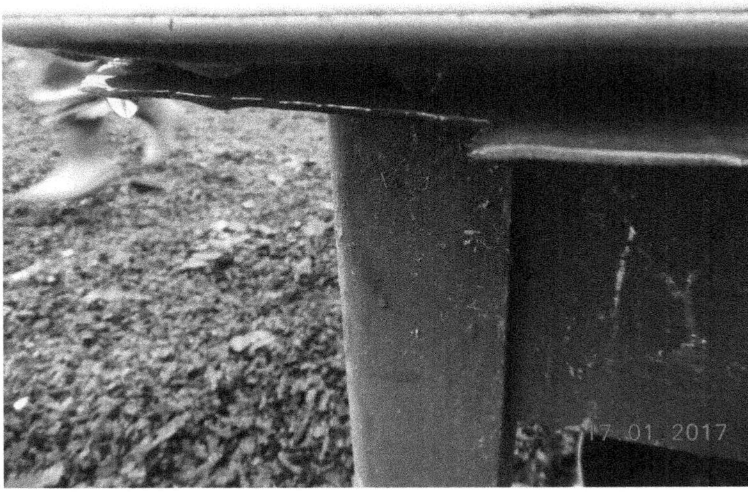

Figure 3: Aistear: An Emergent Curriculum

> Nurturing equality and diversity is important in early childhood. Promoting equality is about creating a fairer society in which everyone can participate equally with the opportunity to fulfil his/her potential. Diversity is about welcoming and valuing individual and group differences and understanding and celebrating difference as part of life. (NCCA, 2009, p. 8)

While ECEC in Ireland is delivered by a range of private (both for profit and not-for-profit), community and voluntary providers, different educational approaches are represented within the sector including for example Montessori, High Scope, Froebel and Steiner (French, 2007). Aistear can be used across each of these relatively diverse approaches while still retaining the unique philosophical and pedagogical methods of the settings choice. Parental involvement is valued and encouraged throughout Aistear and as such is considered influential in positive educational outcomes for children (Barnardo's, 2006).

Following the publication of Aistear, in January 2010 a universal childcare programme to deliver a 'free' (subsidised) preschool year (ten months) was introduced for children of pre-school age (2 years 8 months – 5 years 6 months). The 'Early Childhood Care and Education Scheme' (ECCE) was further extended in September 2016 to two years of ECEC and endeavours to ensure voluntary, equality of access to ECEC for sessions of three hours per day, five days per week, over thirty-eight weeks from September to June. ECEC services are paid a capitation fee by the government for each qualifying child enrolled. Since this scheme was introduced and extended while remaining entirely voluntary, attendance at ECEC has significantly increased (Dept. Children & Youth Affairs, 2019). However, there remains substantial 'systemic challenges' in the Irish ECEC system which stem from inconsistent political will and policy (INFORM, 2020). A strong argument for the development of a universal public ECEC system for Ireland is currently emerging (INFORM, 2020), strengthened by the global pandemic which has exposed serious and irreparable deficiencies in the current system. The right of all children to education and care is at the heart of this argument, while the labour needs and desires of parents and society as a whole are also integral.

Focus on the rights of children have also had an influence on the inclusion of the arts in ECEC. In 2012, the Children's Rights Referendum was held in order to strengthen children's rights as citizens and to enact commitments contained within the UNCRC (1992) into the Irish constitution, in particular 'the best interests of the child and hearing the view of the child' (Children's Rights Alliance, 2012, p. 4). The amendment wording of article 42a states that 'the State recognises and affirms the natural and imprescriptible rights of all children and shall, as far as practicable, by its laws protect and vindicate those rights'. The amendment further states that 'in respect of any child who is capable of forming his or her own views, the views of the child shall be ascertained and given due weight having regard to the age and maturity of the child' (Children's Rights Alliance, 2012, p. 5).

Coinciding with the successful carrying of the Children's Rights Referendum, also in 2012, the launch of the Arts in Education Charter (2012) provides a 'joined-up' approach to art education provision (Coolahan, 2015) and includes ECEC as an important starting point for encountering the arts. Aistear is cited in the Arts in Education Charter (2012) as the core means for the delivery of best practice early years arts experiences in

ECEC, and as such is a valuable resource for both ECEC educators and early years artists alike. The inclusivity of ECEC in the charter is an important commitment to ECEC arts education and highlights how focus on early childhood arts provision has progressed in Ireland within a very short space of time. The nature of this provision will be discussed further in the following section.

Current ECEC Arts Provision

Rapid and diverse improvements in provision of arts education experiences in Ireland have resulted from the publication of the Arts in Education Charter (2012), much of which, as stated, is inclusive of ECEC. The Arts in Education portal for example, was a direct outcome of the charter and is a vibrant online resource managed by Kid's Own publishing company, which provides access to the relative explosion of exciting arts in education initiatives and partnerships which have been funded across the sector (Coolahan, 2015).

Currently there are multiple dedicated arts festivals, individual artists, and early years arts companies (too many to list here) all producing high quality work specifically for early years audiences across music, theatre, dance, film, and visual arts in almost every county across the country. In addition, the Arts Council has introduced and supported a number of awards and commissions for new work focused specifically on early years arts provision and creation. For example, in 2017, The Ark Cultural Centre for Children in Dublin introduced a year-long Early Years Artist Residency programme, funded by the Arts Council, and named after Professor John Coolahan, a long time Ark board member and member of the Benson Report (1979) working group. In addition, many County Council arts offices are currently beginning to direct funding specifically for artists working with young children, however there is of course room for improvement and unfortunately exclusions of ECEC continue to occur. For example, significant recent omissions of early childhood arts include two programs, the now nationwide Teacher Artist Partnership (TAP) program begun in

2017, and the more recent Creative Ireland/Arts Council Creative Schools program launched in 2018. Both successful and ambitious programs have garnered significant investment and together have been inclusive of primary, post-primary, youth outreach, and special education. Both programs have expanded significantly in relation to their funding, and consequently their reach through publicly funded school systems. However, they have yet to move towards providing access for children in ECEC settings. The lack of universal public ECEC system in Ireland enables the exclusion of ECEC from these important national provisions of arts education for children and young people.

While exclusions of ECEC from national programs are significant, nevertheless unfunded and voluntary arts-based activities have in some cases filled the gap and played a role in ECEC arts provision. For example, this research project has developed out of a long term (ten year) community-led initiative between me and the ECEC research site setting. We worked through a barter system, exchanging use of an unused classroom in the building as my art studio space for my time spent in the classrooms developing activities with children and adults. These activities ranged from designing and building installations for play; introducing the children to new materials; making visual documentation; mounting public exhibitions; and facilitating parent and educator training inspired by the Reggio Emilia 'atelierista' model. Our exchange set out on the basis of a shared commitment to children and to community-led learning and collaboration. As the residency evolved I also explored the potential contribution of an arts-based lens within an ECEC setting which ultimately sowed the seeds for my own doctoral research.

Irish ECEC Art Education Research

Although research interest in ECEC arts provision in Ireland is relatively recent, and although the framework of Aistear presents a foundational interest in the concept of 'emergence', nevertheless arts-based research tends to lean toward making claims of the cognitive and developmental benefits of art in education. This follows an approach to evaluating the impact of art education as used by the OECD (2012). To date then, the argument for the inclusion of art experiences within ECEC in Ireland has been advanced on the basis of the relevance of arts-based activity in ECEC to specific learning, cognitive development, or improvement across other areas of the curriculum.

For example, in 2013 the Arts Education Research Group (AERG) at Trinity College in collaboration with Fingal County Councils Arts Office, designed and delivered a fully funded action research project entitled 'Artful Dodgers' in two ECEC settings in Dublin, with two artists in residence. The aim of this arts-based research was described as an effort 'to investigate the impact of this engagement on the children's early development with particular focus on literacy and numeracy skills' (Hayes et al., 2013). Further, the Arts Council's foundational publication 'Early Childhood Arts: Three Perspectives' (2013) also makes claims as to the developmental benefits of engagement with the arts in early childhood,

> We now know without question that high quality early childhood education and care reaps measurable gains in thinking and social skills for all children. Early childhood arts therefore have a significant role to play in children's learning and development. (French, 2013, p. 24)

In the same document however, Rogers notes that while the indissoluble connection between education and care have been foundational the more recent shifts toward an emphasis in focus on education is marked by the change from ECCE (Early Childhood Care and Education) to ECEC (Early Childhood Education and Care), from EU policy to teacher training and education (Rogers et al., 2013, p. 3). This shift also represents the dominance of the argument for developmental benefits in relation to art education by way of justification, as presented for example, in research which assesses,

> the impact of arts education on a variety of skills by critically reviewing all the existing research on these questions. Its rich and nuanced interpretation of the results leads us to conclude that caution is needed when making statements about the impact of arts on non-arts outcomes and on transfer of skills more generally. (Winner, Goldstein & Vincent-Lancrin, 2013, p. 3)

Difficult to measure aesthetic sensibilities and experiences while acknowledged as important are portrayed in these reports as elusive, vague, or not sufficiently scientific (Dowling-Long, 2015) and are consistently overshadowed by the apparently weightier prize of either cognitive development or numeracy and literacy advancement. The enhancement of aesthetic sensibilities is noted as a bonus rather than an aim, where,

> In the event that arts education did not contribute to innovation, arts education would have a place in our schools given the importance of art as a human experience. I would indeed have difficulties imagining a good life without the arts and some cultural awareness. (Ischinger, in Winner et al., 2013, p. 3)

The consequence of this position of aesthetic experiences in education is by inference, its potential disposability in light of the more highly desired achievement of accountability to measurable quality and standards. Despite commitments to include art education in ECEC in Ireland (even if still only partially achieved), and the acknowledgement of the improvements in 'human experience' that it can bring, its diminished position is nevertheless established by attempts to measure its value using tools which prioritise cognitive and developmental progression. However, while of course cognitive development and progress are undeniably important, it has been argued that for young children in particular, this emphasis in ECEC installs a system of norms against which children may be measured (MacLure, 2013b; Snaza et al., 2014; MacRae et al., 2017). Inevitably, with this approach, some children will be found to be deficient as it sets in motion a model of achieving norms which, whether intentional or not, as a consequence, suppresses difference.

I suggest that the processes of evaluating the arts in ECEC are not adequately served by using a developmental lens, rather, the arts in education become dangerously diminished. I believe that the Posthuman ethico-aesthetic paradigm which I explore and present here is better equipped for understanding the potential and potency of aesthetic experience in ECEC, primarily because it begins from the argument 'that difference is the natural state of things' (Strom, 2020).

A Posthuman ethico-aesthetic paradigm which develops from Spinoza's philosophy of immanence, can attend to the rapidly changing social, political, technical, and environmental changes through which young children are living and to which it is imperative for education to adapt. A fundamental aspect of this imperative is the inclusivity of children with different experiences of the world and with different competencies and knowledges to offer.

An approach is required which also enables diverse knowledge forms to be made visible and to flourish within a paradigm which facilitates a wider view of intra-activity, by bringing the material world with/in which children grow and learn, more clearly into view. This is of particular importance when the stability of the material world and 'Nature', of which humanity is a part, can no longer be assumed. In the following section I will consider further the relationship between humanity and the material world through a discussion of the global context of the Anthropocene.

The Global Context – The Anthropocene

> As human beings we inhabit an ineluctably material world. We live our everyday lives surrounded by, immersed in, matter. We are ourselves composed of matter. (Coole & Frost, 2010, p. 1)

The interconnectedness between humanity and the material environment is of course undeniable, and these intimate interconnections are unfortunately also borne out through the unravelling complexity of the era, known as the 'Anthropocene' (Crutzen, 2006; Crutzen & Stoermer, 2000). The term defines the current widespread and irrevocable 'ecological disequilibrium' (Guattari, 2000) generated by the effects of human activity in relation to non-human species and planetary bio-spheres, and through excessive material production, consumption and waste. Multi-layered and asymmetrical social and ecological power relations are a further cause and consequence of this situation, where deep injustices which have become embedded, inevitably impact children's everyday lives and futures (Guattari, 2000; Braidotti, 2013; Haraway, 2015, 2016; Trafí-Prats, 2017; MacCormack, 2018; Malone, 2018). It has been argued that the global pandemic arose due to 'humanities relentless incorporation of animal life into our food chain … like the climate crisis, epidemics are not merely accidents of nature. They have anthropocentric drivers' (Tooze, 2020). Clearly human modes and approaches to engaging with the world require reassessment, not least in education contexts (Snaza et al., 2014). Envisaging materials and environments as tools for human advancement and learning in education is no longer appropriate or sufficient. Ethical perspectives which begin from an acceptance of entanglement *with,* rather than separation *from,* are helpful in this regard. The rapidly changing ecological conditions of the Anthropocene further motivate the necessity for working with research paradigms which are capable of considering the evolving complexity of human/material entanglement.

Although the basis for ecological degradation has appeared in scientific literature for a century (Syvitski, 2012) the term 'Anthropocene' first formally appeared in 2000 when ecologist Eugene Stoermer was joined by the Nobel prize winning chemist Paul Crutzen to propose it as a new geological term for a new era (Crutzen & Stoermer, 2000), where the negative effects of human activity on the planet have become inscribed. Crutzen and Stoermer suggested that the Anthropocene, originated with the invention of the steam engine by James Watt in 1784, when humans first began to aggressively mine and transform natural resources into energy to run machines, escalating into the current hydra-headed state of environmental toxicity of multidisciplinary concern (Syvitski, 2012).

While the fore fronting of 'Anthropos' indicates the human species as central to the cause of the situation, this generates the notion that all humans are equally responsible which is clearly not the case. Haraway suggests that to begin to understand this complexity, that a 'litter' of terms is required to highlight the origins and implications of the Anthropocene (Haraway, 2015). For example, the 'Plantationocene' (Tsing, 2015) holds industrialised agriculture to account, while the 'Capitalocene' (Moore, 2015) finds capitalist economic and political structures to be the root cause. Haraway's own term the 'Chuthulucene' is derived from the ancient Greek word for 'Earth', evoking a medusa like earthbound creature with multidirectional extending tentacles. Other variants of the term continue to emerge including the 'Anthrop-obsecene' (Parikka, 2015), the 'Technocene' (Nancy,

2015) and the 'Plastic-ene' (MacFarlane, 2016). This proliferation points to the diverse conglomerations contributing to its development while the argument as to its initial cause ranges from the primitive human control of fire to the first nuclear bomb detonation in 1945 (Lewis & Maslin, 2015).

Academia has fortified use of the term, examining the Anthropocene through interdisciplinary seminars, research, and publications while research funding has also been abundant. For example, the website of the Arts and Humanities Research Council of the UK states that the £1.5 billion Global Challenges Research Fund announced by the UK government in 2016 'will be key to building more sustainable futures in the Anthropocene' (AHRC, 2020). However, many scholars agree that the scholarship (and funded research) is dominated by white western voices which are silencing important discourse on the effects on Indigenous communities who have been disregarded and excluded from the debate (Todd, 2015). According to Bignall, Hemming and Rigney (2016) this omission is a grave mistake because Indigenous peoples 'have always managed their environments without exploitation' and thus 'they are pertinent exemplars for learning how life can be sustained today in the Anthropocene' (Bignall et al., 2016, p. 472). However, Yunkaporta (2019) points out that the message is often over-simplified in relation to the valuing of Indigenous knowledges which are persistently peripheral where,

> We rarely see global sustainability issues addressed using Indigenous perspectives and thought processes. We don't see econometrics models being designed using Indigenous pattern-thinking. Instead we are shown a dot painting and implored to make sure we include Indigenous employment in our plans. (Yunkaporta, 2019, p. 19)

Indigenous knowledges that are grounded in philosophical thinking follow and understand the complex relationalities between apparently divergent entities (Bignall et al., 2016; Akomolafe, 2019; Yunkaporta, 2019). These perspectives are highly relevant to the current global pandemic, where the intense, and frequently toxic interconnections between what may otherwise appear to be independent (such as political and economic strategies, loss of biodiversity, animal welfare, and human health for example) have become shockingly visible. Nigerian philosopher and member of the Yoruba people of West Africa, Bayo Akomolafe points out that,

> The Yoruba have always understood that everything is a crossroads – not just an intersection of other things but relationships resisting absolute determinacy. Things are assemblages. Provisional, multitudinous, spread out. Like rhizomes. (Akomolafe, 2019)

Davis and Turpin find that the multiplicity of voices and cross fertilization of disciplines are necessary to productively address the 'environmental concerns, aesthetic predilections, epistemological limits and ethical aporiae' (Davis & Turpin, 2015, p. 3). While the majority of these concerns appear human centric, Haraway suggests that the term potentially generates a 'species question' and risks missing the foundational disproportionate power relations that are the results of the continuous transformation of the earth via the maxim of profit above all else and declares that 'system collapse is not a thriller. Ask any refugee of any species' (Haraway, 2016, p. 161).

Haraway argues that the term 'Anthropocene' is in danger of being used to restate political allegiances rather than as an incentive to address the difficulties it poses and suggests that 'the dithering' may be a more appropriate title for exposing political indecision and hesitancy (Haraway, 2016). The dramatic spike in human population of the past five decades is also of concern. Haraway's call to 'make kin not babies' (2016) is supported by those for whom ultimately, human extinction is the inevitable solution (Gray, 2002; MacCormack, 2012) however Haraway states that 'I think of making kin as a way of being really truly pro-child-making babies rare and precious- as opposed to the crazy pronatalist but actually antichild world in which we live' (Haraway in O'Neill-Butler, 2016).

Politically, the Anthropocene has given multidisciplinary urgency and credence to Ecosophies, the first strands of which appeared through the Deep Ecology Movement led by environmental philosopher and activist Arne Naess (1912–2009) and through contributions from Green parties throughout post war Europe (Dolphijn, 2018). It is argued however that inputs on the issues from these sources, risk promoting what Braidotti terms as a 'humanisation of the environment' (Braidotti, 2006, p. 116) where human concerns override other species. An alternative perspective within the ecological movement was developed through the influential work of biologist Gregory Bateson (Bateson, 1972) and of philosopher Felix Guattari (Guattari, 2000). Ecosophical theory emphasises the urgency of radically inclusive sympoesis (Haraway, 2016), as making and becoming-with all other bio/geo/techno entities with which humanity complexly co-exists. These ideas have laid the ground for the recent development of posthuman theorising in education.

Braidotti and Hlavajova (2018) generate a social justice analysis of the Anthropocene, and refer to the consequences of hierarchical humanism where 'the status of depreciated naturalized "others" whose existence has been cast outside the realm of anthropocentric thought' (Braidotti & Hlavjova, 2018, p. 3). Innumerable 'depreciated' people have suffered under hierarchical regimens. The effects of colonialism continue to reverberate globally, as exemplified by the recent 'Black Lives Matter' protests. In Ireland, in relation to children in particular, the Industrial School system and the 'Mother and Baby Homes' are also undoubtedly part of the legacy of hierarchical humanism, whereby dehumanisation and shame became the tools of a regimen which discriminated between and against human beings according to social circumstance and the moral standards of the time.

While hindsight may provide a clarifying lens for understanding the hierarchies imposed by some humans to the detriment of others, the situation is becoming increasingly complex. Scientific advances are blurring human, biological and technological boundaries, to the extent that Bird Rose claims that we are 'being overtaken by processes that are unmaking the world' (Bird Rose, 2013, p. 2). Davis and Turpin argue that this is an aesthetic process in so far as human 'sensorial and perceptive systems are being refashioned at rates that we can barely keep up with' (Davis & Turpin, 2015, p. 11) while Boetzkes argues that we must 'recalibrate our sensorial systems to adjust to contradiction, catastrophe, and ecological volatility' because the Anthropocene 'has altered the terms and parameters of perception itself' (Boetzkes, 2015, p. 272).

Conclusion

In this chapter I have tried to argue, that there is a need for an alternative paradigm to underpin arts-based research, to provide space for complexity, critical thinking, and difference. Spinoza's philosophy theoretically underpins a posthuman ethico-aesthetic lens, which is capable of considering the complex relational activity generated between human and non-human bodies. This necessarily expansive inclusivity shifts beyond dominant human-centric and developmental approaches to art education and is motivated by the ethical concerns presented in the converging contexts described in this chapter.

It should be noted of course that many aspects of this paradigm are already closely aligned to the origins of ECEC. For example, Kindergarten pioneer Friedrich Froebel (1782–1852) has been described as 'being the first posthumanist thinker in early childhood' (Urban, 2016, p. 117). Froebel situated the human, not as centre stage, but rather as always being in relation to the non-human, and to Nature. However, as has been discussed, the context of the Anthropocene demands, that ideas of what constitutes Nature, and for that matter the Human, need to be critically reassessed. Spinoza (1632–1677), also a revolutionary thinker, presents a radically inclusive philosophy which enables approaches to re-considering the relations between Nature and Culture; body and mind; subjectivity and objectivity. Spinoza inspires critical posthuman theorists by leaving behind reliance on installing hierarchical binaries which generate both implicit and explicit exclusions. I suggest that this paradigm also enables arts-based research in ECEC to fulfil its potential and purpose.

Outside, Iris has hidden some inflatable plastic packaging in the T-pee for the children to discover.

The mound of silent, air-filled plastic is found by a small group who are initially puzzled and then very excited.

Their excitement attracts others.

The children instantly engage by throwing, shrieking, bashing, sitting on, standing in, and wearing the strange-shaped objects, which quickly infiltrate the entire outdoor space, while being tested as shoes, hats, vessels and occasionally missiles.

CHAPTER 2

Theory Matters

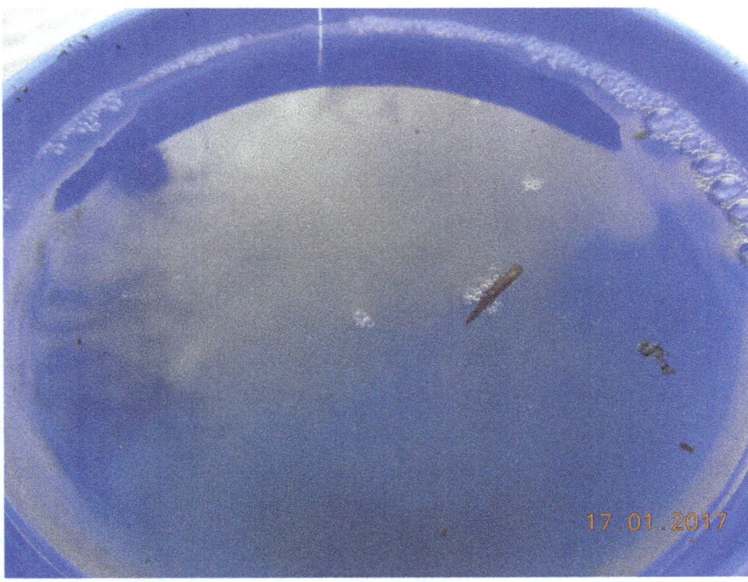

Figure 4: Theory Matters

Posthumanism: An Ethico-aesthetic Paradigm

In this chapter I want to try to clarify what I mean by an ethico-aesthetic paradigm. To do this I need to explain what constitutes an aesthetically oriented paradigm. I also need to describe how this paradigm produces an ethics that is capable of being indiscriminately inclusive and therefore always more-than-human.

In aesthetic practices the material environment is considered not just for its symbolic or representational possibilities but it is also understood as profoundly integral to events, conditions, and phenomena. One of the first things art students learn is how to consider 'negative space' in relation to the construction of a composition of a painting or drawing. This means that everything that will be within the frame of the paper or canvas needs to be considered for the part it plays in the overall image. Paying attention to the shapes and qualities that negative spaces create is considered equally as important to the composition as the positive objects being represented. This means paying as much attention to the shapes of non-solid objects which may be created as the result of relationships between things (which also depend on the unique perspective of the viewer) as to the more obvious physical objects and forms in the composition. If these relational shapes are neglected the artist risks creating distortions which are very difficult to rectify, particularly if the negative spaces have not been seen or acknowledged from the outset.

Similarly, an aesthetic theoretical paradigm requires an expansive view which acknowledges the contributions of all possible entities (environment, materials, child, adult, policy, imagination, pedagogy, etc.) where all entities are acknowledged as potential participants, each contributing their own unique temporal positionality and capacity to generate powerful affects. This expansiveness is also the foundation of an ethico-aesthetic paradigm.

In proposing this paradigm for Irish ECEC art education research, my aim is to align with alternatives which resist dominant developmental perspectives of young children's learning through art experiences. In exploring the possibilities of this paradigm, I have found that when Spinozist ethics and aesthetics join forces, they can resist measurement focused agendas which exert multifaceted pressures on education. I have also found that within an ethico-aesthetic frame, ethics, and aesthetics both reorientate and counterbalance each other's potentially negative tendencies. For example, aesthetics predilections for purity, beauty, and exclusivity are held in check by an affirmative ethics that is radically democratic, particularly through its diverse openness and availability to everything. In turn, aesthetics dilutes ethics desires to survey, police, regulate or control, and instead offers, through its capacity to trouble-make and create interruptions and disturbances as part of its enlivening purpose, a route to taking and spending time along-side others, carefully, modestly, generously, ethically.

Trafí-Prats and Canton describe an ethico-aesthetic paradigm as one which focuses on affect and intensity (Trafí-Prats & Caton, 2020). This means that through this lens, moments of material encounter which matter to children can come into clearer focus and attention because, even though they may not be coherent or even deemed meaningful, such moments are nevertheless replete with affective intensity. Perceived through an ethico-aesthetic lens, moments that matter to children are not put at risk of being overlooked by more powerful pedagogical desires and impulses of adults. In everyday practice this means paying attention to the intensity of moments as they emerge and unfold, deepening that intensity through the act of paying attention and resisting the need to capture moments within definitive meanings. It also enables a much wider view of the diversity of possible participants in events which might include humans, materials, objects, environments, policy, imagination, pedagogy, sound, temperature, microbes, atmospheric pressure, insects (and, and, and). A posthuman ethico-aesthetic paradigm demands valuing complexity and so in many ways, the unfathomable depths of sensory ways of knowing (Dahlberg, 2016). As put by Dahlberg, we need 'to open ourselves up to change and to the unexpected – to non-knowledge and to that which puts difference in motion' (Dahlberg, 2016, p. 129).

Spinoza's monistic philosophy forms the foundation of a Posthuman ethico-aesthetic paradigm by providing both inspiration and an ethical compass that is capable of responding to the immense complexities of the Anthropocene. It does so by actively seeking out and working against inherited hierarchical thinking which has become so deeply ingrained that in many ways, it has been rendered invisible. Unpicking and moving beyond structural hierarchical thinking is enabled by Spinozist posthumanism.

At this point it is necessary to begin by introducing the concept of posthumanism more generally. I will follow this with an introduction to Spinoza and a detailed discussion of how his foundational idea of 'The Affects' paves a way toward hyphenating ethics and aesthetics and can help to rid us of unhelpful hierarchies when we are considering young children's learning and being with and alongside the world.

Posthumanism/s

> We need to devise new social, ethical and discursive schemes of subject formation to match the profound transformations we are undergoing. That means that we need to learn to think differently about ourselves. I take the posthuman predicament as an opportunity to empower the pursuit of alternative schemes of thought, knowledge and self-representation. The posthuman condition urges us to think critically and creatively about who and what we are becoming. (Braidotti, 2013, p. 12)

The term posthuman is a plural, umbrella term which has been developed through multiple fields and disciplines including the arts, humanities, science and technology with different implications and aspirations, and as such is 'a concept in motion, an active theoretical assemblage' (Taylor, 2016, p. 21). Spanning a spectrum of scholarly and scientific applications that range from the Critical and Cultural Posthumanities to Transhumanism, this polarity demonstrates its differing genealogies but also its impetus as a theoretical movement.

The posthumanities share as a starting point a criticism of the assumptions which surround the term 'human' as inherited from the ancient Greek. 'Anthropos' the Greek word for the human was an exclusionary term, which bracketed humans by specifically referring to educated, adult, Greek, males and determinedly excluding all others which at that time, included Persian/Barbarian, uneducated/slaves, females/children, non-human animals/deities (Ferrando, 2016). The term human today presumes a far greater inclusivity however it is argued that it has retained a veiled ethos of exclusion at its core and as such is deeply problematic (Braidotti, 2013; Hayles, 2017). Posthumanism then is a rejection of this conceptualisation of humanism as stable, idealised, or aspirational, and as such as a category that remains beyond the reaches of many, including children.

Braidotti and many others (Hayles, 1999; MacCormack, 2018; Snaza, 2013; Snaza et al., 2014; Wolfe, 2010) argue that the concept of humanism as it stands generates an identity binary produced between belonging and otherness, so that criticism of the category of the human is deeply political. Snaza finds that 'the political importance of posthumanism's reconceptualisation of 'the human' is most clear in relation to the history

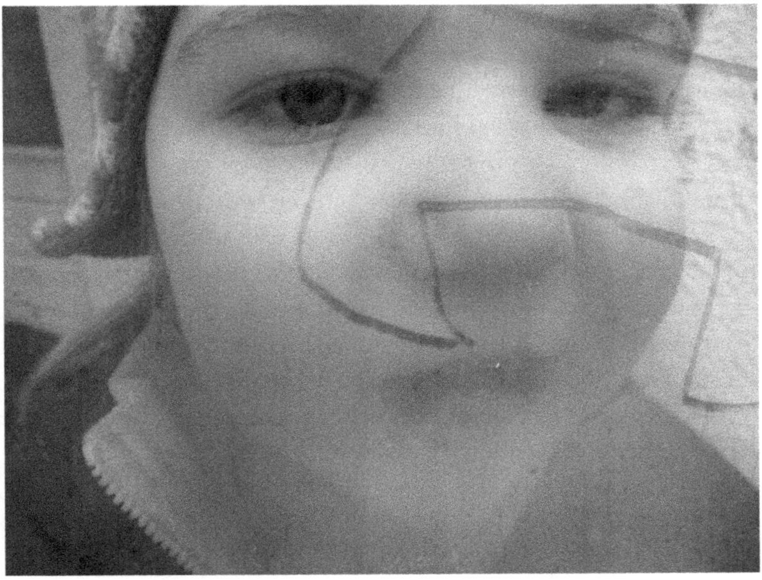

Figure 5: Posthumanism's

of dehumanisation' (Snaza, 2013, p. 48). The 'post' of posthumanism then, indicates a moving beyond the exclusionary construction of 'humanism' towards an open notion of the category.

The terms post-dualism and post-anthropocentricism which are shared across many posthuman theoretical positions require some clarification. Post-dualism argues against the oppositional binaries set up through the hierarchical systems inherited from the European enlightenment, and the resulting separations constructed between body and mind, and further, between nature and culture. Post-Anthropocentricism proposes the need to decentre humanity as a species in order to take a wider view of the relationality and co-dependence between multiple species and ecologies. This position tends to read humanity as an entire species and is less concerned with the specific inequalities generated for different groups of humans by environmental breakdown and the consequences of differing political and economic responses.

Moving beyond a fixed notion of the human is therefore represented by a broad spectrum of positions. On the one hand, transhumanism's which are informed by science, technology, and cybernetics, focus on machinic and technological human enhancement and degrees of availability. Transhumanist's broadly claim that we have not yet achieved posthumanism, but that moving beyond the limitations of the human will be achieved through technological and scientific enhancement, and so the focus of transhumanist's remains determinedly anthropocentric.

In direct contrast to the transhumanist agenda, the philosophical, critical, and cultural posthumanities are driven by an environmental and social justice stance. This position is productively enhanced by critical academic theories which originated with the deconstruction of the human through poststructuralism. As stated by Braidotti,

> The human of Humanism is neither an ideal nor an objective statistical average or middle ground. It rather spells out a systematised standard of recognisability – of Sameness – by which all others can be assessed, regulated, and allotted to a designated social location. The human is a normative convention, which does not make it inherently negative, just highly regulatory and hence instrumental to practices of exclusion and discrimination. The human norm stands for normality, normalcy and normativity. (Braidotti, 2013, p. 26)

Cultural, critical, and philosophical posthumanism's are motivated by a critique of the definition of the human from a western point of view, rather, they explore the plurality of the human in a postcolonial, technological, and globalised world. This has undoubtedly opened scholarship up to the multiple previously unrepresented voices of 'others' which have begun to emerge in academia. Through the developments brought about by this determined inclusivity and the diversification of theoretical positions, posthumanism strongly objects to the idea or idealisation of a unified subjectivity as represented by the universal image of 'Man', inherited from the European Enlightenment. Posthumanism seeks to offer 'a more complex and relational subject framed by embodiment, sexuality, affectivity, empathy and desire as core qualities' (Braidotti, 2013, p. 26). This premise derives from Spinoza's ethics which envisages an expansive, emergent, and complexly connected world where subjectivity becomes reconfigured as radical difference that is integral to all lives, human and non-human (MacCormack, 2018). Philosopher of childhood David Kennedy finds that this more complex understanding of subjectivity formation is such that,

> The subject-in-process as opposed to the subject-as-substance is always being produced in a process involving contradiction and struggle. (…) The subject-in-process recognises and honours difference in the world because it recognises difference within itself and works for coordination rather than unity. (Kennedy, 2006, p. 10)

Criticisms of Posthumanism

Criticism of posthuman theory which has recently begun to emerge presents important considerations. For example, posthumanism has been derided as yet another 'post', theoretically related to postmodernism and its propensity for uncomfortable abstractions and claims of 'newness' (Rekret, 2016; Petersen, 2018). These criticisms serve as a welcome warning against the use of language which may be vague or jargonistic, and against immodest or polarising binary claims which unhelpfully set the past against the future, or the old against the new.

A further criticism of posthumanism is focused on the 'turn' to materiality. For example, Paul Rekret (2016) writes that 'it has become a veritable doxa in certain circles of the humanities and social sciences today to invoke an appeal to humanities 'entanglement' with a vast non-human world as the basis for posthumanist ethics and politics' (Rekret, 2016, p. 225). Rekret grounds his criticism in a quote by Lucio Colletti (1972),

> To say, therefore, that an object is material is still to say nothing. Materiality as such does not specify, it is rather a generic attribute, a property common to all things. (Colletti, cited in Rekret, 2016, p. 225)

However, in many ways this is precisely the point, not to say nothing of course, but to draw attention to shared commonalities. Materiality also offers a different, other than human starting position from which to begin to question the position of the human in relation to others and to the world. Aligned to this however, another major criticism of the material turn has developed as the assigning of agency to matter which has provoked a mocking tone. Petersen (2018) writes in criticism of an article which assigns agency to data which in this case is generated by city air, 'did the air agree to being represented as an agent who found the researchers? The verb 'found' seems very active and purposeful to me in this context, and how does the air feel about that?' (Petersen, 2018, p. 11). However, while derision may to some minds be deserved, in more generous terms the speculative approach applied by Posthumanism permits a seeping of playfulness and necessary experimentation into theory. While this may cause offence, given the productivity of play and the rigorous requirements of experimentation, it may however help to produce new and challenging perspectives. Pushing beyond set boundaries in writing and theory requires bravery, and tolerance. As put by Braidotti,

> What I find praiseworthy on the part of my critical theory teachers is the extent to which they are willing to take the risk of ridicule by experimenting with language that shocks established habits and deliberately provokes imaginative and emotional responses. The point of critical theory is to upset common opinion (doxa), not to confirm it. (Braidotti, 2013, p. 87)

A more frustrating criticism however is the fact that the term Posthuman itself, as an umbrella term with a broad diversity of starting points and aims (as discussed above) has generated confusion and frequently produces the conflating of differing positions. Posthumanism, sitting as it does between antihumanism and transhumanism, at times becomes misunderstood as closely aligned with these positions. For example in his book chapter entitled 'A Critique of Posthumanism' Pawel Majewski writes 'the term "Posthumanism" in the sense assumed here has a synonym – "Transhumanism"' (Majewski, 2018, p. 181).

Philosophical, critical, and cultural posthumanism's are distinct from the anthropocentric aspirations of transhumanism (Ferrando, 2013) which is primarily interested in human enhancement in the light of technological advances. Philosophical, critical, and cultural posthumanism's which have emerged from feminism, critical race theory, indigenous theories, and queer theories amongst others, are interested in how we consider the 'human' as a question that is undoubtedly affected by technological advances, but also by postcolonialism and globalisation. Philosophical, critical, and cultural posthumanism's advocate rather, for an understanding and acceptance of complexity in relation to justice, difference, diversity, and inclusivity. In this way, posthumanism is not a leaving behind of the human but rather a gathering in of all possible 'voices' (and ways of producing 'voice') in the consideration of what it means to be human in what has been termed the Anthropocene.

In the next section I will discuss Spinoza's ethics and how this comes to underpin the posthuman ethico-aesthetic paradigm, particularly through the reliance on the central concept of 'The Affects'.

> We move back inside for 'work time' where I try to find an unobtrusive place to make notes in my book, but it is impossible not to engage with the charms of the curious children. 'Kasia' who has moderate English, asks to use my 'cheese' – she means the camera, exposing how the meanings of things can easily become tangled to create new images.
>
> Animals and babies enter the classroom assemblage. 'Alice' has a glittery white polar bear on her top and we talk about how it reaches around her back. She asks me to draw it into my notebook, so I do. She decides to draw a picture of a cat 'I can do cats and my name and a 5 and a heart'. I tell her about the new kitten I have in my house.
>
> The ideas and images of the two cats and the bear enter our temporary shared space. More 'invisibles' enter in the form of stories about two babies. A new week-old sister, (whose name is difficult for her brother to remember) will arrive in school next week at collecting time. Another baby enters as news of a mothers' pregnancy.
>
> These 'invisibles' seem as important a force as the sunlight, magnets, shadows, sounds, actions, lunches, chatter, water, paint, glitter, chairs, tables, glue, cake, sweeping brushes, and, and, and.
>
> They enter the assemblage as connected to all of these different elements, forming a picture of moments spent together.

Affirmative Ethics

> Posthuman Ethics is not concerned with the application of a universal moral code (how one ought to live), but is enmeshed in everyday practices and encounters, working with ever present power relationships to co-create empowering relationships

> and to counter constraining forces that limit the capability to thrive (how one might live). (Lester, 2020, p. 148)

Posthuman philosopher Rosi Braidotti states that the social, environmental, political, and technological complexities of the Anthropocene (as described in Chapter 1), generate ethical questions which must be addressed if research, theory, and practice are to be 'worthy of our times' (Braidotti, 2006). In educational contexts this represents a requirement to reconsider and extend the function, position, and meaning of ethics itself. Education philosopher Sharon Todd suggests,

> shifting the focus from education as a scene where one ought to apply this or that principle, to a scene where the conditions or contingencies of ethicality may be found, (…) means no longer simply thinking about education in relation to ethics; rather, it means thinking about ethics through education. (Todd, 2001, p. 437)

Posthuman affirmative ethics is grounded in the philosophy of immanence of Spinoza (Deleuze, 1997) which avoids an approach to ethics that is 'in the mode of indebtedness, vulnerability, and mourning' (Braidotti, 2006, p. 3). Rather, for Spinoza it is 'not by obligation, by coercion – not as a hostage of the other – that man becomes responsible' (Juffé, 2007, p. 17). Posthuman theorists espouse a materialist, bodily approach to ethics that is attentive to sensation and singularity. The inspiration Spinoza provides in this regard is for a new theorisation of subjectivity, as stated by Braidotti 'a post-humanistic and nomadic vision of the subject can provide an alternative foundation for ethical and political subjectivity' (Braidotti, 2006, p. 1). This is made possible by Spinoza's idea that all bodies and minds, both human and nonhuman, are equally and fundamentally part of his conceptualisation of Nature (Bennett, 2010; Murris, 2016) so that,

> Rather than celebrating human will and transcendent ideas, Spinoza directs our attention to the body and the *movement* of thought, emphasising how thought is nonhuman and how all matter has the power to affect and be affected in varying degrees. Rather than subscribing to a morality of transcendent values, Spinoza proposes an ethics of encountering without judgement, and affirmation of joy. (de Freitas, Sellar & Bang Jensen, 2018, p. 2)

Spinoza's Ethics

Written during the Enlightenment and published posthumously in 1677, Spinoza's major work 'The Ethics' effectively upended the dominant Aristotelian-Cartesian principal, that the universe is comprised of distinct substances and their changeable attributes. While Spinoza built on Descartes philosophy he argued that the prevailing notion of multiple individual self-contained substances was wrong, and found instead that reality is made up of a single substance that is equivalent to Nature, God or Substance as infinite being, described as 'absolute affirmation of existence' (Spinoza, 1996 [1677], P8S1). By geometrically configuring God as Nature or Substance, and therefore logically within, rather than outside of everything that exists, Spinoza was ostracised as an atheist by his Jewish community and subsequently lived his life in exile.

Where Descartes considered mind and body as separate and different kinds of substance, for Spinoza mind and body are two attributes of the one Substance/God/Nature (monism). This means that 'the mind loses its status of substance, which has been so crucial for Descartes, and becomes a mere mode' (Lloyd, 1994, p. 9). As a result, Spinoza's monism represents not only an equating of Nature as Substance with God, but it also emphasises inevitable porous affective relations between things, because Nature in its infinite diversity is indiscriminately and logically part of everything that exists, as 'Substance', not just what is usually considered to be exclusively 'Natural'.

As a consequence of monism (where everything exists as part of one single Substance / Nature / God) for Spinoza mind and body become the two available modes of existence through his theory of parallelism. This necessarily rejected the prevailing idea of the supremacy of mind over body, which to a large extent has endured in education. For Spinoza all entities both living and non-living, exist through the modes of 'mind' as thinking (which also refers to an idea of a thing) and 'body' as extension into the world as part of it. 'The Ethics' states that 'a body cannot cause a mind to think, and a mind cannot cause a body to be in motion or at rest or in any other state (if there are any others)' (Spinoza, 1996 [1677], III 2).

This explains how mind and body function together in parallel as distinct modes, but nevertheless connected as part of a single Nature/Substance. Spinoza clarifies that every entity exists to infinitely varying degrees of complexity and capacity for 'motion and rest' through the modes of both extension and thinking.

> The things we have shown so far are completely general and do not pertain more to man than to other individuals, all of which, though in different degrees, are nevertheless animate ( ) And so, whatever we have said of the idea of the human body must also be said of the idea of anything. (Spinoza, 1996 [1677], P13S)

This way of thinking profoundly challenges hierarchical systems and presumptions of human exceptionalism. It does not suggest that objects, insects, or plants all either think or have active bodies that function in the same way, or in ways that are measurable against the human. Rather, it means that the mode of thinking is as infinitely diverse and various in relation to degrees of complexity as are modes of bodily existence, and consequently thinking is not confined to the human/animal brain. Thinking may also refer to an idea or awareness of something as a mode of mind. This generates an expansive inclusivity in relation to the activity of mind as a mode through which everything that exists participates or intra-acts (Barad, 2007) with the world.

Equally, for Spinoza 'bodies' are understood as referring to infinite difference rather than bounded entities encased by fixed containers. Bodies may come together for mere moments before breaking apart to create new relations and formations. This reconfiguring of the idea of the body also produces a reconceptualising of subjectivity as a 'nomadic, transversal assemblage' (Deleuze & Guattari, 1987) that is 'bonded by affirmative ethics' (Braidotti, 2019, p. 33). Rather than an ethics that is based in vulnerability or debt of a subject as distinct from 'others' it encounters (and so effectively installing a hierarchical system based on power and lack of power), posthuman affirmative ethics via Spinoza is accountable through Spinoza's concept of 'The Affects' which relates to the potential in all encounters between entities for the increase in the power to act (where power is *potentia*, or power to, rather than power over) so that,

> ultimately posthuman ethics seeks relations based on imperceptible and infinite difference, that is, not based on anything in advance and based on all possible expressions and affects. (MacCormack, 2018)

Lloyd (1994) finds that Spinoza's monistic philosophy presents an affirmative ethics by clarifying and emphasising the intimacy between humanity and all things that exist and Nature / God. The outcome of this radical integration proposes that if 'God itself is not extra-*natura*, even less can man be: He does not constitute a kingdom within a kingdom' (Lucero-Montaño, 2012, p. 2). In this way, Spinoza presents the necessity to reconsider the ways in which phenomena are understood as fundamentally relational, where diverse entities are credited for their unique participation in phenomena and the ways in which they affect one-another. This is a radical opening up to the necessary consideration of unexpected and previously unconsidered entities in relation to how experience and phenomena emerge as always complexly more-than-human. Spinoza's ethics therefore radically relate to the body rather than the human, where a body can be any entity which exists (as part of Nature/Substance) human and non-human, living and non-living.

Spinoza strongly urged that the dominant humanist ethics of good and evil, be replaced by the concepts of good and bad, traceable through 'The Affects' as potential measures of the increase or decrease of any entities power to 'act' or, its ability to continue to thrive in its particular mode of being. At this point, a clarification of 'The Affects', as foundational to Spinoza's philosophy of immanence is required to clarify the ways in which they relate to and activate a posthuman ethico-aesthetic paradigm.

The Affects

> The body constantly interacts with other things which change and affect it. Some of those interactions preserve the body and enhance its ability to act; others decompose the body and obstruct it from acting fully. The ways in which external things enhance or obstruct our body's activity – and, in parallel, the ways in which the ideas of those

> things enhance or obstruct our mind's activity – are the ways in which external things affect us. The affects are the 'affections', or changes, of the finite body by which its power of acting is increased or diminished. (Lord, 2010, p. 86)

For Spinoza, conceiving of humans as part of, rather than as separate from nature is essential to his construction of ethics. Affects as 'pre-personal' forces (Massumi, 2002) are generated through the activity of encounter between entities in the world, both living and non-living. In this way, affective activity includes but also goes beyond human-centric emotions to include an infinite myriad of diverse entities which affect and are affected by a myriad of others. As noted by Jane Bennett,

> What is needed is a cultivated, patient, sensory attentiveness to nonhuman forces operating both outside and inside the human body (…) without proficiency in this countercultural kind of perceiving, the world appears as if it consists only of active human subjects who confront passive objects. (Bennett, 2010, p. xiv)

As part of nature, the affects are not conceived as being under human control, however, for Spinoza, we may learn to live well through a clearer understanding of them. Affects as explained by Beth Lord, 'push and pull us in different directions, determining our actions and behaviour' (Lord, 2010, p. 83). In 'The Ethics' Spinoza describes in detail the many powerful affects which impact entities in terms of either 'pleasure' or 'pain' which may appear human-centric but in fact relate to everything,

> Pleasure is an emotion whereby the … power of activity is increased or assisted. Pain on the other hand, is an emotion whereby the … power of activity is diminished or checked. Therefore, pleasure in itself is good (and pain in itself is bad). (Spinoza, 1996 [1677], E4p41dem)

The universality of the affects becomes clearer through the most fundamental of all 'passions', which according to Spinoza, is that of the desire to persevere in being or 'conatus', which once again applies to everything not just the human or even the living, 'whereby a thing endeavors to persist in its own being is nothing else but the actual essence of the thing in question' (Spinoza, 1996 [1677], EIIIPVII).

Lucero-Montaño (2012) explains further that the essence or conatus of everything that exists is moved by good and bad affects where, 'for Spinoza, the good affects are those that favour the originating conatus of life, towards its expansion and perfection, that is to joy and happiness. The bad affects on the contrary disturb the being's impetus' (Lucero-Montaño, 2012, p. 4). Affects can therefore be described as defining or locating the intimacy between intra-acting bodies, both human and non-human where, as described by Teresa Brennan 'the transmission of affect, if only for an instant, alters the biochemistry and neurology of the subject. The "atmosphere" or the environment literally gets into the individual' (Brennan, 2004, p. 1). Louise Boscacci (2019) points out that atmospheres are 'both thing-like (a spatial presence with qualities, conceived as ecstasies, and able to be encountered as a resonance), and subject-like, in that they belong to bodies – they are sensed/created by bodies' (Boscacci, 2019, p. 200). This implies an essential porosity between entities which is affirmed by Teresa Brennan where she writes that 'the transmission of affect means, that we are not self-contained in terms of our energies. There is no secure distinction between the individual and the environment' (Brennan, 2004, p. 6). Through an affective lens, aesthetics becomes 'the discipline through which the organism and its environment become attuned' (Berardi, 2009, p. 130). This creates openings for conflating aesthetics with affective activity, enabling the consideration of everyday events which need not necessarily be consciously constructed or set in motion by human protagonists, but may be altogether more like spontaneous everyday ordinary events which can occur with or without human involvement.

The affects then relate to how we can come to understand how entities relate, intra-act and affect each other either positively or negatively. In order to think about the application and relevance of Spinoza's idea of the affects in relation to ethics for contemporary life, as more-than-human, as materially embedded and available to everything as described by Spinoza, environmental philosopher Maria Puig de la Bellacasa (2017) suggests that we can think of the ethics of care as 'a generalised condition that circulates through the stuff and substance of the world' (2017, p. 122). Puig de la Bella

Casa examines through posthuman theory, inclusive and expansive human and non-human affective, ethical entanglements where,

> Caring, or not caring, however, are ethico-political problems and agencies that we mostly think as they pass from humans towards others. But thinking care with things and objects exposes that the thick relational complexity of the intratouching circulation of care might be even more intense when we take into account that our worlds are more than human: the agencies at stake multiply. (Puig de la Bellacasa, 2017, p. 122)

Thinking of the circulation of care through affective material encounters, is facilitated by Spinoza who states that 'the order of causes is therefore an order of composition or decomposition of relations, which infinitely affects all of Nature' (Spinoza, 1996 [1677], II 28, 29). This becomes the route to unlocking human-centric morality from ethics and envisaging ethics and care, as 'a generalised condition' (Puig de la Bellacasa, 2017, p. 122) that encompasses everything that exists as part of Nature. This understanding of ethics and care as more-than-human domains has of course long been confirmed by natural scientists. For example, through his work on avian extinctions, Thom van Dooren (2016) writes,

> Empathy, consideration, care, even various form of ethics have never been the privileged possessions of humanity, and they certainly did not arise as part of the civilizing emergence of cultured humans radically distinct from a nature that is "red in tooth and claw". Rather these kinds of affective engagements – these ways of being meaningfully with others – are products of a long and complex inheritance that undermines any simple distinction between the 'biological' and the 'social'. (Van Dooren, 2016, p. 40)

In considerations of ethics and care in relation to non-living entities and objects, philosopher Graham Harman (2007) finds that art and aesthetics, as more-than-human phenomena, also have important implications for broadening the understanding of ethics beyond human-centric morality. Harman finds aesthetics to be a mode of touching without touching or communication through proximity which is also available to everything. This presents the potential for ethics to be located in affective aesthetic experiences of material connection between all things in the world, irrespective of human intent or involvement (Harman, 2007). However, this is of course not a straightforward argument. Puig de la Bella Casa finds in her explorations of the complexity of touch that,

> One insight often advanced about the specificity of experiencing touch (often supported by references to Merleau-Ponty's phenomenology) is its "reversibility": when bodies/things touch, they are also touched. Yet here already I wonder: to touch or to be touched physically doesn't automatically mean *being in touch* with oneself or the other (...) So maybe we have to ask what kind of touching is produced when we are unaware of the needs and desires of that what/whom we are reaching for? (...) This resonates with the appropriation of others through caring. (Puig de la Bellacasa, 2017, p. 99)

Posthuman education theorists are interested in working with such entangled, complex relations between aesthetics, affect, and ethics to produce critical, more-than-human perspectives of ethics and care. This is motivated by the need to rethink ethics beyond human-centric morality, which cannot be meaningfully applied to everything, and which largely holds a static or simplified western-centric view of humanity.

Affective aesthetic inquiry also may be understood as intrinsically politically charged, as put by Loveless (2019), 'how might the world be organised differently? is a question that matters urgently, and it is a question that art (...) asks in generative and complex ways' (Loveless, 2019, p. 16). In relation to children's modes of being in the world, particularly through play and everyday aesthetic engagement, this theoretical lens offers what Lester (2020) has called,

> a different way of thinking about playing as an expression of children's desires to affect and be affected by the world in ways that produce moments of pleasure and the sense of life being better. This is an affirmative position rather than one of lack. (Lester, 2020)

In the following section, returning to the implications of an ethico-aesthetic paradigm for children more specifically, I consider through a posthuman ethico-aesthetic lens, the ways in which Spinoza's ethics and core concept of the affects, can help to reconfigure how the phenomenon of learning is understood.

At the end of work time and tidying up there is a change of orientation of bodies from verticality to crawling or rolling across the floor to the large group time mat, where the children lie side by side for a few minutes of guided meditation.

They are asked to close their eyes and lie as still as they can while a magic stone (a glitter sticker) is placed on their forehead by Christine (educator).

There is a lot of variety in the stillness of bodies. Some feet need to continue rocking while some lay flat on the floor with knees raised while some are raised towards the ceiling.

Some hands also jiggle and struggle to stay still. At the end, the goodbye song and parents begin to come into the room while children seek out the mirror to look at the sticker on their foreheads.

Another change of orientation for some children who are lifted up by their parents ("You are getting big!") and carried out of the room to get their coats.

Constructivism and Social Constructivism

There has been longstanding dominance in ECEC policy and practice of constructivist and social constructivist theories. These theories both acknowledge and centralise young children's sensory modes of learning, particularly through psychologist Jean Piaget's (1896–1980) stage-based theory of children's learning development which remains influential today (MacRae et al., 2017; Aslanian, 2018). Piaget's image of the child is predominantly that of the 'cognitive child' (MacRae et al., 2017) who follows a relatively linear stage based route towards adulthood or maturity. The social constructivist theory of psychologist Lev Vygotsky (1896–1934) emphasised the child and learning as mediated through social and cultural activity which prioritises language, social interaction, and abstract representation as the central modes to achieving understanding of the world, which is 'amenable to analysis and interpretation through a process of discursive de-construction' (MacRae et al., 2017, p. 8). This approach developed as a way of attending to what was perceived to be missing from Piaget's previous constructivist theories, namely the child's social and cultural milieu. However, within this scheme as in Piaget's, knowledge is still construed as ideally moving away from material and bodily ways of knowing and toward cognitive and abstract representation of things in the world as stable, knowable, and unchanging. From sensory modes of engagement with the world, the child is understood to move gradually towards idealised abstract thought, producing what has been criticised as 'a normative framework through which to understand the child' (MacRae et al., 2017, p. 5).

Posthuman ECEC theorists argue that these analyses of processes of learning substantially diminish the potential for understanding the dynamism of the material world, and the complexities of children's learning with it. It is further argued that a significant implication of the prioritisation of language and representation in particular, in coming to know the world, produces a notable distance between 'knower' and 'known', and so between child and the world (Barad, 2007; Hultman & Lenz Taguchi, 2010; MacRae et al., 2017). There is an inherent implication that (the human) 'knower' is active, while the (material world) 'known' is rendered passive.

Using a posthuman ethico-aesthetic paradigm in education moves toward what physicist and philosopher Karen Barad has called 'ethico-onto-epistemology – an appreciation of the intertwining of ethics, knowing and being' (Barad, 2007, p. 185) which flatten the hierarchies that have been generated in relation to language, expression, non-verbal, and bodily modes of understanding. Prioritising competency in language use as a marker for the achievement of knowledge has the potential for generating exclusions both of less competent users and of obscuring tacit 'bodily logic' (Olsson, 2009, p. 3) or knowledge forms, which are beyond the reach of language. Page describes these forms of learning as 'material pedagogies' (Page, 2018). Material pedagogies are those numerous examples of 'knowing in being' which Page describes as the modes through which 'we learn through and with embodied histories and pedagogies but also with matter. It is the intra-actions, the between of bodies and matter that is pedagogic' (Page, 2018, p. 6).

Nevertheless, logocentric literacy development in young children's learning is of primary concern in ECEC. The undeniable pleasure in the processes and achievement of becoming text literate are not to be undermined, and the aims of such literacy development are understandably, universally defended (UNESCO, 2006; NCCA, 2012; OECD, 2012). However, it is argued that literacy remains tethered to a normative concept and to being used as a measurement tool. Political theorist Claire Colebrook writes,

> Normative notions of literacy (whereby populations are measured against a single standard) operate in terms of extensive multiplicities. There is a linguistic standard deemed to be crucial to effective communication and the transmission of sense; the project is to include as many persons as possible within this standard. (Colebrook, 2012, p. x)

Of course, literacy needs within wider society are far from static, and understandings of what constitutes literacy have morphed across multiple disciplines (Geerts & Van der Tuin, 2016) to the point where for some, it is in danger of becoming 'over-coded' (Masny & Cole, 2009) or 'devalued' as a term (OECD, 2012). There has been a proliferation and bleeding of formerly clear boundaries around language, into multiple new disciplines. Furthermore, while literacy development aspires to function so as to liberate and socialise (Freire, 2005), posthuman theorists suggest that by affixing to the achievement of normalcy, literacy harbours tendencies for establishing unacknowledged yet systematic exclusions (Colebrook, 2012; Hackett & Somerville, 2017; Snaza, 2019) and is shadowed by an insidious preference for neuro-typicality while installing biases which act against neuro-diversity (Manning, 2016).

Although literacy in education is predominantly associated with language, it may also refer to any form of representation where meaning is conveyed or construed (Eisner, 2002). In this way, artistic practices become included in the expansion of the understanding of literacy in pedagogy. Posthuman ethico-aesthetic approaches to re-conceptualising literacy practices are being explored within education (Taylor & Hughes, 2016) and particularly within ECEC (Ceder, 2015). Posthuman literacy research (Kuby & Roswell, 2017) extends concepts of literacy beyond text in early childhood by using starting points other than language. Numerous explorations of a multiplicity of literacies and artistic processes of learning through sensory and non-verbal modes are emerging in posthuman research and practice (Holmes & Jones, 2016; Kind, 2014; MacRae et al., 2017; Odegard

& Rossholt, 2016; Trafí-Prats, 2017). Hackett and Somerville (2017) use everyday movement and sound created by young children as starting points which offer non-verbal openings through engagement with material objects and bodies stating that,

> For us, posthuman readings of early childhood literacy offer the possibility to shift the narrative, to reconceptualise emergent literacy in ways that reconcile with young children's being in the world. (Hackett & Somerville, 2017, p. 389)

Colebrook (2012) argues that despite the numerous threats posed to logocentric literacy and reading attention spans through visual and screen-based modes, multiplicities within literacies are crucial, to counter the tendency toward normalcy. Posthuman theorists attend to the difficulties with discussing artistic practice's as a form of language, or even as form of communication (Kindler, 2010), particularly where creative, aesthetic, and affective modes of engagement are antithetical to normative standards. An emphasis on the affective bodily understanding of art is facilitated by posthuman theory where the affects generated by experiences of art are understood as contingent on the highly specific conditions of particular bodies. Through her concept of 'affective pedagogy' Hickey-Moody (2016) finds that art as a non-human body/object/experience which functions primarily as a producer of affect, is in itself a posthuman pedagogy, which significantly shifts the understanding of literacy beyond the delivery of sense through language. Hickey-Moody states that,

> The way an affect is experienced, and the way(s) in which an affect works, will always be specific to the body in question. Indeed, whether or not a work of art is perceived as having affect at all, is always specific to the body in question. (Hickey-Moody, 2016, p. 261/2)

Spinoza's Three Forms of Knowledge

As suggested above, considering young children's everyday ways of experiencing and being in the world, in relation to emergent literacy, it is helpful to consider how learning might be conceived to occur within approaches where standardisation and normalcy are resisted, such as in posthuman theory.

Art education theorist Denis Atkinson (2018) examines Spinoza's three forms of knowledge where affect and affirmative ethics are centralised, as being useful in this regard. Spinoza's ultimate aim was that we should come to understand ourselves in relation with the world as part of it, through activity and reason, and not through being passive to experiences, which can easily overwhelm and lead toward that which diminishes the ability to act. To this end, Spinoza's defines three forms of knowledge as, to begin, 'inadequate' knowledge, followed by the development of 'common notions' and finally the third, and highest form of knowledge which leads to a 'self-authoring life' (Atkinson, 2018a).

Spinoza's first form of knowledge is described as 'inadequate' in that it is formed through experience without a clear understanding of causes or relations and connections to others whereby,

> We are in a condition such that we can only take in 'what happens' to our body, 'what happens' to our mind, that is, the effect of a body on our body, the effect of an idea on our idea … in short the conditions under which we know things and are conscious of ourselves condemn us to have only inadequate ideas, ideas that are confused and mutilated, effects separated from their real causes. (Spinoza, 1996 [1677], EII 28, 29, cited in Deleuze, 1988)

This form of knowledge theorised by Spinoza as 'inadequate' would seem in many ways to be the primary realm of children. However, in reality, all new experiences and learning opportunities for adults and children alike are a form of inadequate knowledge in that the connections to their wider causes and contexts may take time and different perspectives and approaches before they are fully exposed or absorbed by the body and mind. As explained by Atkinson,

> The first kind of knowledge is inadequate in the sense that what we experience are affections stemming from relations with other bodies or things without comprehending the broader picture of causation, of ourselves and of the other; where the fuller picture is obscured. (Atkinson, 2018a, p. 45)

Nonetheless, Lord clarifies that there is a fundamental value in 'inadequate' knowledge as it is necessary to build deeper 'adequate' knowledge,

> Without experiential encounters with other bodies, we would never build up the common notions that enable us to become rational. Indeed, we must seek to encounter a wide variety of other things, experiment with them and learn about them, in our search for common notions and rational knowledge. We develop rational knowledge *through* experience and imagination. (Lord, 2010, p. 81)

This means that the continuous, diverse variety and richness of ongoing encounters with the world, which children seek out through experimental engagement and play with everyday materials and environments, are understandable as a central mode of knowledge formation through aesthetically and attentively 'being in the world' (Hackett & Somerville, 2017, p. 389). Connections can be formed through fine tuning and comparison between experiences. As such, these playful empirical experiences with the world for both adults and children, become the foundation of all learning. This does not mean however, that sensory experiencing of the world is a stage or phase that one moves away from, as in developmental psychology or stage-based learning theories. Rather, empirical experiences in the world are continuous, specific, and unique to all bodies and situations, regardless of age or ability, however children are undoubtedly advantaged by bringing novelty and curiosity to that which adults have become habituated (Gopnik, Meltzoff & Kuhl, 1999; Gopnik, 2009).

The second form of knowledge is Spinoza's conception of the building of reason which he calls 'common notions' (Spinoza, 1996 [1677], II P40 Schol. 2) as explained by Atkinson,

> The second kind of knowledge concerns the attempt to comprehend our reasons for acting or responding in a particular way and so building a picture of our world and of our capacities and those of others. (Atkinson, 2018a, p. 46)

Common notions are described as 'adequate' because they are generated through efforts to understand and learn about the world and its relations, to generate and understand connections and difference, that further expands the ability to both think and experience. A deeper, albeit still relatively incomplete understanding of the world can be achieved through engagement either with ideas or physical things or both, where knowledge of the underlying structures and relationships between things are developed and made clear in relation to difference.

According to Spinoza, the affect of joy is generated through encountering an idea or body that increases understanding or the ability to act and think. Through this highly engaged and active state one can be released from the passivity of being overwhelmed by that which decreases or limits a body's ability to think or act. The function of experiencing the infinite differences in the world is the development of rational understanding 'which leads to a third kind of knowledge that we might call a self-authoring of life' (Atkinson, 2018a, p. 47). It is here where the concept of responsibility also becomes activated as response-ability (Haraway, 2016) or the ability to act (respond) appropriately according to informed considerations. Spinoza's third form of knowledge also concerns a distinctly aesthetic understanding of the self in relation to Nature, as composed through intensities, infinities, and immanence, as a part of Nature. Spinoza's third form of knowledge is described by Atkinson as enabling,

> the ability not only to establish ways of living and thinking, but also to work and transform oneself – in relation to others – as if 'the self' was a continually evolving work of art. (Atkinson, 2018a, p. 50)

With this in mind, the following section will explore Spinozist Posthuman subjectivity in relation to the reconstruction of the notion of the child as 'Posthuman child' (Murris 2016).

Novelty attracts. Interesting shapes, edges, colours. Paint goes beautifully onto turnip. It's hard to put it onto bread, the bread GETS HEAVY but delicate. We can wash paint off cabbage and potato but not off bread. Just putting paint onto a surface holds interest. Joanna seeks out the table as her group is late out, so others have already started although there is an easier pace and energy, less urgency than previous sessions. Joanna stays at the table for the full hour as she has begun to do for every session. Her English is moderate, so she doesn't chat but likes to work in a self-contained way. She just stops what she is doing when I approach, it's clear I am disrupting her, and she waits for me to move away before she continues. She alternates dark brown with specks of turquoise onto a turnip slice. She spins it with her paint brush. It's clear she is not painting a picture like Tomás. Joanna seems to be fascinated by where and how the colour moves from one surface to the next, from palette, to brush to turnip to back of her hand to edge of table to water basin. She follows and encourages the movement of paint across surfaces. I am fascinated by my own position in this activity, as inhibitor of her pleasure and thought process and relationship to the paint and surfaces. I recognise my own studio practice in her movements with the paint, I understand the instinctive protection of the engagement from outside influences or disturbance of privacy. When I come too close she stops all movement. A student educator also regularly approaches the table to make some comment on what is happening. Joanna does not encourage engagement but waits for the adult to move away before she continues her activity with the paint. I am overwhelmingly grateful to the slices of turnip and bread, that they can offer Joanna a point of engagement and interest that is open to her movement and control, unimpeded by knowing, teaching, and commenting by adults relatively unknown to her, so that she can draw her own conclusions based on her sensory experiences with the materials she is engaging with. This seems like the least violent form of education imaginable which is very affecting. My relationship with Joanna is of no interest to her. I may try to make friends, but she is much more interested in the turnip.

Posthuman Child

> The first step would be then, a deconstructive one: for adults to come somehow to recognise the categories they are imposing on children, just as one comes to realise that one has been wearing a pair of glasses without knowing it. Once we realise that what we see as simply there is in fact an interpretation of what's there, our whole approach to the work with children changes, and we are able to rid ourselves of any positivistic notions of expertise (Kennedy, 2006, p. 8).

Philosopher of childhood David Kennedy (2007) argues that for every crisis of subjectivity throughout history, images of children and of childhood have been reconstructed. This argument is borne out by the table of historical figurations of childhood as presented below (see Table 2), devised by posthuman philosopher Karin Murris (2016). As has been explored in previous sections, posthuman theory resists approaches to children as a 'knowable' category. The implications of this for ECEC and for children begins by generating the concept of the 'posthuman child' (Murris, 2016). At the centre of this deconstruction as suggested by Kennedy in the

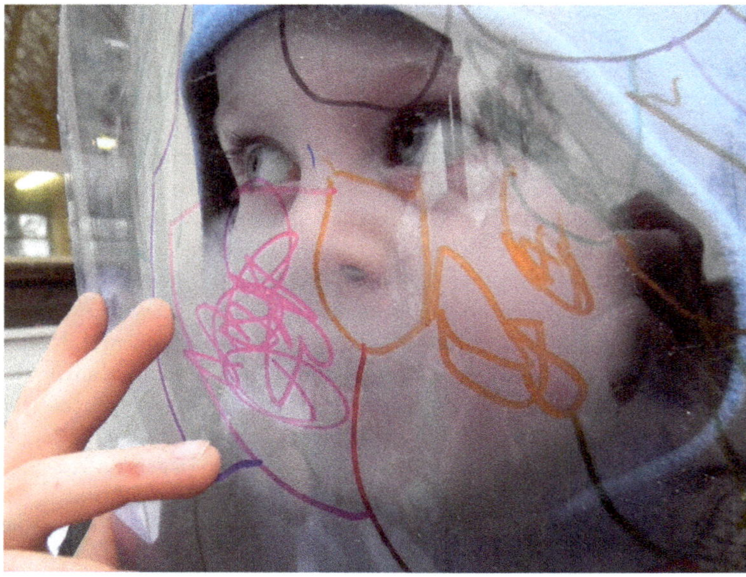

Figure 6: Posthuman Child

quote above, is a vision of subjectivity itself as nomadic, 'subject-in-process' (Kennedy, 2006; Braidotti, 2013; Ferrando, 2014; Murris, 2016), whereby 'subject positions are hybrid, multi-layered, often internally contradictory, interconnected and web-like' (Murris, 2016, p. 108). Crucially, the implication of this is that in turn 'postmodern children are inscribed in multiple and overlapping identities, in whose construction they are active participants' (Dahlberg, Moss & Pence, 2007, p. 57). This claiming of space for the inclusion of children in the construction of their own complex and often conflicting subjectivity generates a new approach to constructions of childhood than those which have come before.

Figurations of Child

Table 1: Figurations of Child: Summarised from Murris (2016, p. 109)

Figurations of Child	Theoretical influences	What child lacks by Nature	What culture needs to provide child
Developing child	Aristotle, Darwin, Piaget, Vygotsky	Maturity	Maturity, guidance
Ignorant child	Plato, Aristotle, Locke	Rationality, experience	Instruction, training
Evil child	Christianity	Trustworthiness, natural goodness	Control, discipline, inculcation
Innocent child	Romantics (Rousseau)	Responsibility	Protection, facilitation
Fragile child	Psycho-medical scientific model	Resilience	Protection, medication, diagnoses, remediation
Communal Child	African philosophies	Social relationships, norms, and values	Socialisation by elders, inculcation

Posthuman theorists highlight how humanist philosophies such as those captured in Table 1 above, never entirely considered children as part of the 'fully-human' category (Kennedy, 2006; Braidotti, 2013; Murris, 2016; Lester, 2020). Posthuman theory is thus 'critical of humanism's view of the child, consigned … to an inferior position as lesser beings, outside the charmed circle of fully developed adult person' (Moss in Murris, 2016, p. xi). Posthuman theory seeks to constructively critique the inherited structures through which children are envisaged and from which education systems have been designed. To do this Murris (2016) suggests addressing these structures from the understanding that they derive from a focus on 'negative difference',

> It is when we focus on negative difference that deficit models of child and childhood emerge: child is still developing, not complete and is unfinished, immature. Child is compared to adult, that is, the 'transcendental signifier': mature, developed, complete … Positive difference, by contrast, is about difference within bodies (not as compared to something 'outside itself' like adult). But because of the differences made by the connections within and beyond other bodies, a child always already finds her/himself as part of the world. (Murris, 2016, p. 60)

Child as Paradigm

Kennedy (2006) argues that this analysis of difference radically alters the position of children and childhood, generating welcome distance from previous ideas of childhood, and moving towards a situation where the vision of subjectivity itself becomes child-like so that adults are also always in the process of becoming and ultimately 'the child's forms of life become paradigmatic' (Kennedy, 2006, p. 10). This in turn indicates how caring for and working with children might be reenvisaged,

> The traditional child-rearing project is to render the difference represented by childhood into the "same" of adulthood. The post-modern child-rearing project is to recognise and honor and learn from the difference, not just individual genetic difference, but the generic differences between adults and children – differences in perspective, in perception, in temporality, in the dynamic relations between the plural elements of the self, in ontological and epistemological convictions, in forms of the human imaginary. (Kennedy, 2006, p. 11)

The construction of the 'posthuman child' then is underpinned by Spinoza's ethics of affirmative difference and an understanding of child and of childhood as always intensely complex and relational. It resists at all costs reductive and universalising imaginaries of children and the assertions of developmentalism, that children only develop complexity with time, and under adult supervision. This reconstruction and effective 'decolonisation of childhood' (Murris, 2016) requires a radical adjustment to ways of thinking about children, particularly in education.

Child-centredness

One of the most difficult consequences of the idea of the posthuman child is the necessary sacrifice of the recently established concept of child-centredness, which has been so hard won over the past two centuries of ECEC (MacRae, 2019). For posthuman theorists, there are several difficulties with child-centredness. The first is with repeating the patterns of human-centredness or anthropocentricism, where the intent is to guide children toward what is considered to be 'fully-human' in the mode of contemporary adults. Also problematic is a view the child as 'autonomous agent' potentially isolatable from their complex social, technical, material, and environmental contexts. Peter Moss explains that,

> Posthumanism is not only critical of human-centeredness but of child-centeredness, turning away from the idea of the child as autonomous agent and turning toward the idea of child as enmeshed in an immense web of material and discursive forces. (Moss, in Murris 2016, p. xi)

However, child-centredness has come to be understood as a marker of 'quality' in ECEC practice driven by the best intentions of care. As such, advocates of child-centeredness have rightly aimed to fully recognise and elevate the societal status of both children and of childhood (MacRae, 2019, p. 3). While these objectives are entirely understandable, the concept of child-centredness relies on and perpetuates a modernist construction of a clear and fixed notion of the child as a starting point which is no longer applicable or useful in this complex and rapidly changing postmodern world. For child-centred pedagogies, knowledge and the world are necessarily stable, knowable, transferable, systematic, and hypothetically identical for all, regardless of any of these complexifying conditions (Dahlberg et al., 2007).

For posthuman theorists child-centredness risks enacting a form of reductionism by obscuring the wider complex circumstances which crucially influence the unique situations and environments in which children both live and learn (Pacini-Ketchabaw, Taylor & Blaise, 2016). Posthumanism's insistence on the de-centralisation of the human subject finds that both knowledge creation and subjectivity are complexly relational and are context and materially dependent. To this end Karin Murris states that 'thoughts are not created in mind space, but are created in the relational and dynamic process of interaction itself' (Murris, 2016, p. 6). In the same way, agency is construed as not contained by the isolated human body but rather 'it is always 'in' the space 'between' the person as embodied organism and the material world' (Murris, 2016, p. 6). Child-centredness is replaced by posthuman child because,

> The problem is that the idea of child as autonomous agent (...), that is, self-governing, is a metaphysical illusion that does not do justice to the 'immense range of causal factors', the many 'chain of events', that cause an action (Frost, 2010, p. 161). This is the case for all human and nonhuman animals, including child. Doing justice to children means taking into account a much greater complexity of 'causal' factors when 'reading' their actions. (Murris, 2016, p. 105)

Inner Creativity

Where reading children's actions in developmental pedagogies is reliant on an image of the child as autonomous agent, in turn, in relation to art education, this generates the idea of inner creativity, posthuman theorists argue that this imposes limiting and diminishing perceptions of both childhood and art (McClure, 2011). In developmental pedagogies, creativity is construed as contained or possessed by the individual, rather than understanding creativity as an enactment between entities. As a consequence, inner creativity within developmental pedagogy is construed as easily contaminated, most usually by adult involvement so that adults can frequently feel hesitant about when or how (if at all) to intervene in children's art making processes. This resulting reticence can in turn have an undermining effect on educators. Christina MacRae discusses a deep sense of unease in relation to assisting children in their artistic endeavours (in representational images in particular), as this runs contrary to early childhood educators training (MacRae, 2008). Berger notes that it is in this way that child-centred pedagogies can also enact a veiling of the complex work of educators,

> Early childhood pedagogical creed has leaned heavily on a child-centred practice that situated early childhood educators in semi-passive roles such as unobtrusive observers and facilitators of the developing child (Langford, 2010). To a large degree, these pedagogical traditions relegated the educators pedagogical work (and its complexity) to the background and often rendered the early childhood educator invisible. (Berger, 2017, p. 180)

Child-centred pedagogies also risk obscuring the role of the material environment. As acknowledged by Tara Page 'not only do we – learners and teachers – make matter and meaning, it also makes us, we are entangled, co-implicated in the generation and evolution of knowing and being' (Page, 2018, p. 8). The implication of this is such that what is learned, created, or said is always both socially and materially infused. The de-centralisation of the human exposes the learning relationship with the material environment as always more than a clearly visible, knowable resource. Posthuman theorising understands the more-than-human contribution to human creativity, experience, and learning, as largely unacknowledged, where the relation is often complexly asymmetrical in favour of the human, rather than based in notions of mutuality.

Voice

This complexity of the relation between human and material environment also makes the idea of voice difficult to attribute or ascertain. Verbal language remains dominant in the idea and construction of the voice of the child within child-centred education, which is bound up with ideas of visibility, representation, and aims of doing justice to children. Hillevi Lenz Taguchi (2011) argues that the focus on language has the effect that 'children who are not verbally adept are not acknowledged in a way that makes their strategies central' (Lenz Taguchi, 2011, p. 47). Kennedy further argues that when children do verbalise their ideas and learning, that 'listening to children as childhood is constructed by developmental psychology and mainstream pedagogy means already knowing what is being said, and is thereby a form of ventriloquism' (Kennedy, 2006, p. 7). There is within this frame therefore, always the latent danger that the intention of attending and listening to children 'can all too easily become a thin veneer of quasi-democracy covering a will to manage and control' (Dahlberg & Moss, 2014, p. xi).

Emergent Listening

In the preschools of Reggio Emilia in Italy, children are envisaged as having 'one hundred languages' (Malaguzzi, 2000) as a way of accounting for the multiple and variable modes and unknown potentials of communicating, which can also attend to the not-yet known, for both children and adults. Bronwyn Davies calls this 'emergent listening' (Davies, 2014a) which she describes as requiring processes of being with children and a willingness to potentially become lost (Davies, 2014a, p. 23), or, in other words, not know in advance what might be being said, but attuning and listening all the same. For Reggio Emilia preschools, Carla Rinaldi writes that emergent listening 'requires a suspension of our judgements and above all our prejudices' (Rinaldi, 2006, p. 65). As a result, the concept of child-centredness as a pedagogical vision of the child as autonomous agent, is replaced by a focus on the conceptualisation of ECEC as 'an integral living organism, a place of shared lives and relationships' (Malaguzzi, 1993). While individuality and unique differences are understood to be part of an infinitely complex set of relations, centralising the child is considered to generate the effect of blurring the social, cultural and material context of which each unique child is a part (Filippini & Vecchi, 1996). The material environment inhabited by children and adults alike can therefore also be understood as contributing to the construction, expression, and movement of voice. John Shotter (2015) lyrically describes the activity between human bodies and material environment where,

> As spontaneously responsive living beings, intimately related to our surroundings, we live immersed within a world of ceaseless, intra-mingling currents of activity (…) which, to repeat, influence us as much, if not more, than we can influence them. Buffeted by the wind and waves of the social weather around us, we inhabit

> circumstances in which almost everything seems to merge into everything else; we do not and cannot observe this flow of activity as if from outside. (Shotter, 2015, p. 10)

This description of activity relates strongly to the idea of Spinozist affect, as previously discussed, while the envisaging of affect as weather also resonates with the posthuman consideration of the emergence of voice as responsive to events within the environment. This also connects to Donna Haraway's concept of sympoesis, meaning making-with, as a concept essential to navigating life in the Anthropocene (Haraway, 2016). Each of these elements relate to the reconstruction and decolonisation (Murris, 2016) of the child, toward the notion of posthuman child which, as stated by Peter Moss above, envisages children as 'enmeshed in an immense web of material and discursive forces' (Moss, in Murris, 2016, p. xi).

At this juncture, I want to begin to think about how activity and specifically, engagement with materials through play in early childhood, might be conceived within a Spinozist posthuman frame as discussed above. In the following section I will examine play and movement in relation to posthuman theory through affective, aesthetic and material focused pedagogies (Hickey-Moody, 2016; Page, 2018).

> Time to go outside.
>
> Coats and boots and hats are negotiated once more.
>
> I remain in the classroom to notice it emptying and the movement of the sound out into the hallway. Still focused on the sound qualities of the building, the first thing I am drawn to outside, a soundless sponge ball being kicked on the concrete awning.
>
> The next is the sound of a balance plank being sprung by the weight of children on it and the next is of a child in conversation with his shadow.
>
> The conversation involves movements where boy and shadow touch to form a single shape, one side three dimensional colour, the other two-dimensional monochrome.
>
> The next sound is of falling water making its way through obstacles.
>
> I am led to this by Ellen who brings me to sit with her foot near the water source: melting frost making its way erratically down a drainpipe through blockages of brown leaves.
>
> The sound is distinct and pleasing so we record it together.

Posthuman Theories of Play and Movement

The phenomenon of play has been extensively theorised historically and is of course considered to be of significance to human and animal alike. The various lenses used to understand play have been dominated by psychological, sociological, and anthropological interests (Shields, 2015) and have focused on describing and defining forms of play in order to understand its purpose. Before making claims as to what play is or its function, play theorist Brian Sutton-Smith suggests that there are seven forms of rhetoric produced by play theorists which need to be taken into account because, he states that 'when it comes to making theoretical statements about what play is, we fall into silliness' (Sutton-Smith, 2006, p. 297). Sutton-Smith defines the rhetoric's surrounding play in order to emphasise the diversity of play scholarship and plays adaptability to differing perspectives. By focusing, not on what play definitively is, but rather on the perspectives and positions taken by different theorists, Sutton-Smith exposes what he calls the essential 'ambiguity of play' (Sutton-Smith, 2006). Sutton-Smith's seven forms of rhetoric in relation to play are summarised in Table 2, while also noting the hybridity within each of the rhetoric's described.

While each of these positions represent distinct forms of play and players, philosopher Rachel Shields finds that theorists largely 'do not think that play transcends human activity and culture' (Shields, 2015, p. 298), and that this represents the loss of a valuable alternative perspective of play. Following a thesis that play exposes 'a profoundly aesthetic quality' (Huizinga, 1949, p. 18), Shield's works with Spinoza's conceptualisation of affect so that play can also be thought of as an 'affective experience that cannot be fully conveyed using conventional language' (Shields, 2015, p. 298). For Shields, play is a force that emerges and exists as more than an expression of human/animal behaviour, which exposes,

> play as existing at least partially outside the human experience of it and instead understands it as a fundamental force that drives not only the emergence of human

> culture and history but also of the natural and physical world in which human beings find themselves. (Shields, 2015, p. 299)

Shields begins with the Spinozist posthuman conceptualisation of the body as the site for theorising play as an affective experience which always moves beyond known and knowable forms of experience. By starting with the posthuman notion of the body, Shields considers play at the molecular level rather than something which is socially or culturally derived

Table 2: Play Rhetoric's: Summarised from Sutton-Smith (2006, p. 304)

Play as progress	Based on assumptions related to children and animal development. In educational theories Sutton Smith finds that play is valued for its association with social, physical, and cognitive development, more so than for enjoyment.
Play as fate	Associated with games of chance, and therefore linked to a largely outdated human relationship with the supernatural.
Play as power	Team sports and representation of distinct groups through playing together as one representational grouping, also linked to some ancient forms of conflict resolution.
Play as cultural identity	Community celebration and festivals, expressing community identity through culturally derived approaches to ritual and costume for example.
Play as supporting development of self	In solitary activities or hobbies, where attention is given to the satisfaction of the individuals personal well-being and enjoyment etc.
Play as fantasy	Prioritises creative and imaginative forms of play. Sutton Smith finds in modern thinking that this rhetoric of play as the imaginary also connects with ideas of play for self-development and of play as progress.
Play as frivolous	Running counter to idea of the 'work ethic' and linked to the classical notion of 'the fool'.

or produced and finds that play can be understood as 'an inherent element of molecular events' where,

> The brain at both the molecular level and the level of consciousness may be thought to be engaged in a ceaseless form of play. Neurons firing by chance, but also according to some set of rules, are 'acting' playfully, and the thoughts they produce are at some level highly contingent and given over to the chance outcomes of neuronal activity moment by moment (…) Consciousness in this view is play at its most basic level – we have no real control over it, it is fluid, shifting, multi-layered, mysterious, pleasurable, whirling, overwhelming. (Shields, 2015, p. 306)

Taking up this molecular exploration of consciousness as a form of play presents an opportunity for thinking about play as a more than human phenomenon which exceeds human and animal consciousness. This enables a move towards the inclusion of other forms of life, growth, and modes of adaptation (in plants or fungi for example) in considerations of participation in play.

Posthuman conceptualisations of play then clearly connect to Spinoza's concepts of affect, ethics and aesthetics as discussed previously where, within all intra-action's entities can increase or decrease each other powers to act, which have been considered here at a molecular level. With this in mind, to work with Posthuman theories of children's play and movement with the materials and environments they play with/in, it is necessary to understand the human and the child as de-centred subjects-in-process, and as being complexly, and playfully, in relation with their material environments, or, as 'naturecultural' (Puig de la Bellacasa, 2017; Hodgins, 2019). To de-centre the human in this way it is helpful to begin with the understanding that, as key to Spinozist posthuman ethics, the affects consider all bodies, human and non-human, to create,

> A new model to replace conscious thought: the body … The point of using Spinoza's model of the body is that it can make us not overestimate consciousness … it can make us focus on the specific potentialities in every situation. (Olsson, 2009, p.152/3)

Beginning with 'the body' in Spinozist terms means thinking of all and any bodies (human, animal, plant, microbial, technological, mechanical, ideational, atmospheric) as worthy of consideration in the analysis of phenomena. This enables a side-stepping of perhaps being blinded by the glare of conscious human intent as a value system in relation to play. Rather it opens to the potential of what else might be happening or considered as constituting play as a complex more than human process which encompasses potentially both enhancing and diminishing activity.

Material Agency

One outcome of decentring the human in considerations of intentional conscious forms of play is the required reimagining of the notion of agency. In posthuman theory agency is understood as not emitted from or contained by a human body but rather as distributed and produced through the activity of all bodies within the event as it unfolds, as stated by Karan Barad 'agency is a matter of intra-acting; it is an enactment, not something that someone or something has. It cannot be designated as an attribute of subjects or objects' (Barad, 2007, p. 178).

For Posthuman theorists focus on the activity of the material environment produces the concept of 'material agency' (Coole & Frost, 2010) which envisages the material world as an active participant in phenomena. Of course the concept of material vitality is not in fact new, but rather extends as far back as the ancient atomists and to Epicurean philosophy. In his poem 'De Rerum Natura' ('On the Nature of Things') Lucretius (estimated b.99BC) draws attention to the material/bodily realities of invisible forces where he writes,

> Let me draw your attention to other particles which, though invisible, have undeniable reality (…) we smell the various odours of things, even though we never see them approaching our nostril; we do not observe seething heat, nor can we discern cold with our eyes, nor do we see sounds, and yet all these must be of a corporeal nature, since they have the power to act upon our sensory organs. For nothing can touch or be touched, unless it is corporeal. (Lucretius & Ferguson-Smith, 1969, p. 41)

Lucretius also crucially pointed out the essential porosity of everything in the world 'no matter how solid things may appear to be, they are in fact a porous consistence' (1969, p. 43). Where Spinoza defined the affective body through the capacity for movement and rest, similarly, Lucretius found that movement in any form is only enabled by the idea that 'the universe is composed of two things, namely matter and the void in which matter is located and moves in every direction' (1969, p. 45). Crucially, this produces an idea of all movement, human and non-human, as dependent on the infinitely variable activity of Nature rather than agency. Spinozist posthuman theory therefore presents a different lens for understanding and valuing children's play, movement and learning with objects and materials. Through Spinozist posthuman theory, learning and play are understood as activated through processes of sensitised improvisation, attunement, and movement with the material environment as part of it as put by Stuart Lester,

> Children's play, rather than being an exercise in progress towards autonomy and rationality (the adult common sense of play), becomes momentary spacetime in which life cannot be reduced to what has already been produced and marks the potential to create and work with difference. (Lester, 2020, p. 160)

Conclusion: An Ethico-aesthetic Paradigm

In this chapter I have discussed in detail the multiple considerations which comprise an ethico-aesthetic lens as produced through Spinozist Posthuman theory. In Chapter 3, I will examine how an ethico-aesthetic paradigm differs from the dominant pedagogical perspectives in ECEC of both Constructivism and Social Constructivism. A materials-focused approach to the literature will demonstrate how, although materials have been central to ECEC pedagogy since its inception, the paradigms and perspectives of 'active' learning have differed, each in turn with implications for how young children are understood.

Jonny is one of the first to approach the table and wants my help to create a structure. We stick a tall twig with clay to the table and bend it over to form an arch. We stick the other end to the table to make it stable. This structure gets repeated by Jonny while also deviating into smaller connections. Simon, (Jonny's twin) is working at the other end of the table on his own structure which he then wants to connect to Jonny's.

p. 73

Oran and Natalia chat excitedly in Polish. Oran wants to collaborate on a structure. He uses small lumps of clay stuck to the table to balance his structure which quickly grows vertically with a long piece balanced across like a see-saw. He shows his excitement by making sudden bursts of jumping moves careful not to topple his structure. Natalia works on her own piece which they then connect together through two long sticks touching both pieces. They want to be photographed in front of their combined work which Noreen (educator) does for them.

p. 74

Tomás is also working at the table, where he stays for almost the full hour. He has been watching Jonny's system of working by stabilising the structure and creates his own which he wants to connect to everyone else's. There is awareness of the delicacy of the structures, but surprise at how the clay fixes unlikely combinations. The main impetus is to use the linearity of the sticks to join with favoured friends' work. Permissions to join are given or not given, and so the request becomes an emotionally charged declaration of allegiance. Rain is also affecting the clay, loosening its 'glue'.

p. 75

The clay begins to spread over the table, forming small muddy pools and rivulets of brown water. This process is helped by Jane who gathers a little cup of water, filling it in the nearby bucket and spreads it over the clay. She is very reluctant to leave and remains outside at this activity as long as she possibly can. The connections become loosened with the addition of water.

p. 76

I try to 'rescue' as many of the structures as I can from toppling over and replace them on a small clean table for parents to see at home time. My intervention radically alters the structures, they now appear to be substantially less lively having been cleansed of the messiness of children and weather. The new configurations appear as hollow shells of the mornings vibrant and complex activity. I have drained the life from them by trying to make them 'presentable'.

CHAPTER 3

Material Matters

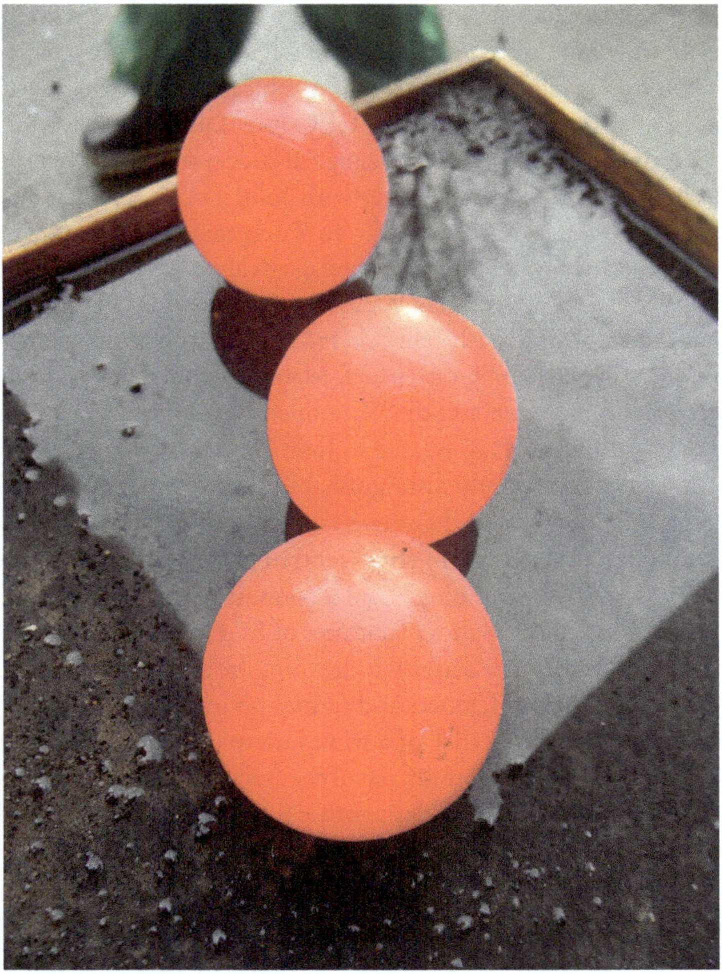

Figure 7: Learning Objects

Introduction: Learning Objects

It is of course widely acknowledged that 'early years education and care is inextricably linked with objects' (Jones et al., 2012, p. 1). Since antiquity, materials and objects and have been used as devices for designing and directing young children's learning through numerous pedagogical systems and philosophies. The term 'learning objects' describes the tangible materials which are ubiquitous in ECEC classrooms. In his analysis of the historical development of learning objects, Zuckermann (2006) categorises various movements in ECEC (see Table 3), each associated with learning objects based on pedagogical concepts and 'active learning' approaches to materials. Beginning with John Locke (1632–1704) and philosophical empiricism, according to Zuckerman 'learning by doing' was developed through three key pedagogical movements as follows; the 'Experimenting' movement focused on 'Construction and Design' and was related to Friedrich Froebel (1782–1852); the 'Intelligent Hand' movement focused on 'Conceptual Manipulation' related to Maria Montessori (1870–1952); and the 'Simplified Reality' movement was focused on 'Reality Role Play' related to John Dewey (1859–1952).

These categories are also distinguishable by their use of materials, their pedagogical emphasis, and their understanding of processes of learning. Each of them has in common: child-centred philosophy, developmental pedagogy, cognitive psychology, and a commitment to active learning. There is established throughout centuries of ECEC multiple methods of leading children through activity to learning from the manipulation of objects. Despite their differences and various philosophical positions, this acknowledges the importance of a wide variety of materials and objects within ECEC. However, within each of these systems, materials have been consistently considered as predominantly useful for the purposes of human advancement 'with the object rendered docile in the service of 'learning' from it' (MacRae, 2012, p. 123). This has established an approach to materials, which as Lenz Taguchi (2010) points out, results in an inevitable and fundamental separation between human/learner and the world where,

Table 3: Learning Objects, Adapted from Zuckerman (2006)

'Experimenting'	'Intelligent Hand'	'Simplified Reality'
FROEBEL (1782–1852)	**MONTESSORI** (1870–1952)	**JOHN DEWEY** (1859–1952).
Construction & Design	**Conceptual Manipulation**	**Reality Role Play**
Froebel Gifts	Montessori Materials	Baby Dolls
Paper Weaving	Shape Puzzles	Food Play
Pattern Blocks	Shape Sorting and Stacking	Household Play
Unit Blocks	Colour Matching	Kitchen Sets
LEGO® Bricks	Cuisenaire Rods®	Dress-up Costumes: Pilot, Chef, Doctor, Nurse
Lincoln Logs®	Number Tiles	Doll Houses
K'NEX®	Alphabet Blocks	Trains

> The world and matter is understood as important to interact with for learning to be constructed, it is basically, a "tool" and something passive, "out there" to construct knowledge about the world. (Lenz Taguchi, 2010, p. 46)

More recently, posthuman theorists point to new ways in which 'matter comes to matter' (Odegard, 2012) in early childhood classrooms, that extend understanding of materials and their value in education beyond (adult) directed or intentional learning programs. For example, Liz Jones and colleagues (2012) point out how particular objects chosen and loved by children can become 'imbued with children's everyday lives' (Jones et al., 2012, p. 4). A materialist perspective of ECEC may also bring to light those unnamed or less visible materials which also populate children's lives and classrooms but are missing from Zuckermann's categories listed above.

A multitude of materials move with children's everyday activity and are largely unaccounted for in developmental or cognitive pedagogical strategies and curriculum. Nevertheless, learning, movement and change also occurs through and with this universe of 'hidden' materials. Materials are part of children's everyday lives both indoor and out, in school and at home, and when attention is drawn to them they can be seen to contribute to children's rich experiencing of the world, both with and without adults, or trajectories of progress. However, certain materials are synonymous with ECEC and so to begin to examine the literature, the following section will trace the uses and understandings of 'natural materials' in ECEC.

> Both materials invite different sensations and body movements, even though both are approached via a paintbrush. Orla is definite about not liking seaweed once it has been established that this is in fact what is on the table. Christine asks, "what is it you don't like, is it the feel of it, the smell, the colour?", "The colour". A group of eight children have gathered, each works calmly, there is no urgency or clamour. The selection of stones is varied through colour, shape and size and allows enough differentiation to generate preferences. The seaweed is difficult to paint, its spring and slipperiness makes it difficult to attempt to cover any large area, but the paint goes on well and the change in colour from brown to bright blue is dramatic and easy to register instantly. The movement required is different, however some stones also prove difficult. Some stones move with the paint action, some don't. It is easy to mix paint on the stones, their surfaces accept the colour. The most striking aspect is how the act of painting onto the objects is absorbing, it slows bodies down substantially, it also slows down chatter and sharing, it invites an insularity that is undisturbed or separate from all other activity and busyness around. Several children spend long periods of time.

Natural Materials

Natural materials have long been a feature of early childhood education systems, most notably perhaps in the pioneering theories of Pestalozzi (1746–1827), Froebel (1782–1852), Steiner (1861–1925), Montessori (1870–1952), John Dewey (1859–1952) as well as Loris Malaguzzi (1920–1994) through the Reggio Emilia approach, and the numerous education systems that they have each influenced. Educators have understood the value of paying attention to natural forms and their innate complexity and beauty through various modes and practices, from drawing to imaginative play. Natural materials have been used widely across philosophically diverse educational methods spanning from the determinedly democratic, to practices where concepts of purity and perfection have been espoused.

Pestalozzi's method was founded on learning from primary contact with natural objects (such as shells and leaves) to develop observational skills and ultimately, autonomous critical thinking and reasoning. Pestalozzi's object lessons involved the relatively scientific, sensory exploration of various objects (Soëtard, 1994; Pestalozzi, 2008). Objects were named, described, and gradually complexified through a program of observation, drawing and dialogue between teacher and children so that a gradual progression toward reasoning might be achieved. According to Pestalozzi, 'sense impression of Nature is the only true foundation of human instruction because it is the only true foundation of human knowledge' (Pestalozzi, 2008, [1894], p. 200). Pestalozzi's pedagogical approach resonates strongly with Spinoza's contention that primary sensory experience builds both reason and knowledge.

Drawing was an important part of object theory, the purpose of which was to develop a personalised awareness of the complexities of simple forms which could gradually be built upon, and was closely linked to teaching measurement, mathematics and aesthetic appreciation so as to 'try to sharpen the child's eyes' (Pestalozzi, 2008, [1894], p. 331). Despite his pragmatic approach however, Pestalozzi's method did not provide a definitive bridge between theory and practice through a systematised teaching device, rather, it was open to adaptation and the varying preferred emphasis and styles of individual teachers and mothers, where Pestalozzi stated 'examine everything, keep what is good and if something better has come to fruition in your own minds, add it in truth and love to what I am trying to give you in truth and love in these pages' (Pestalozzi, cited in Soëtard, 1994, p. 6). While this openness to interpretation, and trust in parents and educators may have been a central part of its appeal and longevity, subsequent object lessons of the nineteenth century became more didactic, undoubtedly more closely attuned to the prevailing pedagogical systems of the times.

An influential later British adaptation of Pestalozzi's method was Elizabeth Mayo's 'Lessons on Objects' (1832), which itself was subsequently further adapted to eventually exchange Mayo's interpretation of the Pestalozzi method, from emphasis on engagement with tangible natural objects, to the use instead, of pictures of those natural objects. This of course denied the sensory tactile experience so important to Pestalozzi, however it ensured the desired regularity and uniformity of pedagogy particularly across the British colonies where they were implemented. Sengupta (2003) finds that the replacement of objects with pictures was also driven by the strong theological convictions of the British Christian colonisers, who equated fixations on objects with tendencies toward childish, primitive, and idolatry practices.

In sharp contrast to Pestalozzi's original method which encouraged mothers and teachers to develop their own compatible processes as they saw fit, these later adaptations provided replicable models for dialogue between children and teacher. This produced the rote learning effect of nineteenth century object lessons, satirised by Charles Dickens in 'Hard Times' (Dickens, 2003) (see, e.g. Chapter 2 'Murdering the Innocents'). This is poignantly remembered by educationalist Margaret McMillan, who describes her childhood memories of object lessons, which she associated with classroom cruelty and fear where children 'were filled with anxiety and distress' (McMillan [1927] in Nutbrown, Clough & Selbie, 2008, p. 45). Sengupta (2003) also points out that in these later object lessons, classification of objects was paramount, where the 'proper ordering' of the material world was applied in parallel, to language. Sengupta states that 'embedded in this popular pedagogic technique were powerful cultural and epistemological assumptions that were fundamentally informed by Britain's imperial identity' (Sengupta, 2003, p. 98). Object lessons developed in this way, were considered important devices for educating non-literate populations, both children and adults, 'for training what colonial officials thought of as 'childlike Indian minds' (Glover, 2005, p. 544). The discrimination of objects through ordering and language may well have built upon Pestalozzi's own clear preference for the use of natural objects, which he described as 'pure' (Glover, 2005).

The use of natural objects as pedagogical devices was also foundational to much more loving educational methods in the nineteenth century in Europe, also influenced by Pestalozzi. Froebel (1782–1852) visited

Pestalozzi's school in Switzerland and was deeply inspired by his methods and ideas. Froebel also understood nature as essential to the holistic education of the child and emphasised the links between play and learning, highlighting children's necessarily intense relationship with the objects and materials with which they play, where he wrote,

> The child would know himself why he loves this thing; he would know all its properties, its innermost nature, that he may learn to understand himself in his attachment. For this reason, the child examines the object on all sides; for this reason he tears and breaks it; for this reason he puts it in his mouth and bites it. We reprove the child for his naughtiness and foolishness; and yet he is wiser than we who reprove him. The child would know the inner nature of the thing. (Froebel, 1974, p. 73)

Froebel's pedagogical objects which he called 'gifts' consisted of specifically designed materials and objects to be introduced through a series of stages, largely made from natural materials including wood and wool. Using universal forms such as spheres and cubes encapsulated Froebel's educational philosophy based on a process of developing an 'ideal purity' (Froebel, 1974, p. 232; Pine, 1996, p. 91) always through play which Froebel stated as the 'purest' product of the child (Froebel, 1974, p. 55; Flannery Quinn, 2013, p. 2).

For Froebel, although his philosophy was (as of its time) deeply Christian, it was also an essentially pantheistic philosophy which emphasised the interconnections between things, both animate and inanimate. Froebel's philosophy resonates with contemporary concerns for environment and for those interested in sensory modes of learning. It has been suggested that Froebel's philosophy was feasibly influenced by his early experiences as both a forester and mineralogist (Provenzo, 2009) and that his progressive theories describe a humble acknowledgement of humanities equality with all surrounding things within the environment, both living and non-living, which aligns strongly with Spinoza's monism. Froebel wrote that,

> This instruction is conducted not so much in accordance with the nature of man as in accordance with the fixed, clear laws that lie in the nature of things, and more particularly the laws to which man and things are equally subject. (Froebel, 1974, p. 95)

Other spiritually leaning educational philosophies (which are still widely in use today) also tend to espouse a trajectory towards 'purity' using natural learning materials, most notably those of Steiner (1861–1925) and Montessori. Steiner's educational beliefs which he named 'anthroposophy' (human wisdom) rely on an aesthetic understanding of both children and nature to the exclusion of all things other than those which are naturally derived. Digital technology, plastic and any other non-natural tools and materials are thus strictly excluded from Steiner learning environments both inside and out. Steiner play and learning objects are also aesthetically pleasing, open-ended and multifunctional to promote creativity.

Montessori's approach also held a preference for natural materials based on her educational philosophy of 'Cosmic Education' (Grazzini, 2013). For Montessori there is 'the inorganic world which is ecologically linked in innumerable ways with the biosphere which, in turn, is linked with human beings or the psycho-sphere' (Grazzini, 2013, p. 108). In this way Montessori envisaged complex interconnections and relationships at play whereby the child, using their 'inner' sensibilities, selects developmentally appropriate, aesthetically pleasing (natural) materials with which to work and play. However for Montessori, within this learning scenario 'the important factor is not the external object, but the internal action of the soul' (Montessori, 2014, p. 69), exposing the fundamental prioritisation of human development above 'matter', despite the understanding of profound ecological (and 'cosmic') connections.

Relational pedagogies (Papatheodorou & Moyles, 2009) and social constructivist theories prioritise the importance of human relationships within processes of learning. However, despite commitments to understanding the connections between children and their material environments within each of these child-centred pedagogical approaches, posthuman and new materialist theorists find an over-riding anthropocentricism which misrepresents the relationship between humanity and the material world (Barad, 2007; Bennett, 2010; Braidotti, 2013; Coole & Frost, 2010; Dolphijn & Van der Tuin, 2012). Lenz Taguchi argues that such pedagogies,

> do not manage to include in their equations the material world as an agentic producer of meaning. They show in their writings that the material and the body are

> merely discursive in these views of learning, and remain passive objects upon which discourse is inscribed. (Lenz Taguchi, 2010, p. 46)

This, it is argued, produces power structures and divisions between humanity, the material world and nature, with which, for posthuman theorists, humans are intimately entangled (Barad, 2007). Lenz Taguchi suggests that instead 'as humans we must understand ourselves as material objects of the world, just as any other beings and matter' (Lenz Taguchi, 2010, p. 47).

Much of the posthuman, new materialist, and feminist ECEC research and practice occurs in the theorisation of the quiet spaces of children's small everyday interactions with all kinds of materials which attract children's attention, which may or may not be 'natural'. Paulina Rautio explains that human autotelic behaviours, or those that occur without any apparent meaning or purpose but simply to enjoy experiencing materials, demonstrate a kind of being lost in the moment, or flow (albeit one that lacks the ambition and future focus of what Csikszentmihalyi's flow (1997) has come to represent in education and business models for example). This state can be read as not entirely driven by human intent, but also as necessarily motivated by material circumstances (Rautio, 2013, p. 7). Rautio notes how when children carry stones in their pockets for example, this simple and overlooked activity, as one of many, may also be read as a politically inflected practice whereby children and nature may become reenvisaged, where,

> for children, intra-action with stones provides a political niche: a virtually irrelevant material (unless used to break windows or causing washing machines to bread down) lends itself to be carried, collected, moved, exchanged, valued and worked with through means that children possess, on their own, without adult help supervision or acceptance. When we carry stones, for no particular reason, we engage with a practice that celebrates also being in the present rather than only knowing for the future. (Rautio, 2013, p. 12)

Similar interests in processes of tacit knowledge building through bodily sensation and hand movements are explored by MacRae (2020) when she uses posthuman theories and slowed down filmed data, to facilitate her thinking about children playing with sand. MacRae's research finds that 'slowed film of hands in motion draws our attention away from words, towards a (re)cognition of a sensed intelligence' (MacRae, 2020,

p. 90). The approach of de-centring the child in visual data analysis such as this was introduced by Hultman and Lenz Taguchi (2010) who previously used a photograph of a child playing (also with sand) to examine how diverting the 'habitual anthropocentric gaze' in research analysis of visual data has the effect of understanding 'the child as emergent in a relational field where non-human forces are equally at play in constituting children's becomings' (Hultman & Lenz Taguchi, 2010, p. 525).

Pacini-Ketchabaw, Kind and Kocher (2017) also explore natural materials such as clay and charcoal for example through posthuman, new materialist research and practice. Clay is theorised through movement with and against children in what they call an 'ecology of practices' (Stengers, 2005) through which children come to understand themselves as belonging, as part of the world, and always in relation to the materials they encounter.

> The responses of clay and child are never predictable, because ecologies of practice are always emergent. Movements are not intentionally performed: they emerge. Clay responds to children's movements as they work with it. Yet sometimes it resists and refuses to stay still in one shape. It is impossible though, to predict these resistances. (Pacini-Ketchabaw et al., 2017, p. 65)

Similarly, when working experimentally with charcoal Pacini-Ketchabaw and colleagues (2017) discuss the surprisingly destructive and disruptive qualities of the material. Charcoal led children to blacken their hands, bodies, faces and classroom, and so to experience the intensity of 'risky' learning and responsibilities (Pacini-Ketchabaw et al., 2017, p. 43). This in turn led adults and children together 'to rupture the romance of experimentation, of the beautiful, of the exotic' and to follow Atkinson when he writes that 'allowing oneself to become undone is a crucial condition for learning' (Atkinson, 2011 p. 165 in Pacini-Ketchabaw et al., 2017, p. 40).

Rooney's (2019) posthuman, new materialist ECEC theorising is also drawn towards sticks, but the more common, uncharred kind. Children's universal attraction to sticks and twigs, (like stones) gathered haphazardly on outdoor walks, are discussed, where Rooney points out how children perceive them as living things (Rooney, 2019, p. 47). Vygotsky also previously noted, in developmental psychology terms, how children become open to transforming found objects such as sticks into their lively games and imaginative play, where he wrote,

> A child who sits astride a stick and pretends to be riding a horse; a little girl who plays with a doll and imagines she is its mother; a boy who in his games becomes a pirate, a soldier, or a sailor, all these children at play represent examples of the most authentic, truest creativity. Everyone knows what an enormous role imitation plays in children's play. A child's play very often is just an echo of what he saw and heard adults do; nevertheless, these elements of his previous experience are never merely reproduced in play in exactly the way they occurred in reality. A child's play is not simply a reproduction of what he has experienced, but a creative reworking of the impressions he has acquired. (Vygotsky, 1990, p. 11)

While developmental psychology is interested in how children may be enamoured of adults in their drive to progress toward becoming them albeit through playful and imaginative means, Rooney on the other hand, through a posthuman lens, notices how children also bring attention to sticks as living things, in both animist ways as described by Vygotsky, but also in realist ways. For example, she explains how children pay attention to sticks as homes to small creatures such as spiders, or provide surfaces for lichen and plants, and sometimes refer to delicate peal-able bark as 'skin'. Rooney also notices how sticks bring children toward braver explorations of the world where they are used instinctively as 'prods' easing children toward uncertain places or things they may be curious or nervous about, allowing an 'arms-length' extension to the child's body. In these ways, without being taught how to, children find for themselves processes of working and being with materials which enable much more than mimicry of adults.

> The table rapidly descended into quite a chaotic mess. The powder paint dust spread quickly onto clothing, shoes, table, and ground … it seemed to be everywhere very quickly. Water was being mixed into the dust at different rates, some pots produced thick gloopy mixtures, but most had too much water and a lot of brightly coloured spills ensued. A particularly violent gust of wind lifted several of the cardboard sheets on the table knocking over almost full bowls of water, creating pools of liquid on the table and piles of card I had set up. No-one seemed particularly interested in painting. The main activity was mixing, stirring, pouring, sprinkling, and searching for more powder and liquid to add.

Learning Environments

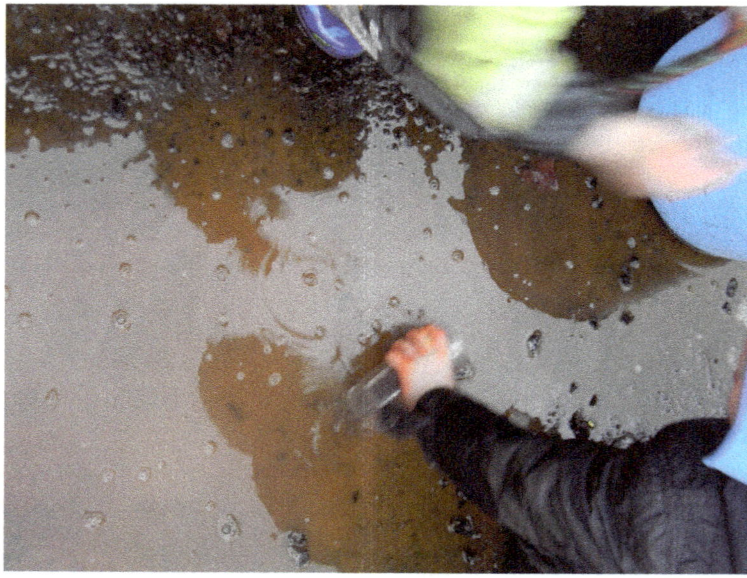

Figure 8: Learning Environments

Throughout the history of ECEC, theorists have found early childhood environments to be more than worthy of consideration in relation to young children's experiences of learning. The aesthetics and organisation of classrooms for example, were, and remain, fundamental to many pedagogical approaches, distinguishing one from the other and emphasising unique philosophical values. Multiple ECEC pedagogical approaches concur with the current Irish National Curriculum Framework, Aistear, which considers the learning environment as integral to young children's modes of learning. For example, John Dewey's educational philosophy has been significantly influential in terms of ECEC environments and classrooms (Zuckerman, 2006). Dewey stated,

> I believe that education, therefore, is a process of living and not a preparation for future living. I believe that the school must represent present life – life as real and

> vital to the child as that which he carries on in the home, in the neighbourhood, or on the play-ground. (Dewey, 1897, sec. 2)

Dewey believed that 'real life' provides excellent learning materials and objects once these 'everyday' objects are of the child's scale. Today, this has created classrooms filled with miniaturised 'real' objects such as cookers and kitchen accessories as well as dressing up uniforms from 'real' adult jobs such as nurse or chef.

Montessori also considered child-scale as an important factor for children to feel 'at home' within carefully designed school classrooms. Montessori's child-sized chair is firmly associated with her philosophical approach and is now standard within the majority of educational settings for young children (Bone, 2019). For Montessori, like many other child-centred pedagogical approaches, child-centred learning environments are understood to support children's independent exploration and learning, with the aim of promoting competency and confidence in children as they navigate their classroom spaces and ultimately the wider world (Pope Edwards, 2002, 2003; Montessori, 2014).

In the Reggio Emilia approach the environment is considered to be the 'third teacher' (Tarr, 2001) and thus a crucial support to the human teachers in the classroom, where specific criteria are fundamental to the design aesthetic and layout. For example, horizontality, transparency, and flexibility of indoor spaces are all important considerations where,

> The school environment must lend itself to manipulation and transformation by adults and children alike, and be open to different ways of use. The school should be able to change during the day and during the year to be continuously modelled and redesigned as a result of the experimentation of children and teachers. (Ceppi & Zini, 1998, p. 38)

The work of biologist and anthropologist Gregory Bateson (Bateson, 1978, 1985) was influential in the philosophical development of the Reggio Emilia approach, particularly Bateson's conceptualisation of aesthetics (Vecchi, Chieli, & Reggio Children, 2008, p. 138). Through this influence Reggio educators value the relational and ecological importance of environments in terms of children's learning and creative capacities, so that

Reggio classrooms are now world renowned, and made distinctive by their impressive aesthetic emphasis (Ceppi & Zini, 1998). Loris Malaguzzi wrote,

> Here we consider the environment to be an essential constituent of any theoretical or political research in education. We hold to be equally valuable the relationality of the environment, its capacity for harmonious coexistence, and its highly important forms and functions. Moreover we place enormous value on the role of the environment as a motivating and animating force in creating spaces for relations, options, and emotional and cognitive situations that produce a sense of well-being and security. It has been said that the environment should act as a kind of aquarium which reflects the ideas, ethics, attitudes and culture of the people who live in it. This is what we are working toward. (Malaguzzi, 1997, p. 40)

The focus on the learning environment as an aesthetic entity relies heavily on nature as visible and active within Reggio schools and on natural elements such as light to enhance the atmosphere of the space (Ceppi & Zini, 1998). Pedagogical engagements with the changeability of natural elements such as seasonality, weather, animal, and plant-life for example are emphasised to deepen children's connection to nature.

Beginning with Froebel's term 'kindergarten' (child's garden) the valuing of the connection to nature is accentuated in ECEC above all other levels of education however, as pointed out by Osgood (2019), the enabling learning environment within ECEC is,

> Enabling only to the extent that adult educators make it so through their human endeavours; the framework prompts educators to consider how they can use the environment, organize and place material resources to optimize child development; the emphasis is entirely anthropocentric. (Osgood, 2019, p. 113)

Further, many ECEC philosophies are also founded on uncritical understandings of nature as a consistently positive entity that is a necessary good for children to experience, particularly through the movement of 'returning childhood to nature' (Louv, 2005). As pointed out by many new materialist and posthuman theorists (Taylor, 2013; Taylor & Pacini-Ketchabaw, 2019; Trafí-Prats, 2017) this overlooks issues of ecological and environmental degradation and injustice as the 'real world' which children both live in and are to inherit. The drive to 'return' to nature rather reinforces a modernist nature/culture binary where nature is perceived as exterior, static, passive and therefore separate from children and humanity in general (Blenkinsop et al., 2018). Posthuman theorists point out that this obscures the fact that 'for some children who live in threatened and threatening places, the prospect of spending time outside is not a positive one' (Trafí-Prats, 2017, p. 327). Further, Malone (2019) states that over one billion people on the planet currently live in slum conditions where children are,

> exposed to a range of risks in their precarious environment: polluted air, dirty water, traffic accidents, flooding, potential landslides, forest degradation and the impact of lack of sanitation, and the stench of garbage surrounding their homes. (Malone, 2019, p. 8)

The recent global pandemic which saw the enforcement of, and compliance with stay at home 'lockdowns' world-wide further reinforces the idea that venturing outdoors, however counter-intuitive, may be risky. The drive to insist on the benefits of nature further excludes and overlooks consideration of children for whom natural materials and environments, through illness or additional needs for example, are problematic. The concept of 'ChildhoodNature' has emerged in recent years as a response to the awareness of children's complex relations with natural environments and attempts to acknowledge these real-world circumstances within pedagogical systems.

ChildhoodNature

Across the fields of education, sociology, children's geographies, environmental education and activism amongst others, researchers and theorists are confronting the idea that children are always already part of nature and it's instability, complexity and flux, and in close relation to the difficult and urgent challenges presented by the Anthropocene (Crutzen, 2006; Crutzen & Stoermer, 2000). This has produced important and insightful research and pedagogical practices which forefront the complex relations between children and the geo-bio-techno-social factors and forces which intimately impact them and their multiple environments (Rautio & Jokinen, 2015; Pacini-Ketchabaw et al., 2016; Trafí-Prats, 2017; Masny, 2018; Malone, 2019; Taylor & Pacini-Ketchabaw, 2019).

The concept of ChildhoodNature arises as a reaction to long entrenched and persistent assumptions of human exceptionalism, which, many believe have been perpetuated through systems and practices of education (Rotas, 2015; Snaza et al., 2014; Snaza & Weaver, 2016; Taylor & Hughes, 2016). As clarified by environmental education theorist Karen Malone (2019), these assumptions are namely; that humans are superior to all other life forms and have rights above all else; that humans have individual power to control their own futures and fortunes; that nature is an endless resource for human use; and that the human story is fundamentally about economic and technological progress. Through her environmental education research spanning three decades, Malone finds alternatives which are based in an ecological paradigm which proposes that,

> (1) Humans may be exceptional species in some respects; however, they still depend upon other life forms for their survival; (2) human affairs are influenced by social processes; however, they are also influenced by the biophysical environment which often reacts to human activities; (3) the biophysical environment imposes constraints upon human affairs (e.g., human health and survival are possible only under certain environmental conditions); and (4) no matter how inventive humans may be, their science and technology cannot repeal ecological principles; there are limits to the economic growth of human societies. (Malone, 2019, p. 14)

ChildhoodNature considers the fundamental interconnections and often messy shared vulnerabilities between nature, children, and learning environments and understands that much of the complexity of the relation becomes evident during the unpicking of prior assumptions and understandings of 'Nature'. As put by Masny 'creating the concept of childhoodnature-as-one invites a reading of blurred boundaries of childhood and nature but also unpredictability, complexity, and messiness' (Masny, 2018, p. 6).

Increasingly, there are compelling examples of research and practices which explore and extend the potential and implications of the concept of ChildhoodNature and children in relation to materials, place, and other species. For example, Rautio and Jokinen's research on children's relation to 'more than human worlds' while playing in snow piles in Finland become the material and conceptual anchor to explore how,

> When snow, children, woolly mittens, scarves, boots, snot, rocks, ice, frost, dark nights, and lampposts to name but a few partaking elements convene, they produce a shared deterritorialization. As a result, the children in the midst can be thought of as if freed from being viewed as individual representatives of a developmental phase, freed from being viewed as "growing up," and freed from one's doings viewed as "meaning" something other than what sustains the activity. (Rautio & Jokinen, 2015, p. 2)

Further, multispecies ethnographic research reveals new understandings of the significance of children's co-evolving relationships with animals, birds and insects (see, e.g. Haraway, 2016; Hohti & Osgood, 2020; Hohti & Tammi, 2019; Kummen, 2019; Rautio, 2019; Schulte, 2019) while questions of relationship to place in which issues of inclusion, colonialism and diversity are also examined under the umbrella concept of ChildhoodNature (Knight, 2019; Rotas, 2015, 2019; Trafí-Prats, 2017).

Complex, contemporary, and 'impure' materials are also considered by posthuman and new materialist researchers in relation to children's processes of learning and being in the world. 'Junk' or recycled waste materials for example, are explored theoretically to generate new knowledges and understandings of children and their relationship with nature. Some of these materials are discussed in the following section on 'open-ended' materials.

Marcus was particularly interested in mixing and stirring. From his movements with the paint and tools it is clear to educators, from what they know about him, he is using his love of cooking at home with his parents. He stays at the table for the full hour, using the powder like seasoning, carefully adding precise amounts to the bowl of liquid. The fluorescent powder paint I have brought is very attractive when it floats on top of murky colours. His blue mittens become soaked in soupy paint.

Open-Ended Materials

'Open-ended' materials in ECEC are understood as those materials which are endlessly adaptable to children's inventiveness and imagination. Aistear, the Irish Early Childhood Curriculum Framework advocates that open-ended materials and resources be offered to children to support creativity and exploration (NCCA, 2009, p. 11). This section discusses a sample range of open-ended materials and their treatment through posthuman theory in the literature.

Junk Materials and Glitter

Improvements in environmental awareness have led to an increase in the use of recycled materials in education settings. Of course, for decades, packaging waste such as cardboard boxes have been reimagined by children through creative art and play activities, however in posthuman, feminist new materialist, ChildhoodNature, and arts-based research, these practices are also being taken seriously theoretically, as part of the larger ongoing social concerns regarding management and use of waste products in relation to children and education. In ECEC in particular the 'Remida' of Reggio Emilia (Reggio Children, 2005) have been influential in this regard. Remida centres store, grade, collect and distribute waste materials from local industries such as clean paper, plastics, card, and fabrics. In the Republic of Ireland the first such centre was the Travellers Resource Warehouse in Dublin, set up in 1989 (Fay & McCabe, 2015). Currently there are two other such centres; 'Re-create' in Dublin, operates professionally to supply education settings with recycled materials, as well as offering professional creative training workshops. The Connaught Creative Resource Centre was run and maintained by service users of Western Care for almost twenty years. Western Care is part of the national health system which is responsible for providing working opportunities for adults with intellectual disabilities and has generated a strong community around this not-for-profit facility (it is this centre which is local to the research site school). Unfortunately, this facility is now closed.

Odegaard and Rossholt (2016) situated their research in one such Remida in Norway. They created a 'Black Box' space within the centre where children visited and played with recycled materials curated by the artists and researchers. The research found that posthuman theorising and methodology facilitates fore fronting the movements of children and materials together. Having lost their previous association and function through the process of recycling, the materials potential for creative use by children appears inexhaustible. Odegaard and Rossholt look to MacRae's (2011) earlier research with children and junk materials, which works with Foucault's use of the term heterotopia as 'a space of difference' (MacRae, 2011), or that which resists interpretation and representation. MacRae finds that this resistance, which is facilitated by junk materials, encourages new, unexpected, intuitive connections to be made, and also enabled her to see this at work through other art processes such as drawing. MacRae notes that,

> a thing that had registered as formless, whether a junk model or a mark on a page, took on new value (...) This ability to build new kinds of relationships with objects, objects that are lively and have a life of their own, can be valued as a different way of thinking and looking at the world. (MacRae, 2011, p. 111)

Carefully recycled materials used for the purposes of creative activity can however become 're-contaminated' through artistic processes. Card gets covered in drippy paint or stuck to plastics with tape, staples, and string, to be eventually returned sticky, mixed up and crumpled, to landfill, demonstrating how the upbeat mantras of using recycled 'junk' materials in art education can conceal less virtuous realities.

Other theorists have taken up the complex movement and trails of materials beyond their brief encounters with children and artists in homes, studios, and classrooms. Osgood (2019) for example, explores the materiality of glitter which is closely associated with children's creative art practices and ECEC classroom environments, declaring that in wider society it is 'everywhere'. Osgood asks 'not just what it is or what it comes to symbolise in a discursive sense but materially how it functions, mutates, contaminates, circulates and scatters' (Osgood, 2019, p. 118). Osgood traces the recent realisation of the environmental impact of glitter and notes how a wave of ECEC settings have decided to ban its use on environmental grounds. Osgood also points out however how the impact of the search for more 'natural' alternatives have produced other equally complex and dark realities (e.g. using child labour in mica mines in India (Bhalla, Chandran & Nagarai,

2016)). Thus tracing the materiality of glitter aims to 'challenge habitual ways of thinking and being in early childhood' and finds that 'making space to consider glitter as generative can lead to investigations into uncharted territories and so heighten our worldly sensibilities' (Osgood, 2019, p. 131).

Fabric

Other posthuman theorists have found similar strategies of following materials to be productive in revealing new understandings about children's ways of learning and being. MacRae for example has her attention drawn by a red blanket in an outdoor 'rough and tumble' play event between boys in an ECEC setting. MacRae uses the concept of the 'minor gesture' (Manning, 2016) 'as a way to resist more normative accounts of play, where play is coupled to cognitive and social stages of development' (MacRae, 2019, p. 1). The red blanket becomes caught up in the playful movements of the children which leads MacRae to reconceptualise play as a way of being in the world (MacRae, 2019, p. 1) rather than a practice of mastery (of materials) or mimicry (of adults), or explainable on a developmental scale. Manning's concept of the minor gesture works to enable the exploration of play as it unfolds, which in turn leads to a closer form of '*care for the event,* by giving it more fully our attention. This allows us to hover over its indeterminate character, rather than using it as a retrospective explanation' (MacRae, 2019, p. 5). MacRae uses video filming to gather data, which also allows her to slow down both the film and her own approach to it, and pay attention to how it helps her as participant researcher 'to think and act, rather than setting out to attribute meaning to children's actions' (MacRae, 2019, p. 6). Focus on the bodily materiality of the event, initially through the attention to the red blanket the children are enjoying moving with, but also other materials they collide with in the environment, helps MacRae to avoid the anthropocentric gaze (Hultman & Lenz Taguchi, 2010) and to think differently about the event as it unfolds. Attaching the concept of the minor gesture to the red blanket play event produces new possibilities for understanding play as an act of sensing, or a bodily way of knowing and being in the world with others. Kind and Argent (2019) also find that following the movements of children and fabric generates various forms of choreography. In this case they work in an indoor atelier or studio space that has been specifically curated, where,

> The studio is a fabricated space; that is, it is a carefully composed, curated and created space. It is not merely a background to children's experimentations or a container for art explorations but an emergent space itself always in the making. As a curated space, the studio brings different elements into relation with each other so that they touch, provoke, intra-act and encounter each other and create previously unrealised possibilities. (Kind & Argent, 2019, p. 35)

The fabric in this cared for space, produces possibilities for artistic experiences that emphasise touch and movement, which envisages the fabric as entering into play. The fabric evades form, rather it fluidly shifts through multiple forms in response to the movements around it. Kind and Argent note that their fabric activity in the studio space generates a new arena for thinking about children's art practices, where often they are framed and valued as either process or product. Here however, fabricating or making with a material that refuses to be fixed or 'finished' creates opportunities for unexpected play and movement that for a while moves into the theatricality of an improvised game devised by the children. Kind and Argent find that 'in the intertwining, in the play of making, there is a mutual co-composition' (Kind & Argent, 2019, p. 41).

Back inside, after lunchtime, some children choose to work in the art area. An idea to build a structure spreads among three children who each work on their own designs with help when they ask for it. Negotiation of sellotape and pieces of white card help to materialise their structures, one a triangular tent shape, another a tent shape but with end sections for doors that open and close and the third is a square shape. During the work the sun beams in low to the ground and creates exciting shadows of hair and sellotape and hands working which two of the children notice and play with for a little while.

Paper: Drawing and Painting

Children's drawing as both process and product, have long been valued within the fields of psychology and pedagogy for relaying information to adults about what, how and when children think, or, as 'windows' into children's knowable minds (MacRae, 2008). Drawing has been considered as indicative of cognitive development, as moving through definable stages, from scribbling through to visual realism. As such, analysis of children's drawing has also been used to 'understand the progressive nature of knowledge itself' (MacRae, 2008). This has produced a normative course of development and maturation that is codified and interpretable, for example, by locating recognisable evidence of particular schemata in children's drawings, which are considered as a form of 'universal language used by all children as they grow' (Knight, 2013, p. 255). The dominance of this understanding has been underpinned by the popularised interpretations of Piaget's learning theory as discussed previously, in which the child is characterised as moving from sensory-motor (bodily) stage through a gradually progressive sequence toward the operational (cognitive) stage. This encapsulates learning development as moving progressively away from bodily or sensory knowledge, toward the more valued capacity for abstract thought,

> Although the infant starts to know the world by actively engaging with objects, such knowledge evolves progressively, so that ultimately the object that was initially manipulated by the child's body is constructed through rational thinking. For Piaget, once the child is able to think operationally, the body is no longer important and the object ceases to exist out there. The child's drawing of an object for Piaget, then, indicates the degree to which that individual is able to conceptually produce the object as an object of thought. (MacRae, 2008, p. 276)

Piaget's (1971) theories on pattern in cognition were further extended by Athey (1990) who described a number of definable schema, for example 'Dynamic Circular', 'Dynamic Vertical' 'Enveloping and Containing Space', 'Going over and Under' (Athey, 1990). These schemas are subsequently traced through all modes simultaneously so that the practice of mapping recognisable schema in drawing is also applied across children's interests, movements, play and other creative work. However, as pointed out by de Rijke (2019),

> Schemas are both visually and physically predetermined, carrying the assumption that all children, whatever the diversity of their personal, cultural, social, physical or aesthetic circumstances, will 'fit' somehow (or adults will find a fit) and thus – conveniently enough – the children will be testable by those measures. (de Rijke, 2019, p. 159)

Even if schema are not used as a method of measurement or assessment, as defined and recognisable patterns of behaviour (Nutbrown, 1994) they are nevertheless encouraged as a means for adults to construct further learning possibilities for individual children. Although this may appear useful on some levels, it nevertheless supports a focus on comprehensible 'behaviours' in children, which in turn reinforces the idea of children as users and producers of simplified and knowable ways of being and knowing (as noted by Knight above).

Adaptations of Piaget's stage based learning theories have of course been much criticised (Aslanian, 2018), particularly since the rise in popularity of Vygotsky's (1978b) social constructivism which considers the child's social environment to be influential in processes of learning. Social constructivist pedagogy considers children's meaning making through conversation and narration during process of drawing to be of importance. For example, drawing in Reggio Emilia is considered to be one of children's 'hundred languages' (Malaguzzi, 1997) where the process of drawing makes visible, complex discursive and social meaning making amongst children. The subsequent evaluation of drawing as significant in its capacity to support the expression and generation of meaning, learning, and understanding for and of children, again appears to prioritise cognitive outcomes over bodily forms of knowledge building. However, drawing also generates scribbles, where meaning and cognitive value are confounded. Scribble has been scrutinised within the fields of psychology and pedagogy in order to impose or generate meaning and as a result of its resistance (to meaning), has been consigned to the lower orders of 'sensory motor', 'babbling' and 'pre-writing' stages of development in children (Tarr, 1990; de Rijke, 2019). However, as a domain of both young children and artists (see the work of Cy Twombly for example), much more of interest is to be found in scribble, when a less hierarchical, more artistic, and philosophical perspective is applied,

> Scribbles, as evidenced by the fact that they are nearly always thrown away, resist 'being-there' as they are tracings of 'becoming' (…) The line takes time and IS time as a temporal trace; thus, scribble is a form of 'becoming', or growth rather than development, and as such, it remains unfinished, always. (de Rijke, 2019, p. 173)

Congruous with the idea of 'becoming' and growth rather than development, Piaget's (1952) earlier work had focused on the child as biological, material organism, where he states, 'the organism is a cycle of physico-chemical and kinetic processes which, in constant relation to the environment, are engendered by each other' (Piaget, 1952, p. 5). For Piaget, drawing was also materially focused, in that the environmental, biological, and bodily processes at work in children's drawing, makes the interconnections visible. However, locating scribbling in a bodily phase where the optimum trajectory is toward cognitive abstraction has a devaluing effect. De Rijlke notes that other early analysers of children's drawing, such as Rhoda Kellog, 'admitted that her study of over 100,000 drawings and paintings made by children age two to four can 'prove' nothing but that 'all human activity has unity with the physical universe' (Kellog, 1959, p. 124, in de Rijlke 2019, p. 159). These interesting findings however have largely been subsumed by the prioritisation of 'the biological processes of aging, the mechanisms of learning, cognitive, social, emotional change or adaptation' which, de Rijke warns when 'taken too literally, they become a kind of trap' (de Rijke, 2019, p. 170).

In posthuman and new materialist theorising, the performative, material, temporal, affective and contextual components in children's drawing and artmaking are all considered as potentially productive of new perspectives. In her research on intergenerational drawing methodologies for example, Knight (2013) thinks about children's drawings as related to time rather than stage,

> Each time a child draws, they produce a drawing in reaction to what is occurring – physically through materials, environment, body function, and metaphysically through thoughts and mood, at that moment. Scrutiny of drawings should not therefore

> attempt to determine, fix, indicate a child's developmental or growth 'stage'; rather, drawings should be thought of as momentary pauses, a momentary stillness, not a cemented icon of proof of some predetermined intellectual achievement. (Knight, 2013, p. 255)

This is a liberating understanding of art making practices as mobile, temporal assemblages of material, discursive, environmental, and bodily elements. It also acknowledges that art methodologies are set in both real time and 'in the time of art – a temporal dimension in which one is in dialogue with both 'what is no longer possible' and what has not yet been done, with resources from objects, traditions, ideas and waste distributed – sinking into and emerging from time' (Fuller, 2008, p. 6).

Davies (2014a) thinks with Spinoza's concept of affect in drawing, painting, and telling stories while art making over a number of years with a young child, a neighbour she takes care of in her home. Through the lens of affect, Davies is interested in how the art making processes of adult and child avoid categorisation based on age, but rather focuses on affects as material (physical, chemical, and metaphysical) forces that 'pass between one being and another creating a change of state in which something new might be generated' (Davies, 2014b, p. 11). This potential for newness and surprise that is essential to art, is made available (to both adult and child) when attention is paid to the Deleuzian concept of 'lines of assent and descent' (Davies, 2014a). These are strongly connected to affect, where 'making art is a complex dance between lines of descent (making life coherent and predictable) and ascent (opening up to the new and unexpected)' (Davies, 2014b, p. 12).

Marmé Thompson (2019) is also interested in postdevelopmental approaches to children's drawing where she explores an 'understanding of the process of art-making in early childhood as a microcosm of the process that artists of any age engage, rather than a biologically conditioned and psychologically constrained process of constructing images' (Marmé Thompson, 2019, p. 138). Marmé Thompson finds that children's drawings as objects, are small components of the larger experience from which they emerge, in other words, that they do not reveal the entire complexity of the circumstances of their construction. Drawing for artist and child is understood to be 'infinitely responsive and collaborative, assembling bits and fragments of experience in an improvisational process that is as unpredictable as it is astonishing' (Marmé Thompson, 2019, p. 138).

> At the table, painting of pictures is ongoing on the smaller pieces of paper. Connections and meanings are assigned. Suzanne (child) tells Iris (educator) she has made grey like the sky and we hold her painting up to the sky. Jonny spends time making detailed looped shapes and filling them with different shades of blue. He works quietly. Oran becomes very excited by pouring a lot of blue onto the table making shiny puddles of paint to completely cover a paintbrush. Eric moves from the nearby water pipes to pour water into the blue paint palette and Diana is very happy moving between areas with a stick, a long strip of paper and a wad of tissue testing the movement of the paint by rubbing, scraping, dipping, and chatting happily as she works, often calling 'look at this!'.

Digital Media

Producing drawing that is 'responsive', 'improvisational' and 'astonishing' as suggested by Marmé Thompson (2019) above, may be dependent on the material or medium involved. Young children's use of digital media for drawing is increasingly of interest in research, particularly given the rapidly proliferating availability of digital media, and the pervasive quantity of digitally produced imagery in children's everyday lives (Alliance for Children, 2004). Envisaging the creative possibilities of digital media may be coloured by adult's preferences or anxieties around the highly commodified and mediated nature of the particular media form. In her study on introducing iPads in ECEC for example, Knight found that,

> We became aware of the powerful emotions the public has around introducing digital media such as iPads to the very young and how these emotions seem to circulate around the ethics of exposure, the cognitive impacts on 'natural' development, social impact and the perceived threat to 'real' play. (Knight, 2018, p. 136)

Digital media challenge the perceived 'purity' of more established ECEC art materials and toys, but they also present concerns surrounding the possible limitations of processes which are deemed to be inherently creative. However, all materials present specific parameters which could be perceived as restrictive. To explore this in relation to the perception of digital media, Kucirkova and Sakr (2015) generated a comparative study between crayons, iPads, collage, and a PC in one 3 year old child's creative practice at home, supported by her father. While this research focused on text making practices as well as drawing, it found that both digital and non-digital materials each 'carry a distinct creative potential' which 'has implications for how we support early childhood creativity' (Kucirkova & Sakr, 2015, p. 59). Although accepted as part of everyday lives of children and the growing acceptance of technology for educational purposes, inconsistencies remain in education toward young children's use of digital media. Knight (2018) finds that contrary to adult reservations around the use of digital media in early childhood or ideas that more traditional art materials may be 'under threat', digital media do not overwhelm children's desire to use low-tech materials where, in her study she found that, when given opportunities 'children found ways to merge their paper and digital art in interesting ways' (Knight, 2018, p. 146). Knight states that,

> a child's drawing and writing skills are not tied to particular material objects or procedures. Different objects including paper, pencils, iPads, fingers, glass, binary coding, assemblages and rhizomes collectively and complimentarily nurture the gross and fine motor skills needed for writing and drawing. (Knight, 2018, p. 147)

Knight's core concept of 'digital aesthetics' also relies on a focus on affect and multidimensionality in relation to children's engagement with art and art producing materials. Knight works with Masney's (2006) Deleuzian understanding of literacies as being grounded in desire, transformation, and connection with the world,

> The desiring machines of child, hand, eye, pencil, paper, connect with random singularities of, ideas, thoughts, concepts during drawing (...) Rather than constructing their own knowledge about the world, a child extracts already existing referents from the cosmos to make connections about/to the world, to things experienced, known, conceptualised, imagined. (Knight, 2009, p. 54)

This analysis aligns clearly and closely with Spinoza's theories of learning where experience is uniquely built upon by each individual learner to create meaningful connections and to deepen understanding. Knight's study with iPads explored the integration of technology into children's art processes, showing how they afforded complex and interesting merging of otherwise distinct practices such as drawing, photography and painting. Knight finds that careful and critical use of digital technologies in ECEC can be a positive contribution where,

> digital technologies provide young children with particular opportunities for play-making and for art making that compliment other materials commonly found in a kindergarten. (Knight, 2018, p. 148)

For ECEC educators, technologies, particularly the use of photography and video recording are less controversial or contested as documentation and reflective tools. They can also prove to be rich resources for research and as a means for including children in research processes which aim to 'make learning visible' (Gandini, 2005; Rinaldi, 2006; Fleet, Patterson & Robertson, 2017). For example, the understanding of learning as experimentation, facilitated by movement with the material environment was examined through empirical research with 2-year olds by MacRae (2020), who works with slowed film data of children's hands playing with objects in a sand tray as mentioned previously. MacRae noted that,

> slow-motion viewing brought to my notice how objects set hands in motion in ways that I had not perceived while I was filming. The slowing of film brought into focus a contact zone of continually shifting space between hands, toys and sand. (…) The scooping, scraping and pouring actions of hands in response to sand was also a reminder that sand moves hands differently to toys, or other hands. (MacRae, 2020, p. 98)

MacRae's research is made possible by the unique affordances of slowed down film data. The important research insights were not available to her through visual observation but required both the film camera apparatus as well as the ability to manipulate the film by slowing it down through a computer program. MacRae worked with altered temporalities and alternative understandings of bodies through the concepts of affect and movement, specifically through Spinoza's definition of bodies whereby 'bodies are distinguished from one another by reason of motion and rest, speed and slow-ness, and not by reason of substance' (MacRae 2020, p. 102). Spinoza's philosophical definition of bodies is made tangible but also operational through the computer program that enables both the repeated and the slowed down viewing of MacRae's data of 'bodies' as moving hands, toys and sand in the sand tray. This technologically mediated film data is then used to present findings which advocate for 'reinstating sense as a mode of attention in order to counter a lack that is perceived until children learn language' (MacRae, 2020, p. 90). MacRae's research thus offers the idea that mechanical and digital technologies can be essential tools for adult appreciation of young children's sensory, bodily, complex, and nuanced modes of learning and attending to the material environment. Kind and Argent (2017) agree with this generative artistic approach to video in particular where they are,

> interested in the interpretive and poetic possibilities of video and how the processes of filming, editing, viewing and considering the work together can help us develop deeper attunement and invite more sensitive and diverse ways of knowing, seeing and responding. (Kind & Argent, 2017, p. 86)

These opportunities which technology can provide to develop new intimate ways of seeing and being with the material environment are of course available to both children and adults. This shifts the focus on documentation through technologies such as video and photography towards what Kind and Argent call 'a particular kind of observing, noticing, and documenting. It is not an objective, distanced or evaluative search' because, they state, 'the ways that we attend to things matter' (Kind & Argent, 2017, p. 87). Digital technologies offer children and adults modes of attention which can supplement and enhance ways of seeing and thinking differently, particularly about the everyday, while also affording the capacity for democratic practices of sharing. They can also importantly enable an aesthetic, poetic approach to the everyday environment where,

> By tuning into what is initially hidden by habit or, indeed, by a sense of ordinariness, and focusing on the minute variations that manifest within quotidian practices, we reveal the everyday as a space of invention. (Mitchelmore & Fleet, 2017, p. 62)

CHAPTER 4

Messy Methods

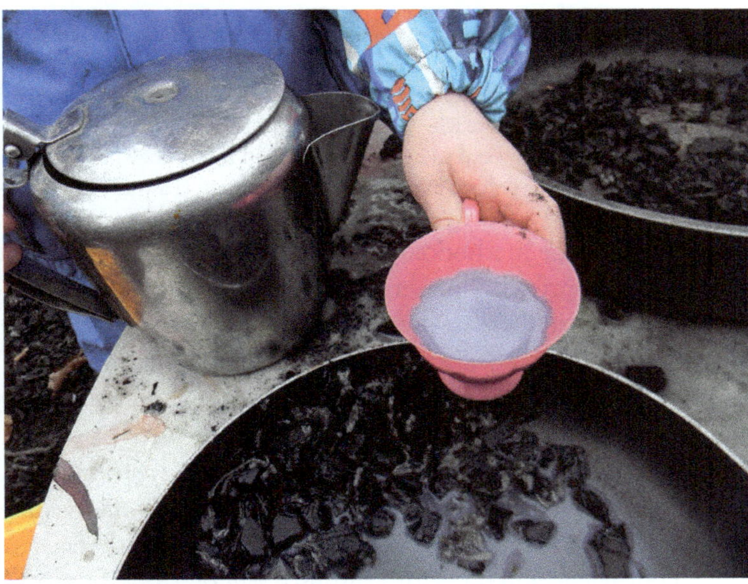

Figure 9: Messy Methods

Introduction

> While standard methods are often extremely good at what they do, they are badly adapted to the study of the ephemeral, the indefinite, and the irregular. (...) this implies that the problem is not so much the standard research methods themselves,

> but the normativities that are attached to them in discourses about method. (Law, 2004, p. 4)

The posthuman paradigm presents opportunities for seismic shifts across all aspects of education research, theory, and practice. As suggested by social scientist John Law in the quote above from his important book 'After Method: Mess in Social Science Research' (2004) this includes a necessary reorientation of research methodologies. Law's argument is summarised in the books prologue as follows:

> Most current methods look for clarity and precision. It is usually said that messy findings are a result of poor research. The idea that things in the world might be fluid, elusive, or multiple is unthinkable. Law's startling argument is that this is wrong, and it is time for a new approach. Many realities, he says, are vague and ephemeral. If methods want to know and to help shape the world, then they need to reinvent their practice and their politics in order to deal with mess. (Law, 2004)

In education, the methodological challenges that posthuman and post-qualitative approaches present are substantial, because 'educators and educational researchers are used to looking at schools as places where humans dwell together to learn what it means to be human' (Snaza et al., 2014, p. 39). Educational research that is challenging humanist assumptions aims to 'try to do away with method/ology-as-usual by opening a wider purview for trans disciplinarity, and by activating *potentia*, with its promise of more ecological modes of being, based on relationality' (Taylor & Hughes, 2016, p. 22). The purpose of this endeavour is so that meaning, as mobile, contingent, and transitory, can also be understood as 'generated among subjects' (Snaza et al., 2014). This includes how young children participate in meaning making.

Post-qualitative research is presented and explored as wholly appropriate for approaching 'vague and ephemeral' aspects of lived experiences, and not as a binary alternative to scientific methods of detachment and objectivity, which of course have an important role to play in knowledge formation and understanding. Post-qualitative education research examines how education theory and practice might best accommodate modes of learning in being, and there is much to be learned from young children in this regard. This chapter discusses post-qualitative research, its origins, rationale, and aims as well as a range of examples of post-qualitative approaches across education. It also presents the postqualitative concept of diffraction, through the methodology of a/r/tography, which offers a variety of interconnected methodological possibilities that are productive and appropriate within the ECEC context.

The Beginning of Post-qualitative Research

Coining the phrase 'post-qualitative' in 2011, Elizabeth St Pierre published a chapter in the Sage Handbook of Qualitative Research entitled 'Post Qualitative Research: The Critique and the Coming After' (St Pierre, 2011). In the chapter, St Pierre acknowledges that qualitative research that had developed since World War II as a reaction against positivism, produced a 'sea change in the social sciences and humanities' (St Pierre, 2011, p. 612). However, over the course of several decades as a result of persistent criticism for not being 'scientific enough' from Scientifically Based Research (SBR) (paralleling also SBR's strident disapproval of postmodernism), St Pierre claims that qualitative research has long been stifled by the need to find defensive positions whereby 'it has become conventional, reductionist, hegemonic, and sometimes oppressive and has lost its radical possibilities' (St Pierre, 2011, p. 613). The author describes post-qualitative research as emerging out of this deep dissatisfaction with 'conventional humanist qualitative methodology' (St Pierre, 2011, p. 611).

Since St Pierre's chapter in 2011, post-qualitative research has gained significant ground and has been published in special issues of several journals including Qualitative Inquiry, International Journal of Qualitative Studies in Education, Qualitative Studies in Education, and the International Review of Qualitative Research (Masny, 2015). As a multi-disciplinary concern, it emanates from, and draws upon, a range of philosophical and theoretical developments including Posthumanism, Postcolonialism, Poststructuralism, Feminist New Materialism, Actor Network Theory, Deleuzian philosophy and Affect Theory. It also finds new starting points to reignite the relevance of concepts drawn for example, from both Speculative and Indigenous Philosophies. Adding to the varied philosophical starting points, an array of scholarship perspectives emerge from further variations between genealogical, political, and ethical emphases (Braidotti, 2013). Post-qualitative researchers describe their work as both post-qualitative (Lather, 2013; Lather & St Pierre, 2013; MacLure, 2013a, 2013b; St Pierre, 2013; Johansson, 2016; Higgins, 2017; Davies, 2018) and posthumanist (Hickey-Moody, 2016; Holmes & Jones, 2016; Jackson, 2013; Mazzei, 2013; Pedersen & Pini, 2017; Taylor & Hughes, 2016; Ulmer, 2017).

The notable advances made by ECEC post-qualitative research in particular (Fairchild, 2017; Ceder, 2015) that 'might unhitch early childhood practices from individualistic and developmental accounts' (Pacini-Ketchabaw, Clark & Hodgins, 2014, p. 752), may be due to a focus on two core critiques: the assumptions and ensuing injustices of humanism in relation to children, and the dominance of language in both research and culture.

The strong critique of the assumptions of humanism that is foundational to posthumanism as previously discussed, extends to post-qualitative research practice, where objection is aimed at the exclusions and distortions that humanist assumptions create. Particularly at issue in academic research, are the notions that humans subdue the world through reason, and that humans alone display consciousness, intent, ethics, and complex, coherent language. Furthermore, it is argued that, within the extensive and varied human species, inevitable measures for degrees of humanism have become embedded, which produce systems of privileging, particularly, the emphasis on cognition over sensation. Although it is acknowledged that phenomenological studies have undoubtedly extended understanding of sensation and affect, the focus of this work nevertheless has been predominantly human-centric. Post-qualitative researchers argue that knowledge and understanding have been limited by the failure to enable a broader range of perspectives, of research positions and of modes of knowledge construction (Rotas, 2015; Taylor & Hughes, 2016; Ulmer, 2017). Post-qualitative research aims to serve the multiplicity of voices representing human minorities, and those positioned at the power-less end of the humanist scale, including children. This is also motivated by the concern that persistently human-centric research is not only insufficient, it is also deeply inappropriate in light of human induced damage to the planet (Taylor & Hughes, 2016; Braidotti, 2013; Haraway, 2016; Wolfe, 2010; Badminton, 2000).

In addition, in relation to the post-qualitative critique of the dominance of language, discourse is understood as producing power structures that need to be acknowledged at a minimum and challenged at best. Post-qualitative research claims that the dominance of language in both research and culture more broadly endangers and side-lines other forms of meaning making. Inextricably linked to the reliance on language is western civilisations insatiable quest for 'meaning' which requires that it be assigned to that which may evade it (MacLure, 2013b). With language perceived as the core cultural carrier of meaning and 'sense' (Colebrook, 2012), that which is inexpressible or inexplicable through language risks misinterpretation and marginalisation (Rautio & Jokinen, 2015). As prolific producers of non-verbal modes of being and knowing, children's ways of constructing knowledge and of being in the world are endlessly open to adult misinterpretation. As discussed in the previous chapters Posthuman considerations of literacy argue for the opening-up of the concept of literacy beyond the logocentric to include diverse, non-verbal, bodily, 'messy' (Law, 2004) ways of learning and knowing.

Reconfiguring Method

Reconfiguring research and knowledge construction through alternative methods has become a necessity because as Weaver and Snaza argue,

> The belief that methods must be selected from existing options and assembled *before* approaching the 'objects' of study is not only a form of *bad science*, it is also deeply implicated in anthropocentric and colonialist politics. (Weaver & Snaza, 2017, p. 1055)

Manning describes method as an 'apparatus of capture, method gives reason its place in the sun: it diagnoses, it situates, it organises, and ultimately it surveys and judges' (Manning, 2016, p. 32). The requirement of scientifically based research to install and maintain an objective distance from its object of research in order to establish validity, cuts to the core of the ethical objection of the post-qualitative position. However, it is only certain strands of positivism creating these incongruous conditions as explained by Lather and St Pierre,

> If we give up the scientism of positivist social science, we can no longer think many descriptors we believe we need to guarantee the value and rigor of humanist qualitative inquiry – for example, systematicity, process, audit trails, the clarity of language, value-free knowledge (objectivity, bias), the accumulation of knowledge, triangulation, coding data, and data itself. Without these, how do we know that what we are doing is science? Does it matter in the new mattering? And who gets to define science anyway? The natural sciences seem to be telling us it has always been about entanglement. Perhaps we are behind and need to catch up! (Lather & St Pierre, 2013, p. 630)

Methodological Challenges

Post-qualitative approaches to research erode the foundational processes of conventional qualitative methodologies, creating a necessity to rethink, rework or reject the terms which have previously been used to stabilise research. Such mechanisms have had a disabling effect on the ability to adapt to rapidly changing social and environmental circumstances. Methodologies, which operate from pre-set methods through terms and procedures including 'observation', 'data gathering', 'interviewing', 'coding', become exposed by post-qualitative researchers as insufficient modes of understanding nuanced, affective, and complexly mobile systems of generating knowledge (MacLure, 2013a; Mazzei, 2013; St Pierre, 2014; Weaver & Snaza, 2017). The concept of 'data gathering' for example, where pieces of information are extracted from research subjects for scientific analysis can require a level of homogenisation of the intimate or personalised specifics of the data in order to achieve 'reliable' generalisations. To post-qualitative researchers, this is disingenuous to the research subject, and to the data itself (Jackson, 2013; Somerville, 2016; Koro-Ljungberg, MacLure & Ulmer, 2018). Furthermore, it is argued that, through scientifically oriented procedures such as coding, qualitative data can become unrecognisable through the process of interpretation into an 'acceptable' form of truth (MacLure et al., 2010; MacLure, 2013b; St Pierre, 2014). Also problematic is the assumption that only a level of distance from the data can produce the truth, as well as the idea that 'data' itself is inert, passive and available for transformation (Koro-Ljungberg et al., 2018). It has been argued that scientifically oriented approaches to qualitative research can tend toward installing and nourishing a colonising relationship between researcher and research subject. However, rather than calling for an end to coding for example, MacLure calls for a coding that is not so gripped by scientism but is rather led by 'wonder' (MacLure, 2013a, 2013b). This involves envisaging a form of attention that, through extensive reading and forming creative connections through the data, produces 'a particular kind of experimental assemblage' (MacLure, 2013a, p. 165). The term 'experiment' is read as distinctly artistic rather than scientific, as explained by Ingold,

> In the art of inquiry (…) every work is an experiment: not in the natural scientific sense of testing a preconceived hypothesis, or of engineering a confrontation between ideas 'in the head' and facts 'on the ground', but in the sense of prising an opening and following where it leads. You try things out and see what happens. (Ingold, 2013, p. 6)

Applying this open notion of inquiry as an intuitive 'art' to educational contexts creates the potential for conceiving of education as a natural space for exploration of unexpected, interdependent, processual, messy, and entangled systems. Exploration of the complex interconnectedness of the world that is continuously composing and decomposing (Sheldrake, 2020; Tsing, 2015), is of course not new, particularly in the natural sciences. However, accounting for this in education research practice most certainly is (Weaver & Snaza, 2017). Taylor and Hughes offer a range of theoretical and material exemplars generated by contributors to their book *'Posthuman Research Practices in Education'* (Taylor & Hughes, 2016). Methodological suggestions range from 'Rhizomatic readings' and 'Cartographic mapping' (Lenz Taguchi, 2016), to 'Multispecies Ethnographies' (Pacini-Ketchabaw et al., 2016), and 'Affective Pedagogy' (Hickey-Moody, 2016), which is by no means an exhaustive list of the possibilities. Posthuman, post-qualitative approaches to research design, practice and analysis then, do not form a unified 'method' rather, they are multiple producers of 'situated, material, interconnected, processual, and affirmative knowledges' (Ulmer, 2017, p. 836). In terms of methodology, Ulmer (2017) suggests that post-qualitative researchers operate in ways that could be thought of as either 'thinking with', 'thinking without', or 'thinking differently'. I take up this suggestion by examining a range of approaches to post-qualitative methodology in the next section. However, I begin with a discussion of the key concept of diffraction which has been used productively by many post-qualitative researchers as a way of activating and attending to difference in, and through, research.

Diffraction as Methodology

> In substituting diffraction for reflection, it displaces the trajectory of Western epistemology and its potent optical imagery. This change of metaphors has far reaching implications for the way in which the practice of knowledge and theory production is conceptualized – precisely because diffraction is more than 'merely a metaphor'. As a method, diffraction incorporates historicity and difference into the practice of theory itself. And in its emphasis on effects it is essentially pragmatic. (Sehgal, 2014, p. 188)

Diffraction, as a metaphor and as a scientific material phenomenon, has been the catalyst to rethinking the foundations of postqualitative and posthuman research, and methodology. A diffractive approach to scholarship was initially proposed by biologist and philosopher Donna Haraway (Haraway, 1997; Sehgal, 2014) and was later taken up by quantum physicist and philosopher Karan Barad (Barad, 2003, 2014; Sehgal, 2014), notably in her book *'Meeting the Universe Halfway: Quantum Physics and the Entanglement of Matter and Meaning'* (2007).

Barad points out that, since antiquity, optical metaphors have been employed in western thinking to frame the relationship between vision and knowledge construction (Barad, 2007, p. 86). However, Barad and many others find that vision centred knowledge production relies on the assumed separation and stability between the knower and the object of knowledge. Barad's (2007, 2014) proposal of diffraction as an alternative methodological approach is based on the reading of quantum physicist Niels Bohr's work on the model of the atom which ultimately led him to reject atomistic metaphysics, Newtonian physics, and Cartesian distinctions between subjects and object.

In physics, diffraction is understood as the way that waves behave when they meet an obstruction by overlapping, bending, or spreading. Given the correct conditions, a water, sound or light wave can display diffraction (Barad, 2007, p. 74). However, particles (as matter or material elements) can also display wave behaviour under some circumstances 'diffraction effects have been observed for electrons, neutrons, atoms and other forms of matter' (Barad, 2007, p. 82). Known as the 'wave-particle duality paradox' of quantum theory, this draws attention to the complex entanglement of states of being which, according to Barad, offers an opportunity to rethink both epistemology (the theory of knowledge), and ontology (the nature of being). Barad writes,

> Bohr explains how it is possible for electrons to perform particle-ness under certain experimental circumstances and wave-ness under others. The key is understanding that identity is not essence, fixity or given-ness, but a contingent iterative performativity. (Barad, 2014, p. 173)

For Barad and posthuman theorists this means that identity formation is always in flux and changes with circumstance, movement, or adversity. It therefore prevents judgements being formed based on fixed notions or assumptions of identity and rather clarifies how identity is reliant on circumstance, making it open to change and adaptability, which demonstrates the essence of the ability to learn, grow and be transformed by and with the environment.

Furthermore, Barad explains that the apparatus employed for seeing or knowing any phenomenon is not neutral or innocent but rather is integral to how atoms perform, concluding that 'wave and particle are not inherent attributes of objects, but rather the atoms perform wave or particle in their intra-action with the apparatus. The apparatus is an inseparable part of the observed phenomenon' (Barad, 2014, p. 180). By taking account of the apparatus and deposing representational reflection (which requires separation), for Bohr and Barad knowledge is constructed through 'direct material engagement with the world' rather than 'standing at a distance and representing' the world (Barad, 2007, p. 49). Diffraction 'entails thinking the cultural and the natural together in illuminating ways' (Barad, 2007, p. 135).

Barad states that 'there is a deep sense in which we can understand diffraction patterns – as patterns of difference that make a difference – to be fundamental constituents that make up the world' (Barad, 2007, p. 72). Haraway's interest in diffraction is as a concept that 'does not map where differences appear, but rather maps where the effects of differences appear' (Haraway, 1992, p. 300).

Diffraction in research practices enables a reading together of texts, concepts, phenomena, events or processes for new thinking and understandings to emerge (Geerts & Van der Tuin, 2016). Rather than setting theories against each another critically, a diffractive methodology, emphasises potential and connection to enable creative, and unexpected outcomes. Crucially then 'diffraction attends to the relational nature of difference' (Barad, 2007, p. 30). Diffraction also has implications for educators where ubiquitous reflective practice 'may lead to reproduction, standardisation and forced universalities' (Myers, Smith & Tesar, 2017, p. 279). Diffractive practices move away from habits of reflecting on the world from the outside towards understanding the world, where it is accepted that the knower and object of knowledge are always entwined or entangled (Barad, 2014; Murris, 2016). However, at the heart of this approach is an acknowledgement of the dynamic nature of matter, so that subjects and objects are understood not as pre-existing entities but emergent through intra-action (Barad, 2007). To this end, Lenz Taguchi finds that diffraction as a methodology is not about uncovering the essence or truth of the data, but is an uncovering of a reality that exists among multiple realities being enacted in an event which have not been previously 'disclosed' (Lenz Taguchi, 2012, p. 275). Diffraction has been discussed as the entanglement of ontology, epistemology, and ethics, because as put by Barad,

> The separation of epistemology from ontology is a reverberation of a metaphysics that assumes an inherent difference between human and nonhuman, subject and object, mind and body, mater and discourse (…) What we need is something like an

> ethico-onto-epistemology – an appreciation of the intertwining of ethics, knowing and being – since each intra-action matters (…) because the becoming of the world is a deeply ethical matter. (Barad, 2007, p. 185)

Thinking Differently

> If much of reality is ephemeral and elusive, then we cannot expect single answers. If the world is complex and messy, then at least some of the time we're going to have to give up on simplicities. But one thing is sure: if we want to think about the messes of reality at all then we're going to have to teach ourselves to think, to practice, to relate, and to know in new ways. We will need to teach ourselves to know some of the realities of the world using methods unusual to or unknown in social science. (Law, 2004, p. 2)

In response to John Law's statement above, of the need to find new ways to think about messy realities, Jackson and Mazzei (2012), explore the potential of different theories and concepts to reinterpret data, to open them up to new readings and understanding. Their approach is demonstrated through the analysis of a single piece of data (a section from fieldwork notes in an American university setting) being reworked through different concepts and theorists including; power through Foucault, desire through Deleuze and intra-action through Barad (Jackson & Mazzei, 2012).

St Pierre suggests that thinking research data with theory or concepts 'instead of with method and methodology' (St Pierre, 2017) offers new ways of seeing empirical events, and therefore offers new routes to thinking about knowledge production. St Pierre (2017) finds that powerful concepts can also be given new life through new empirical contexts. The postqualitative approach to thinking with theory aims to attend to both materiality and theory (discourse) without privileging one over the other. MacLure suggests that qualitative research should give up its habits of representation and interpretation in order to acknowledge and account for,

> The materiality of language itself – the fact that language is in and of the body; always issuing from the body; affecting other bodies. Yet also, of course, always leaving the

> body, becoming immaterial, ideational, a striated, collective, cultural and symbolic resource. (MacLure, 2013b, p. 663)

This emphasises the multiple material and immaterial states of language, and through Deleuze's '*Logic of Sense*' (Deleuze, 2004) opens up to exploring sensation through language, enabled by post-qualitative research. As demonstrated through an example of field notes from a study in an early childhood setting, MacLure finds that 'bodily matters simultaneously demand and defy translation into codes and significations, (and) expose the workings of representation in education and research' (MacLure, 2013b, p. 663).

On the other hand, proposing a form of 'thinking without', Mazzei (2013) suggests the 'voice without organs' as a way to approach conventional interviewing in qualitative research, by working with Deleuze and Guattari concept of the 'Body without Organs' (Deleuze & Guattari, 1987). Mazzei illustrates 'an enactment among research-data-participants-theory-analysis' (Mazzei, 2013, p. 732) which negates the singular (human) subject as the source of knowledge and suggests new ways of thinking about the collective production of knowledge. This contributes to developing research practices which de-centre the human (including the human researcher) as a core challenge for postqualitative research (Sandvik, 2010; Fairchild, 2016). Fairchild also proposes reframing the researcher as another body within the research assemblage where other bodies might include data and theory. Fairchild finds that this 'fluid approach plugs into the assemblage in flux and prevents the foreclosing of ideas, data, and analysis' (Fairchild, 2016, p. 22). Sandvik concurs finding that conceiving of research as a diffractive assemblage loosens researcher control of outcomes (Sandvik, 2010, p. 37).

Posthuman reading of theory and concepts also offers education researcher's opportunities for thinking and doing differently, to find new applications for concepts which may have become fixed within humanist interpretations. For example, Aslanian (2018) reads Piaget's early qualitative work alongside Barad's to find that Piaget's 'focus on biological development has been interpreted as deterministic' (Aslanian, 2018, p. 419) but that the biological material emphasis in Piaget's ideas 'are harmonious with ideas of interconnectivity expressed in posthuman thought' (2018, p. 419). The intrinsic interconnections between human and environment which Piaget based his earliest theories on, thus re-emerge for new consideration through posthuman and new materialist theories which reject developmentalism (Aslanian, 2018). These theories reassign importance to material and the body in knowledge making, however they also include attention to the social, and discursive lives of children, as espoused by social constructivism, because 'research within neuroscience describes the biological and the social as interwoven and the ramification of this interconnectivity is increasingly reflected upon within education research' (Aslanian, 2018, p. 419).

In her study Sorensen (2009) reinterprets Vygotsky's 'Zone of Proximal Development' (ZPD) through a process which aims to 'account for the materiality of learning from a posthumanist stance' (2009), through which she develops the concept of 'liquid knowledge'. Sorensen finds that the generally accepted metaphor of the scaffold in relation to ZPD, is 'structurally immutable' (2009, p. 129) and does not account for the movement that Vygotsky considered so important in supporting children's development. Sorensen states that her description of 'a creature in progress through its immersion in a space of flow with other humans and things (…) better captures the motion Vygotsky implied with the notion of ZPD' (Sorensen, 2009, p. 129).

Through further posthuman diffractive re-reading of theory, Snaza (2013) finds that the emancipatory 'humanising' aims of educational theorists such as Paulo Freire (Freire, 2005), become ensnarled in hierarchical habits of speciesism. Snaza suggests that Freire's 'politics of inclusion' unavoidably affirms, and therefore potentially sustains, the existence of unacceptable exclusions. Snaza proposes that education ought rather to take up Freire's commitment to a politics of love, but differently, in order to develop a posthumanist education that can 'open up love beyond the limits of the human (…) by realising our real relations to other beings in the world, relations that humanism has taught us to disavow' (2018, p. 419). Diffractive approaches applied to ECEC research also enable different thinking about data analysis and documentation practices. For example, through the proposition of 'Relational Materialism,' Hultman and Lenz Taguchi (2010) analyse a photograph of a young child playing with sand to disrupt anthropocentric habits of data analysis (Hultman & Lenz

Taguchi, 2010). By thinking of both the material and the human body as equally performative, diffraction occurs through new understandings of agency (Barad, 2007; Bennett, 2010) where 'with each movement the girl, the sand and the bucket are in a process of transformation' (Hultman & Lenz Taguchi, 2010, p. 38).

In further study, Lenz Taguchi (2011) examines practices of pedagogical documentation to find that anthropocentricism and logo-centricism can become privileged. Although this study focuses on a renowned pedagogical approach which prioritises children's creative learning processes (the Reggio Emilia approach), Lenz Taguchi finds this aim may nevertheless become impeded when 'the child, and conceptual meaning-making, is foregrounded' (Lenz Taguchi, 2011, p. 46). Pedagogical documentation is used as a way of 'making visible' children's learning processes through text and visual means including children's drawings and quotes in the Reggio Emilia approach, however, Lenz Taguchi finds that the focus of the documentation, which is generally selected and collated by adults, promotes human centric attributes which may mask the complex contribution of the material. Lenz Taguchi states that,

> Thinking and learning takes place in between heterogeneous actors, rather than being something localised inside a human superior mind separated and located above the material world and other organisms. (Lenz Taguchi, 2011, p. 46)

In her doctoral thesis Sellers (2009) worked with the Deleuzian concept of the rhizome as a structural tool for thesis writing that does not comply with the traditional format in order to 'interfere with normativities of practice that have come to sanction what is recognisable as academic writing and examinable as thesis text' (Honan & Bright, 2016, p. 732). The aim of this was not as a criticism of work that complies with thesis structures, but to argue against 'over-coded signifiers' including the constraints of the thesis structure itself. Sellers (2009) thesis describes chapters as 'plateaus' which can be read in any order. During fieldwork in a single Australian kindergarten, multiple forms of data were gathered which used what she calls 'rhizomethodology' (Sellers, 2009). This approach relies on arts-based practices such as drawing, map-making, storyboards and poetry to enable play to infiltrate the research methodology and analysis, so that through such diffractions, research with/about children does not become 'adult(erated)' (Sellers, 2015, p. 28). Sellers explains,

> One implication of working with rhizo understandings of children, childhood and curriculum is that it refuses the kind of concretisation that is perhaps expected, such as considering what it might all mean for learning and teaching (…) Conceiving (of) play differently involves finding ways beyond thinking of play as a (nounal) fixed thing or event, rather, it involves thinking of play (verbally), as activity of dynamism and movement … any adventure with rhizoanalysis continues to be about opening (to) possibilities for where we might go in our thinking. (Sellers, 2015, p. 28)

A growing number of examples of research approaches which use diffractive, new materialist and posthuman theories rely on artistic, material, and affective approaches to thinking differently and productively within the context of ECEC. They are each lit by rigorous experimentation and the capacity for artistic thinking and processes to counteract the potential effects of method as a prescribed mode of 'capture' (Manning, 2016). To demonstrate their methodological diversity (and for brevity), I summarise a small sample of these diffractive artistic approaches to ECEC research in particular in Table 4. Each of the examples focus on multiple diffractive, artistic methods and posthuman or new materialist theoretical approaches to research to ECEC.

Crucially, none of the examples found provide a singular definitive method. Rather, the open nature of the theoretical approach makes it both possible and necessary to devise and/or re-use existing methods that are particular to each new study, oriented by posthuman ethics. The next section clarifies how arts-based approaches to research contribute to diffractive research methodology and further why postqualitative methods may be described as 'anti-method'. I also discuss how, in the case of my research, A/r/tography offers a guiding methodological approach appropriate to the Posthuman theoretical framework of my project.

Table 4: Post-qualitative Arts-Based Methods Examples

Methodology	**Researchers**	**Art Based Method**	**Aim/Outcome**
'Nomadic' writing	Holmes and Jones (2016) 'Flickering, Spilling and Diffusing Body/ Knowledge' in Taylor and Hughes (2016) Posthuman Research Practices in Education, Routledge.	Disrupting simplifying tendencies in human-centred childhood studies, by using challenging contemporary artworks alongside concepts drawn from process philosophies of Deleuze, and Whitehead.	To try to 'rethink data as words but also as images, movements, politics, molecules, affect, noise, haecceity and pollution' (Holmes & Jones, 2016, p. 22).
'Thinking with Paint'	Pacini-Ketchabaw et al. (2014), Thinking with Paint: troubling Settler Colonialisms through Early Childhood Art Pedagogies.	Through material/ discursive ubiquity of paint ECEC settings the researchers 'Attend to the properties of paint – its viscosity, smoothness, slipperiness, stickiness, its ability to dry and solidify' (p. 753).	(…) to generate insights, problems, and disruptions in our early childhood practices' (p. 753).
'Research Assemblage'	Sandvik, N. (2010). 'The art of/in educational research: Assemblages at work'	Pays attention to sensations created through the interactions of disparate elements because the 'obligation to contribute in movements towards diversity is increasing' (p. 37).	New ideas can be generated 'without evidence-based approaches as tranquilizers' (p. 38).
'Recycled materials as a pedagogic idea'	Odegard, N., (2012) 'When matter comes to matter – working pedagogically with junk materials'	'to explore the concept of materiality and the idea of working pedagogically with junk materials'	'Junk materials offer a golden opportunity to explore the tension between creating meaning and being part of the transitory' (p. 397).

Table 4: Continued

Methodology	Researchers	Art Based Method	Aim/Outcome
Ethnographic fieldwork in a Remida	Odegard and Rossholt (2016) 'In-betweens spaces. Tales from a Remida'	To explore the pedagogical influences of the 'less than human including light/shadows/ darkness' (p. 54).	'Aesthetic explorations happen continuously, they cross borders and timelines where play and learning are intertwined' (p. 55).
Pedagogical documentation as reflective process Case Study	Penfold and Turner (2020) 'Reflecting on children's play at the Whitworth'	Case study of a child painting at the Whitworth Museum early years art atelier.	'Pedagogical documentation can support a gallery team in exploring the contextuality, contradictions, politics and ethics that shape children's learning' (p. 186).

Anti-methods

In light of the postqualitative approaches to research methodology discussed in the previous sections, postqualitative research methods are devised from within the research process as a way of being capable of responding to emergent events and data. This means that the researcher needs to approach their research with openness, humility, and an ability to develop methods which are capable of 'going along with' events (Ingold, 2013), rather than being decided in advance. For my research, I found both John Law (2004) and Stuart Lester's (2020) approaches to method to be helpful and inspiring, particularly where they too are interested in 'taking account of the everyday' (Lester, 2020, p. 174) and installing 'a commitment to experimenting with different ways of becoming attuned' (Lester, 2020, p. 174). In my research I found arts-based approaches to be particularly adept and useful in this regard while also capable of prioritising the posthuman ethical imperatives that underpin my project.

Lester suggests 'cartography' as a guiding umbrella term which includes a range of performative approaches which can work separately, intra-actively and diffractively (Lester, 2020, p. 181). Similarly, 'method assemblage' (Law, 2004) is the term proposed by Law comprising a range of both new and more established methods. However, as distinct from a mixed or multiple methods approach to qualitative research, postqualitative 'anti-methods' are so called because of their refusal of the advance prescribing of research methodology as a means of capturing data. Rather, anti-methods aim to be open to all appropriate, affective ways of attuning carefully to events as they unfold. This is primarily a difference in perspective where the Posthuman lens provides an ethical orientation which requires that the researcher be willing to adapt so that they can move with rather than in advance of the data offered.

Mobility rather than fixity within post-qualitative research becomes an ethical undercurrent in post-qualitative methods. So much so, 'mobile methods' are suggested as part of a cartographic research practice by Lester (2020). This might involve attention to movement of different bodies and materials at varying speeds. Walking and other movement methodologies such as dance and drawing are further possibilities which can also be augmented and complimented by numerous audio-visual processes. This can contribute important detail to awareness of the sensory dimensions of spaces and the ways they are engaged with by children for example. Video footage can be slowed down, and/or speeded up to offer new creative perspectives of space, time, movement, and play without the sense that 'the truth' of the data is being altered or tampered with, as might be the case in qualitative methods.

Similarly, mapping in qualitative research methods may be oriented toward defining and positioning events in relation to a fixed idea of space or time, perhaps through diagrams and other graphic forms of representation. In post-qualitative research mapping is discussed as 'not about accurate representation between points but a more performative, aesthetic and artistic way of paying attention to the non-linear, indeterminate, multi-sensory lived experience of space' (Lester, 2020, p. 187). Sellers (2009) approaches mapping in a variety of ways which attend to different simultaneously overlapping movements through both drawing and story boarding of play events. Knight (2019) has developed what she calls 'inefficient mapping' as a productive, creative drawing research method which changes and adapts according to the research context as it unfolds. This approach to mapping critically questions the relationship of the cartographer to that which is being mapped and draws attention to the power structures inherent in the practice.

Observation as a key method in qualitative research is still useful in post-qualitative research but crucially the complex, entangled relationships between researcher, research site, materials, data, and all possible participants is acknowledged as influential in the process. Where qualitative observation would have a relatively clear and narrow understanding of positionality of who is participating in the research and their clear roles within it, post-qualitative practices of observation on the other hand requires 'a state of receptive and generous ethical sensibility towards others things and bodies' (Bennett, 2001; Lester, 2020, p. 187). In post-qualitative observation, it is understood that observation and participation are inseparable (MacRae, 2020). Further, the material/affective 'being there' of a researcher has an affective impact that needs to be acknowledged but equally, unexpected non-human elements such as weather or objects can also be understood as entangled and potentially affectively powerful within the research.

Practices of observation in postqualitative research can be enacted through arts-based approaches which also contributes to rebalancing ideas of the overriding importance of words, both spoken and written. This is particularly valuable in education which is concerned with representation through the idea of 'voice' as a rights-based imperative. Arts-based research practices can enable visual, poetic, and fictional forms of voice to emerge which can confound or even refuse meaning. In this way, storytelling is also suggested by Lester (2020) as a postqualitative research method which acknowledges different perspectives and ways of seeing and understanding events and phenomena. Stories of course contain and relay valuable collective cultural knowledges and 'can bring theoretical concepts and policy intentions to life, as they reach beyond the cognitive to the affective and embodied. Stories make and add to history as well as imagine possible futures' (Lester, 2020, p. 189). Story, drawing, movement, and dramatic play for example could all emerge entangled together as creative possibilities in postqualitative observational research practices. This does not mean that this becomes a fixed method applied to gather data, rather creative processes may emerge in response to events that last only for a moment. Postqualitative perspectives accept these moments as valid and valuable and does not require them to have been put in place in advance. This allows research methods also to be spontaneous and playful but still understood as having potential to generate important knowledge.

One such example of an approach that could be described as postqualitative research is a project entitled 'On What Grounds' (Thorp, 2020). This project was devised between the Serpentine Gallery Education department, designer Bahbak Hashemi-Nezhad and the Portman Early Childhood Centre in Northwest London. The project examined how, by moving beyond designated or formalised play spaces such as playgrounds or schools, everyday neighbourhoods might offer surprising materials and spaces for rich, playful, and creative experiences for children. The research site was, 'a 21 story tower block surrounded by wide open spaces hidden corners, vantage points, contrasting scales and surfaces' (Thorp, 2020, p. 188) as chosen by the designer;

> Through the project the site became familiar to the children, but was never static; the interaction between children, adults, objects, and space was in constant flux. We found traces of people on the site each week and these unexpected encounters often shaped the session. A supermarket trolly was repurposed to become a vehicle to move and spin around. The crack in the pavement caused by construction work signaled the presence of a monster or meteorite. A dead pigeon opened up a conversation about injury and death that continued long after we returned to the Portman. (Thorp, 2020, p. 191)

The project used still black and white photographs taken by the designer as one method of documentation, and for discussion points between children and adults. The designer's aesthetic is evident, and the play episodes can easily be read as artistic events. The research also used a form of 'mobile method', by taking the children out of their classroom and accounting for events as they occurred on their walk to their selected research site. During this 'accidental ethnography' (Fuji, 2015; Lester, 2020) observation was also used to assist with suggesting new materials to work with each week. The designer decided which materials to bring to the research site informed by the previous week's observations of play. These included on one occasion, two large wooden planks (which the children helped to carry) and a sheet of plastic on another, with different materials being brought over eleven sessions. 'Storytelling' also became an important method in this cartography of the emergence of play with materials and spaces, as demonstrated in the quote above referring to the drawn-out development of the dead pigeon storying.

A/r/tography

In art education research, 'A/r/tography' also offers potential for diffractive methodology which relates strongly to cartography and method-assemblages as suggested by both Law and Lester. A/r/tography, uses art, research, teaching and writing and has been growing in its potential and application since its initial development in Canada almost two decades ago (a decade before post-qualitative research began to be published). A/r/t/ographic researchers Stephanie Springay and Rita Irwin state that,

> A/r/tographers don't simply research phenomena in the arts using qualitative means; they are artists-and-teachers-and-researchers, who examine educational phenomena through an artistic understanding and inquiry process. (Springay, Irwin & Kind, 2008, p. 87)

A/r/tography aims to find ways for education, art and research practices to converge within inquiry (Irwin & De Cosson, 2004). A/r/tography acknowledges the non-verbal space of making, as an ethical space for thinking and attending differently. The materiality of artistic practices invites sensory ways of knowing and make space for affect to take a central role as part of the research frame. Irwin defines A/r/tography as 'a research methodology, a creative practice, and a performative pedagogy that lives in the rhizomatic practices of the liminal in-between' (Irwin, 2013, p. 199). Through each of the practices of art (A), research (R) teaching (T) and writing (graphy) Irwin and De Cossen state,

> Art is the visual reorganisation of experience that renders complex the apparently simple or simplifies the apparently complex. Research is the enhancement of meaning revealed through ongoing interpretations of complex relationships that are continually created, recreated, and transformed. Teaching is performative knowing in meaningful relationships with learners (…) there are multiple borders diffused again and again. (Irwin & De Cosson, 2004, p. 31)

The emphasis on 'multiple borders' becoming 'diffused again and again' through different research approaches creates the potential for diffraction as discussed previously, whereby each of the approaches to research can bring to light differences that matter, and that may not otherwise emerge. However, A/r/tography is not necessarily postqualitative or posthuman in its outlook, as it originated within pre-existing qualitative methodology. Furthermore, the use of A/r/tography as a methodology in ECEC research is only recently emerging. In her A/r/tographic doctoral research in a single ECEC setting in Norway in 2011 for example, Fredriksen states that 'I did not know of any other study where A/r/tography was applied in early childhood education. Choosing such an approach was therefore an exploratory act – I was taking some chances' (Fredriksen, 2012, p. 42). Fredriksen's study used a largely qualitative methodology that combines A/r/tography with multiple case studies using qualitative practices of data treatment (coding etc.). A/r/tography in Fredriksen's study was used productively to organise and focus on her differing (diffractive) roles as artist, teacher, and researcher.

Post-qualitative approaches to A/r/tography which have recently been emerging demonstrate clear compatibility between A/r/tography and Posthuman theoretical approaches (Sinner, 2017). In a review of forty nine examples of A/r/tographic scholarship, Sinner (2017) notes that postqualitative A/r/tographic research moves away from 'familiar representations' and brings 'together the affects of researcher(s), participant(s), networks of connections, as well as multiple geographies' (Sinner, 2017, p. 56). Sinner suggests that when taking a postqualitative perspective 'A/

r/tography offers the essence of a methodology that we not only interpret, but can continue to actively change through ongoing and persistent engagement, as theorists and practitioners of the arts in educational research' (Sinner, 2017, p. 58).

In the next chapter I will discuss my own research fieldwork site, and how A/r/tography became enacted in my study through different arts-based approaches to gathering and analysing data in postqualitative research.

CHAPTER 5

Theory from Practice

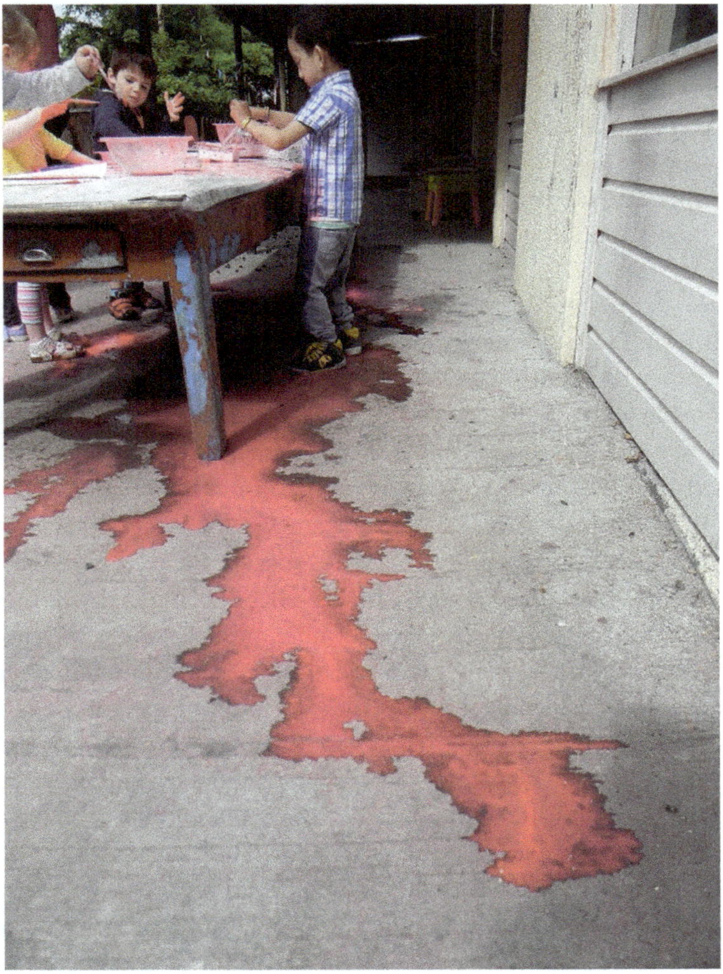

Figure 10: The Research Site

The fieldwork research site for my study is a private, not-for-profit ECEC setting, established in 2007 by two co-owner educators in a small town in the West of Ireland. The original building was a large former primary school building and from 2007, through a barter system arrangement, I became the preschools resident artist. For eight years one of the buildings empty classrooms was used as a painting studio for my art practice, in exchange for working with the children and staff on a variety of different projects. These included public exhibitions of the children's artwork; co-design and delivery of adult education courses; setting up a Saturday art school; documentation projects; introducing new materials into the classrooms and outdoor areas; and building temporary play installations from recycled materials. Due to the school being demolished to rebuild the towns original primary school, the pre-school moved to a substantially smaller building in 2015 without space for a studio. The fieldwork began in 2017.

The settings policy document for that year clarifies its ethos and practices in relation to the importance of relationships between adults, children, and families. As my fieldwork research site however, my own long-standing relationship with the setting needed careful consideration. In conventional qualitative research this embeddedness could be considered a limitation (Jordan, 2015) where issues such as comparison, validity, and bias could arise. In a postqualitative theoretical framework however, it is acknowledged that the researcher is openly always part of the research so that the relationship could also be argued to bring 'a depth of understanding to the research' (Jordan, 2015, p. 14). Furthermore, posthumanism requires decentring the human so as to find a holistic perspective of phenomena, so while the relationships were strong, they were not the specific focus of my study. Rather, I found that the depth and ease of our relationships enabled me to take a position which relied on a highly valued sense of mutual trust. My plain language statement given to parents and educators before commencing fieldwork assured them that the focus of the research was not to either evaluate or assess either the children or the school.

At the time of the fieldwork, the pre-school comprised two classrooms, each with three educators, and one with a special needs assistant (SNA). One classroom had twenty-three children, the other had twenty-two. Each educator leads the same group of either seven or eight children for 'small group' work throughout the year. The children come from diverse backgrounds and for several, English was not the primary language spoken at home. The range of primary languages within the school that year included Spanish, French, Hungarian, Urdu, and Polish. The following short descriptions of the research site are extracts from journal notes and provided here to paint a picture of the preschool as encountered by me, one morning at outside play time:

> Noisy, and excited movement of the children from both classrooms spilling out into the outside area for 'free play' outside time allocated for a minimum of fifty minutes every day. The children are all dressed in clothing appropriate to the outdoors such as wellington boots, raincoats, leggings, hats, and mittens etc. The outdoor space is less defined and ordered than inside. Inside, visual signs, notices, drawn symbols and fixings create organisational spaces, and 'homes' for everything within the High Scope model. Each classroom is defined by activities such as 'home corner', 'book area', 'art area', 'water area' with multiple visual signifiers to define where each object can be found and tidied away by the children during 'clean up time'.
>
> The outdoor space is defined by four different ground surfaces however the activities the areas support is not necessarily defined by these divisions. There is a large sand area which is covered with fishing nets when not in use, a rubber chip play area which is sloped creating a gentle gradient to roll bodies and objects downhill, a grass garden area with large trees, benches and a music wall made by the educators from pots and pans and recycled plastic tubing which is closed off when it is too wet. The concrete awning which is partially covered and runs the full length of the building and is approximately two meters wide is used as a space to move through to get to the other areas or for parents to gather in at home time. Within each of the outdoor spaces, movement and speeds are not restricted in the same way as they would be inside. Inevitably bodies begin to move differently, rolling, running, climbing, dragging, pulling, sliding. Large mature trees surround the entire site, offering sticks, leaves, sounds, shelter, raindrops, hailstones, birds, tree bark, snails, and bugs to drop unpredictably into all of the play areas.
>
> The awning space has partial shelter and no defined purpose prior to this project, and so none of the adults or children or objects particularly 'belong to' or 'own' that space, whereas inside, every inch of space has been claimed as belonging to the objects and bodies that occupy it. The outside play time is also a time when the adults come together to watch without monitoring (writing or taking notes), to play with the children, to drink tea and chat with each other. It seems that in this outdoor environment where everyone is on 'break time', unplanned things can happen, and it

is within this atmosphere that I decide to set up the pilot phase of the research as an outdoor 'atelier' in the awning space.

The fieldwork consisted of bi-weekly visits to the setting over twenty-seven sessions on Tuesday and Friday mornings. I supplied the majority of the materials while the setting supplied regular equipment such as markers and paintbrushes. A small grant was awarded by my university which covered the cost of materials. The twenty-seven sessions were made up as follows:

- Four observation sessions (two per classroom).
- Five 'pilot' sessions in the outdoor atelier space.
- Ten artist/researcher designed sessions.
- Six sessions (one each) designed by each educator.
- Three sessions designed and led by educator pairs.
- A presentation of photographs in a slideshow format for the children and parents delivered on the final day.

Before commencing, formal ethical procedures such as garda vetting; information presentations for educators and parents; plain language statement sharing; consent forms; and submitting documentation for review by the university ethics committee were all necessarily compliant as part of a research study at doctoral level. Being a postqualitative study does not preclude requirements to fulfil ethical standards that do important work in relation to child safety in particular.

My research method was confirmed in this formal procedure as A/r/tography however, I was not entirely sure what methods I would use and had no definitive method plan. Beginning with theory (Spinozist Posthumanism) rather than method as suggested by postqualitative theorists (Jackson & Mazzei, 2012; St Pierre, 2014; Lenz Taguchi & St Pierre, 2017) provided orientation, but also disorientation. At that early stage in many ways, I hoped that my extensive reading would at some point lead me to a definitive 'how to' for the posthuman, postqualitative research which felt so theoretically appropriate to my study. Of course, no straightforward, simple, or replicable research method exists. This lack of clarity in relation to applicable methods created difficulties for my supervision team who were trying hard to guide me toward known, acceptable ways of doing research. However, no existing pre-formed method seemed appropriate to my perspective and arts-based research interests or seemed to fit with the Spinozist posthuman theory I had found so inspiring. Therefore, I mostly felt my way through the data gathering using artistic methods in which each session began with an artistic material invitation for the children. Other data gathering methods included photography and drawing as experimental, sometimes tentative, often instinctive approaches to recording, gathering, collecting, and thinking. Bringing a hardbound sketchbook and camera with a video function were all that I required. While this open, 'feeling my way' approach to data gathering methodology enabled me to observe, play and participate in what felt like a very natural unobtrusive way, it was also for me, constantly infiltrated by doubt, confusion, questioning and general worry as to whether I was doing it 'right'. I now consider this uncomfortable 'not-knowing' to be an ethical position from which to develop research within a postqualitative perspective. Of course, all qualitative research sets out from not knowing however, I think that postqualitative research centralises the discomfort this creates for the researcher so that modesty and humility become barometers. The affective bodily impact of not knowing is a position the postqualitative researcher must bear so as to constantly work to erode any inclinations toward colonisation, and rather move with care, moment by moment with the data as it is offered, and as it emerges in its own space and time.

The Outdoor Atelier

There was an undeniable expectation from adults and children in the setting that my being there as an artist would involve an increase in artistic activity for the children. It was through this expectation that I decided to develop an activity strategy that would fulfil this desire for the children, while also allowing me time to follow rather than lead artistic activity that the children participated in. After the initial observation phase, I had the idea that an outdoor 'atelier' would work well. This would consist of two of my own adapted long tables, joined together under the awning space outside. This idea only became clear after a number of weeks of being in the setting. I do not know why it did not occur to me before starting fieldwork, but when I explained my idea to educators and children and was met with their excitement I became even more certain it was a good place to start.

There were several problems which the outdoor atelier idea resolved. It was important to all of us that all of the children could be understood as voluntary participants in my research even if our aims and interests differed. The children would be free to join and leave the atelier as they wished in a space that was oriented toward play during free playtime, rather than being more structured as may be the case inside. The outdoor area accommodated a greater possibility for spontaneity of movement which meant that the materials were also free to move with the children in ways that would not have been possible inside. For example, paint could be taken to the mud kitchen area or sand could be brought into the atelier space by the children as they wished. But also the materials could move in undetected and unintentional ways, on shoes or in spills perhaps. The outdoor atelier could optimise connections between art and play which I wanted to emphasise. I also wanted for the research to cause minimal disruption to the days schedule which, although flexible, is structured according to the Aistear curriculum to include relatively specific timing for different events and activities such as greeting time, small group time etc. Furthermore, it felt important not to take over the art areas in each classroom so that, should a child not wish to engage with the atelier materials but nevertheless wanted to use other art materials, these would still be available to them. The outdoor atelier also had the practical advantages that the children usually wear waterproof clothing for outside playtime which is suitable for the 'messy' work of the atelier. I would also be able to clean up any mess after playtime when everyone had returned indoors, minimising extra work for educators. The space became what Brent Wilson calls a 'Third Pedagogical Site' (Wilson, 2003, 2007) which is described by Marmé Thompson as a situation,

> in which responsibility, choice and decision-making are shared between adults and children, where children's freedom and choice are maximized within a flexible structure provided by adults. (Marmé Thompson, 2019, p. 138)

The intention was to create a research process that could be pleasurable for the children and the adults alike, a space in which they might respond to materials (or not) as they felt moved to on any given day. I wanted, very simply, to provide opportunities to work and play with materials that had the potential to be artistic and were open to movement and novelty. For the fieldwork process I was also interested in practices which could produce, as put by Marmé Thompson,

> A far more variable image of children who make art, expanding our understanding of the materials, intentions and intensities they bring to that process and helping to dissolve previously inviolate boundaries between artmaking as practiced by adults and by children. (Marmé Thompson, 2019, p. 137)

Educator Involvement

The fieldwork outdoor atelier was designed as a shared, playful, experimental space rather than a specifically pedagogical one. However, while experiencing the process the educators felt that there was pedagogical value in the atelier and decided towards the end of the fieldwork practice that they would like to maintain the atelier themselves, including the bi-weekly routine of bringing in new materials to explore. The fieldwork process had also generated openings for educators to express and explore their own unique knowledges drawn from their everyday lives. It was decided to conclude fieldwork with a piloting of the educators leading the sessions. This phase was not the key focus of the research but was rather another unexpected outcome that was welcomed and supported. A series of six individual educator led sessions were followed by three further sessions of working in teams of two, with one educator from each of the two classrooms. This afforded opportunities to collaborate with colleagues who wouldn't usually work together to extend experiences of sharing approaches and to offer support and enjoyment when introducing new processes. The educators also decided that as 'outside time' normally fell just after 'small group time' it would make it more manageable for each educator whose turn it was to lead the session to begin by exploring it during small group time before the other children came to join in. Educators also hoped this arrangement would facilitate peer learning where those children who had explored the material during small group time could informally introduce it to the other children as they came outside to join in.

Materials

For each bi-weekly engagement I brought a new material proposition to the atelier, often in combination with paint. Materials included: ice; vegetables; fish; toys; sticks; gelatine; and Plaster of Paris. Some of the materials were quite unconventional in that they may not have previously been considered by either the children or the adults as art materials, and some were familiar materials made new by combining with paint and by context of the outdoors and its accompanying weather systems. The materials I introduced were selected for several reasons. First and foremost, I had to ensure that all materials I introduced posed no hazard to the children in terms of health and safety. It was also important that all materials could introduce potential for aesthetic engagement, movement, and playfulness while also being relatively accessible within the locality (e.g. seaweeds, wool, sand, oyster shells, plants, and flowers). Many of the materials were familiar to the children and adults such as paint, clay, and paper, while others were either entirely new (Plaster of Paris, gelatine), or simply new to an artistic context (bread, vegetable slices, fish). Other less familiar items such as medical droppers were sourced from the local Creative Resource Centre or 'Remida', which supplies surplus and waste materials from local industries that are safe to use in creative projects (there are several pharmaceutical factories in the locality which donate materials such as droppers to the Resource Centre). Scale was also a consideration in my material selection, as was the different modes of movement or spontaneity that particular materials could offer. We also enjoyed exploring the transformational properties of a range of materials including Plaster of Paris (hardening); Clay (stickiness); Charcoal (burning); Ice Balloons (melting); Gelatine (setting).

I developed a 'setting the table' presentation of the materials for each session which became like a domestic ritual. This idea was held theoretically by Davies (2014b) who writes about lines of 'assent and descent' in relation to artistic facilitation, whereby 'making art is a complex dance between lines of descent (making life coherent and predictable) and ascent (opening up the new and unexpected)' (Davies, 2014b, p. 12). The regularity and predictability of the table setting, its location and time of the sessions provided predictability, while the new materials and their movement with the children were open to newness as lines of assent or creative possibility. Before they came outside, the children enjoyed predicting and announcing my arrival, and watching the table setting ritual from the large inside windows. The communal focus of the atelier felt convivial and important because, as put by MacRae,

> By emphasizing the *collective* in the composition of a shared moment, attention is spread more evenly across the people and the things that are singularly brought together for a brief moment. (MacRae, 2012, p. 120)

Introducing materials in the atelier space generated overt artistic activity for the children while also producing endless data for the research. However, crucially, I was also constantly drawn to other everyday activity that occurred in the setting, which I also viewed as aesthetic. These 'ordinary' moments were equally valuable to the research process as generative of data and understanding them as aesthetically significant contributed enormously to the development of my thinking. The idea that an aesthetic lens can reveal the infinite complexity and richness of children's learning with materials and environments in which they are always already emersed, goes to the heart of the purpose of my research.

The next section will discuss in more detail the data gathering methods that I used during fieldwork, followed by a description of the post-qualitative processes which I devised for the data analysis.

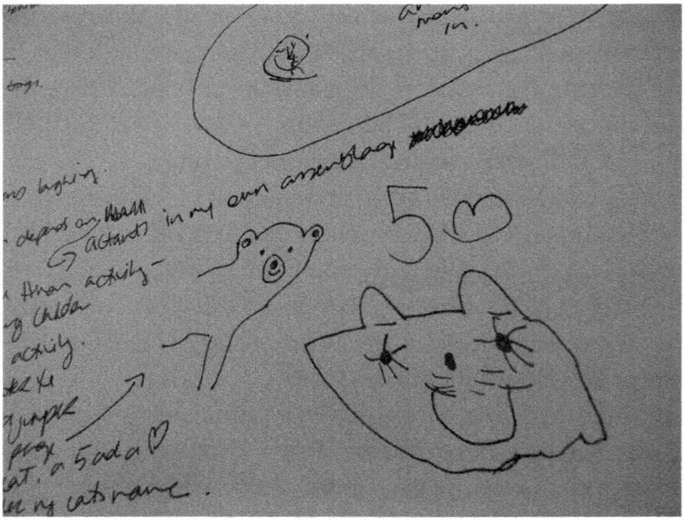

Figure 11: Drawing with Children

Data Gathering Methods in A/r/tography

A/r/tography works in and across the intersections and individual practices of Art (A), Research (R), Teaching (T), and Writing (graphy). The principal methods I used for gathering data moments were photography, video, drawing and writing journal notes. The photographs of the material environment which I took and present throughout this book had an aesthetic which helped to bring attention to the material environment and were also of interest to the children. This interest brought about the introduction of a children's digital camera as another form of data gathering, but from the children's perspective and aesthetic. The children produced a large number of photographs of the environment, their friends, as well as a series of extraordinary 'selfies'. In addition to the process of taking photographs, the aesthetic and affective power of the visual data itself (the photograph as object) produced ongoing opportunities for thinking, writing, and researching. A series of printed photographs were displayed in the setting for the children to see and discuss during the fieldwork which generated interest and curiosity. I also wrote journal notes after each session which felt like a form of storying of the morning's events. I greatly enjoyed taking the time to remember in a necessarily imaginative way, moments that drew my attention while also thinking of how those moments connected with the Spinozist Posthuman theory I was consistently reading and being inspired by. I also used a hardback sketchbook in the setting for taking notes and drawing. In this, I was often joined by children who wanted to contribute their own drawings to mine, which I welcomed. This became a way of having conversations while drawing together with the children.

I experimented with the ideas of following materials and mobile methods. For example, one morning, I decided to follow the movement of a single object (a small hand sized toy) brought to school by one boy over the course of a morning. This developed into ideas of 'following' materials (such as paint) as they spread throughout the wider play area such as into the sand or kitchen areas for example. Walking/moving playfully with the children also produced useful new data moments for theorising with afterwards. Exploring processes of mapping was also useful as a data gathering method. Some data were also produced in the form of audio recordings and transcribed educator interviews. These provided opportunities to discuss different aspects of the research with the educators who were interviewed in individual sessions which lasted approximately an hour each. In hindsight however, I think this approach to interviewing reveals my insecurity with wanting to research 'correctly'. For future discursive data gathering, I would refocus on ensuring an enjoyable process through arts-based collaborative methods or a practice which involved more focus on material and bodily movement. These interviews were nevertheless interesting, convivial, and useful for providing new ideas and perspectives of events from the educator's points of view and focused on the educator's adaptation of an aspect of the research methodology going forward.

Reading theory consistently throughout the entire research process proved essential to orienting my thinking and to understanding the moments I was drawn to from different perspectives. As each of the methods I used ebbed and flowed with the bi-weekly sessions in the atelier, some became more prominent than others. Many methods emerged simultaneously while some were used very infrequently. For each visit to the atelier all that I knew for certain was the material I would bring. After that, my research methods followed activity and movement of the children and materials with the understanding that much would be lost. In trying to understand how arts-based research practices can contribute to ECEC by noticing much of what may otherwise be missed, I had to acknowledge that I too, would never be able to definitively 'capture' the richness in its entirety. The following section will discuss how the data gathered through the various methods described above, was organised, analysed, and theorised within the post-qualitative, posthuman theoretical paradigm of my project.

Data Organisation

Due to the productivity of all of the diverse data gathering methods explored in the fieldwork, organisational mechanisms were necessary to coherently 'see' the data. The research questions which shifted and developed along with the research itself became tools within the analysis process through the key concepts which underpinned them, as Affect, Agency and Care.

The first question asked how can 'small' (spontaneous, unmediated, aesthetic) moments of learning and experience with the material environment, be understood and valued in ECEC and was generated by the consideration of Agency. This occurred by repeatedly asking who and what is involved in producing the phenomena within each small moment, because in order to value and understand the moments, they needed to somehow be assigned to 'participants' or protagonists (human and non-human, visible and invisible, material and discursive) within the event. When agency is understood as co-produced performativity (Barad, 2007) the idea of agency in events becomes multiple and complex.

The second question asked whether an artistic approach to research might offer new perspectives of how learning and experience emerges in an ECEC setting. This was activated the concept of Affect which became a lens for seeing how engagement with the material environment produces enhancing, as well as potentially diminishing affects. The third question explored how such 'small' moments might relate to the bigger challenges of contemporary education. This highlighted the concepts and complexities of Care on both micro and macro levels. A fourth concept of being 'Materials-Led' focused on the arts-based and material aspect of the research. This concept was folded into each of the other three by linking theory, data moments and materials together in the analysis.

Beginning with theories and concepts rather than with a specified method for data analysis as suggested in the literature (Jackson & Mazzei, 2012; Lather & St Pierre, 2013; Lenz Taguchi & St Pierre, 2017) created a data organisation process I called 'mapping the data as a bloom space'. The term 'bloom space' borrowed from Spinozist affect theory (Seigworth & Gregg, 2010; Stewart, 2007), enabled thinking of the diversity of the data as unique events or 'bodies' each holding a temporary position on a 'messy' map inspired by Spinoza as suggested by Deleuze,

> In short, if we are Spinozist's we will not define a thing by its form, nor by its organs and its functions, nor as a substance or a subject. Borrowing terms from the Middle Ages, or from geography, we will define it by longitude and latitude. A body can be anything; it can be an animal, a body of sounds, a mind or an idea; it can be a linguistic corpus, a social body, a collectivity. We call longitude of a body the set of relations of speed and slowness, of motion and rest, between particles that compose it from this point of view, that is, between unformed elements. We call latitude the set of affects that occupy a body at each moment, that is, the intensive states of an anonymous force. (Deleuze, 1988, p. 127)

Bloom space maps provided an open organisational process for multiple forms of data which could infinitely increase, decrease, connect, and disconnect and in multiple directions. They could accommodate the possibility of movement, without erasing any of the detail of the singular events.

My organising process to achieve the bloom space maps began by looking again at all of the data: fieldnotes, transcripts, drawings, photos, and videos and research texts and simply assigning a single colour according to key research concepts. Events or research data that related strongly to Affect were assigned a pink marker, Care was assigned with yellow, while Agency was blue. Orange markers were used for events that related strongly with materials. This also became a visual way of marking texts and theory in books and research materials. I also numbered photographs and videos and the interview transcripts were initialled according to pseudonyms. I mapped all of the data under one of the research question key-concepts. I used the concepts as co-ordinates or location points and as possibilities through which diverse data events and contexts could become connected.

While the data organisation through colour assigning and mapping concepts may appear similar to other qualitative approaches such as grounded theory perhaps, the mapping process here was my attempt to organise the vast quantity of data rather than as a useful way to analyse it. Although my study is undoubtedly 'grounded' by fieldwork data or moments, grounded theory uses systematic processes of segmenting the data (Creswell, 1998, 2003) whereas my approach ensured that each data moment remained intact in its detail. My analysis process was instinctive, aesthetic, affective and diverse. For example some data were analysed alongside art works while others were connected with reading.

In my study, although data were placed according to concepts of Affect, Agency and Care, which were generated by the research questions, every data moment could feasibly be related to other adjacent concepts to produce further perspectives of that data moment. This added to the potential of data to 'bloom' into new thinking and understanding. The mapping process also allowed for a cross pollination between visual, audio and textual data (video could be grouped with transcript notes etc.) which were connected by concepts. In this way, each piece of data remained intact but became intensely complexified and enriched by association with other pieces of data. This process significantly multiplied the potential of each data moment so that eventually I had to accept that it would not be possible to work with it all. Despite my best efforts to apply an organisational process to the data my selection of which particular data I might work with for my analysis was based on the affective impact or 'stickiness' (MacRae et al., 2017) of each data moment, which required and enabled intuitive and emergent analysis processes to take the lead.

Sticky Data

To begin the analysis process, the sheer quantity of data and its complex qualities and potential was overwhelming. I began by working closely with the enormously helpful idea of 'sticky data' (MacLure et al., 2010; MacRae et al., 2017). Sticky data is described as data which cannot be easily figured out, evades assumptions, and stands out as something puzzling but is nevertheless deeply affective. As described by MacRae and colleagues,

> 'Sticky data' sticks out, sticks to and often gets stuck in our thoughts, feelings, in our throat, on the page, in fieldnotes, camera lens, or memory. Not only are they full of molecular reactions and interactions, stubbornly seductive and curiously viscous, such data can jolt or conjure a sense of wonder. (MacRae et al., 2017, p. 3)

Sticky data might also allow other data, theories and processes to cling to it which encourages connectivity and diversity in approaches to analysis. Analysis of such sticky data involves 'staying with the trouble' (Haraway, 2016) of the often complex confusion that the data presents, thinking about it from multiple perspectives, running theory through it, sitting it 'diffractively' alongside art works and noticing what connections or new thinking this might produce. These are diffractive, emergent analysis 'methods' as anti-methods, some of which are suggested by the data event, some by concepts which stand out during the mapping process and some through reading, serindipitous discussion or similar collaborative, connective moments. The emphasis in post-qualitative research is openess to emergent processes while thinking deeply, often through confusing diffractive routes.

My analysis process involved generating affective and aesthetic connections with the data. The idea of analysis being an aesthetic process takes as a starting point, Bateson's definition of aesthetics as being 'responsive to the pattern which connects' (Vecchi et al., 2008, p. 138) which is referred to by Vea Vecchi as profoundly influential in the Reggio Emilia approach. The aesthetic approach to analysis which I took meant beginning from an understanding that the aim of analysis was to seek out creative connections between events, materials, theory, concepts, art and children. The process did not aim to find difinitive or absolute understandings, nor was I interested in finding singular truths. I aimed rather to be inclusive of finding many ways to produce rich thinking and writing which might bring about new understanding and life to the data, developing theory out of and alongside practice. In other words it became a way of paying attention to the data moments by connecting and envisaging them as part of, and held by an expansive more-than-human ecology.

The particular concepts, materials and sticky data selected for analysis are presented in the following analysis chapter which contains the fine detail of a small selection of the data, as the heart of my project.

CHAPTER 6

Storying Small Moments: Agency

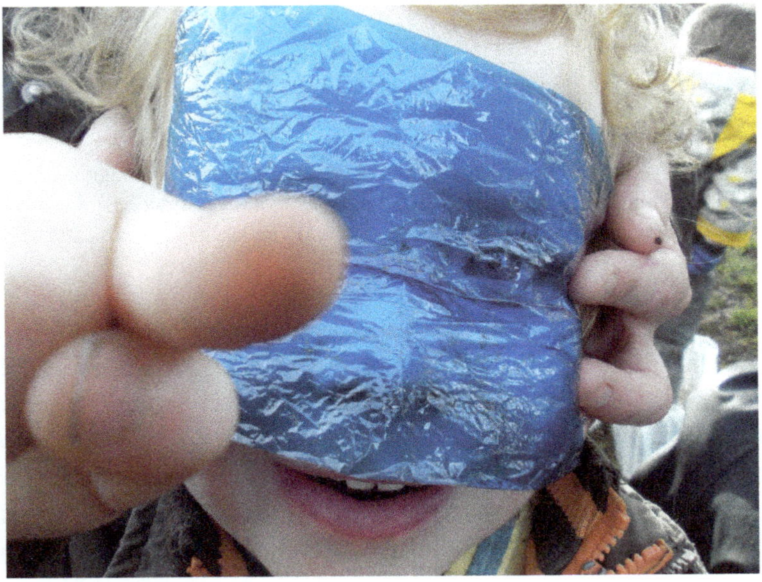

Figure 12: Storying Small Moments: AGENCY

Introduction

In the following sections of this chapter, I present analysis or research stories under each of the concept headings of Agency, Affect and Care. These research stories don't aim to exemplify the concepts however they do demonstrate their potential in relation to finding other understandings of events that are inclusive of the material environment as an active participant in how learning and care events are transmitted. While the concepts provided a focus for approaching the small moments I wanted to work with, I think that the narratives in turn also extend understanding of the concepts in relation to Posthuman theory. I precede each section with a short discussion of each of the key concepts before sharing the narratives to which they relate.

Agency

> Agency is a matter of intra-acting; it is an enactment, not something that someone or something has. It cannot be designated as an attribute of subjects or objects (…). It is not an attribute whatsoever. Agency is a 'doing' or 'being' in its intra-activity. (Barad, 2007, p. 178)

The concept of agency is important to rights-based education theory, policy, and practice, where empowerment, visibility, and equality are of concern (Harper, 1997; Rotas, 2015; Atkinson, 2018b; Ehret & D'Amico, 2019). However through a Posthuman lens, when agency is understood as enactment rather than embodiment, as affirmed by Barad in the quote above, then 'the centrality of the human is displaced and a more expansive and relational concept of assemblages of bodies supports us in thinking about the ways in which we are moved pre-cognitively' (O'Donnell, 2017, p. 7).

When agency is understood as the ability to act that is fundamentally enabled or disabled, enhanced or diminished, by a given material, affective context or environment, this connects directly into the essential impetus of all things to thrive at the most fundamental level, or their 'conatus' in Spinozist terms. In this way, children can be seen as always intimately entangled within their material environments where 'both child and the materials are active agents together in the becoming of knowledges, realities and relationships' (Thiel, Kuby & Spector, 2019, p. 20). A posthuman ethico-aesthetic lens provides ways of seeing, where and how activity (both ideational and bodily) is increased or decreased through relational intra-action between bodies both human and non-human, on a micro and a macro level. This perspective is an ethically motivated orientation because, as put by Manning,

> It is necessary to go to the heart of why volition does not define experience, and to further explore how agency, as tied to intention and will has not served to bestow power but to parse the world into subjects and objects, thereby startlingly disempowering difference. (Manning, 2016, p. 130)

A posthuman ethico-aesthetic lens supports following children's ordinary, everyday intra-actions with materials, with the posthuman understanding that agency is both performative and co-produced, and therefore reliant on multiple participants, human and non-human.

The following extracts from fieldwork are drawn together to explore the concept of agency in relation to the posthuman conceptualisation of it as a-subjective performativity. Through key theorists agency is 'cut loose from its traditional humanist orbit' (Barad, 2007, p. 177) in an effort to fully attend to the vitality of the material world and to children's intra-actions within it through their everyday learning and play.

Agency in this section mutates amongst five sub-concepts, including 'disobedient learning' (Atkinson, 2018a) 'material correspondence' (Ingold, 2013), 'material intimacy', 'agency overflow', 'voice as visual', and 'non-human agency'. Each story is held together by its focus on particular materials or objects, including here, a plastic horse, ice, cake, paint, bread, and fish.

Agency and Disobedient Learning: The Horse Song

> The surrounding noise makes the small song almost inaudible. Paint spreading from the brush onto hand and skin, temporarily merging with the plastic horse she is holding, and then through the imagined horsehair. The gentle horse lullaby appears through the movement of the paint. (Video Data p. 123)

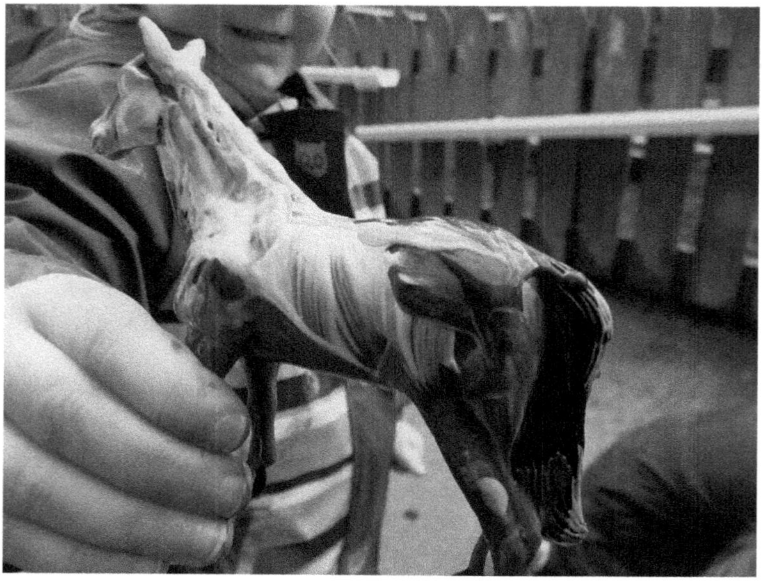

Figure 13: Disobedient Learning: The Horse Song

This analysis works with a short video clip, described in the video data notes above. Filmed during fieldwork, it captures a small song sung by a girl to a plastic horse she is painting at the outdoor atelier. I also consider my own input in framing the event through the camera lens. Making selections of what to film, is both aesthetic and instinctive and directed by the movements of children and materials at play. In selecting what to film, I sense that I am making aesthetic choices, however, like Kind and Argent I 'make no claim to truth or objectivity in what is seen and recorded and acknowledge that we (I) have certain aesthetic, artistic and poetic interests' (Kind & Argent, 2017, p. 89). It is difficult also, to try not to impose any sense of self-consciousness on those the camera is aimed toward. It is, however, important not to film surreptitiously, so that the children are aware of the camera and feel free to object to it whenever they want.

During this plastic animal painting session, there have been no instructions issued to the children on how to engage with the materials and there have been many interpretations during the session. Some children play with the animals and the water, while some create sounds and movement of the imagined live animals as they paint. With this diversity of activity, it can be difficult to know what to focus the camera on. Pacini-Ketchabaw et al. note that,

> Every encounter with materials involves decisions about what, and in what way, to notice. Using a camera means you have to look somewhere. The challenge in photographing and in some way recording children's experimentations is that it is often difficult to know or to recognise what is really happening. Where should I look? At what should I look? How should I look? (Pacini-Ketchabaw et al., 2017, p. 81)

In the video, two children work opposite and independently of each other at the table. Paint palettes are positioned in a row down the centre of the table which requires reaching in to load the brush with paint and yet minimal communication between the children occurs. Both are absorbed in their own painting processes with their own distinct approaches. As I film, the song which has already begun attracts my attention and draws the camera lens to it. While filming I am conscious of the song's delicacy, that it may easily evaporate if disturbed. The song is only barely audible due to other nearby playground sounds, and so was not the initial focus of attention. Filming has made the song noticeable while also preserving it, enabling endless revisiting for the purposes of thinking and writing. As noted by MacRae 'using film accentuates what is in motion and much more closely allows me to attend to the dynamic quality of the event' (MacRae, 2019, p. 5).

My training and experience as a visual artist have a bearing on my selection process. Difference (as displayed by this singular small song), as an ethico-aesthetic element, becomes a marker of interest, throwing up unexpected flares to be followed. Atkinson helps to conceptualise often unaccounted for events such as the horse song, as important instances of what he terms 'disobedient' learning,

> Disobedient pedagogies in contrast to those advocated by Government adopt the Spinozian notion that we don't really know what a body is capable of or what thoughts are capable of being thought, coupled with the notion of a pragmatics of the suddenly possible. Such a pedagogical stance when confronting disobedient objects or aberrant

> ways of learning/practicing may open up to new possibilities for practice and new ways for understanding learning, new ways of understanding art. (Atkinson, 2018a, p. 61)

Framed by the video camera, and my direction of it, the event also conjures what Atkinson calls the 'invention of (a) new world(s)' (Atkinson, 2018a, p. 61) where a horse is miniaturised and can change colour and participate in singing. This also recalls Dewey's work on deepening understanding of the relationship between art and everyday experience where he writes,

> The task is to restore continuity between the refined and intensified forms of experience that are works of art and the everyday events, doings, and sufferings that are universally recognised to constitute experience. (Dewey, 2005, p. 2)

The singer/painter keeps singing to herself/the horse while I film. The imaginative intensity of painting on the toy horse has sparked the emergence of the song. In this way, as the pivot which initiates a spontaneous, aesthetic, and creative act, the plastic toy could be seen as gaining what Bennett calls 'material agency' (Bennett, 2010). Bennett states that 'the locus of agency is always a human-nonhuman working group' (Bennett, 2010, p. xvii).

The toy horse also generates affects of care. While singing, the child places the horse to stand upright on the table and holds the head under the chin. This strikingly gentle gesture is attentive to the horses imagined physical needs, as a creature with a potential for vitality. Reading the significance of the child's non-verbal manual gesture in this way is supported by theorists in relation to pre-conscious thinking and feeling (Wilson, 1999; Dissanayake, 2000). However, this focus risks centralising the human as 'agent'. Rather, when such activity is read as posthuman a-subjective performativity, agency as located solely with the child quickly dissipates. A wider view of innumerable, and unknowable elements colliding to produce this song and act of caring, can be imagined, highlighting what the process of assigning 'agency' might also be masking.

In relation to some of the unknowable elements involved, it is worth noting that songs serve many different purposes and appear through multiple contexts. Even apparently simple songs can be dense and complex.

They may be individual or for communal engagement, perhaps to express love and care, perhaps to ease fear, to demonstrate contentedness or, of being 'lost' in a moment. Deleuze and Guattari note that,

> A child in the dark, gripped with fear, comforts himself by singing under his breath. He walks and halts to his song. Lost, he takes shelter, or orients himself with his little song as best he can. The song is like a rough sketch of a calming and stabilizing, calm and stable, center in the heart of chaos. Perhaps the child skips as he sings, hastens, or slows his pace. But the song itself is already a skip: it jumps from chaos to the beginnings of order in chaos and is in danger of breaking apart at any moment. (Deleuze & Guattari, 1987, p. 311)

As suggested, movement with song such as skipping, swaying, or here painting may be understood as a way of marking time passing or of joining with time and sensing its momentum. A song might travel through its rhythm as a form of measurement. Dewey theorises the harmony and melody of song as movements through time,

> The use of harmony and melody of tone, it introduces incredibly varied complexities of question, uncertainty, and suspense wherein every tone is ordered in reference to others so that each is a summation of what precedes and a forecast of what is to come. (Dewey, 2005, p. 248)

Furthermore, songs are emitted from the materiality of a body, through breadth, throat, belly, mouth and spit so that 'we begin to understand time as felt, as a bodied sense of expansiveness or constriction' (Pacini-Ketchabaw et al., 2017, p. 80). The combinations of bodily movement with painting, may equally have stimulated the songs unexpected emergence.

The horse song demonstrates a spontaneous moment, initiated, and enabled by the materials (paint, toy horse) when art becomes 'the 'perfection' immanent to the making process in which body, ideas and materials interweave' (Atkinson, 2018a, p. 55). The song as an event produced an unexpected, and yet in many ways, unremarkable moment. When framed by an ethico-aesthetic lens however, it can be seen as affirming, and full of affecting care. As an example of a 'disobedient' force, the intimate nature of this small song, which rises almost unnoticed even by the singer, is one which cannot be requested, practised, or suggested. In its singularity it facilitates the creation of a new, imaginative, and captivating 'world' which 'owes is agentic capacity to the vitality of the materialities that constitute it' (Bennett, 2001, p. 34).

Observations: Disobedient Learning

There are several key observations to be drawn from The Horse Song analysis in relation to the posthuman concept of Agency. The movement and activity of multiple participants, human and non-human within the event, reveals agency to be affirmative and co-produced performativity. The perceived or imagined material vitality of the toy horse undoubtedly contributes to the highly specific development of the song as a new creative production, which has also been facilitated by the movement and affordances of the paint and other material elements in the event. Assigning agency to the child alone in this instance, would therefore mask all the other elements which are essential to the appearance of the song. This does not mean reassigning agency to materials, rather it means thinking expansively about what else has contributed to the production of the song as affirmative, enhancing activity. The song does not belong to the child who is almost not even aware of it, rather it belongs the unique combinations of paint, horse, imagination, bodies, hands, brush (and, and, and) which have, through intra-activity, produced a new song. Posthuman agency therefore lies within acts of affirmative productivity, not as an internalised element, for either human or non-human participants. Posthuman agency is also linked to freedom in the moment to move, act, or come together in diverse and unique ways. This can also be understood as movement with time as a component of Nature, in this example, where the movement of the song, may be read as a marker of the rhythm of time. Within this movement, diversity of activity increases the potential and emergence of agency. Difference, and the freedom for it to develop as a form of agency is key, where the unique qualities of the song as it emerges attracts the attention of the camera lens, so that difference becomes a valuable aesthetic marker for attention and thinking. The agency of the event can therefore be understood as an affirmative mode of 'disobedience', or as productive of a unique, unpredictable, and inherently creative act.

Theorist Denis Atkinson has described disobedient learning as fundamental to 'the nature and force of art practice' not as a recognisable form of learning per se, but rather through the experience of art, as a mode of 'destabilisation' (Atkinson, 2018a, p. 7). In the Horse Song fieldwork analysis, artistic activity was shown to capture and direct thinking and attention in unexpected or disobedient ways. Both the child and I became drawn in, emersed, destabilised in different ways, to entirely different effect, through the same small spontaneous, unpredictable event. By allowing materials to take the lead artistically and analytically, means acknowledging that what will and can be learned or produced through an experience, however small and apparently insignificant, cannot be either limited or certain, because recalling Spinoza's contention, 'we do not know what actions a body is capable of, or what thoughts are capable of being thought' (Atkinson, 2018a, p. 27). This has implications for examining the ways in which environments and artistic practices might lead 'disobedient' creative modes of learning and experience in diverse yet deeply inclusive ways. Attention to how and where such openings might arise is crucial for creating, but also valuing spontaneous opportunities for the co-production of agency in ECEC.

Agency and Non-human Agency: Fish

> Noel is very protective of the fish, not wanting it to be hurt or touched roughly. He stands in front of it, telling what he knows about fish, asking other children to be kind. He says he would never eat one, it's not a nice thing to do. Others talk about the taste, fish for dinner, fish-fingers. Slowly the paint starts to get put onto the fish flesh. Its strong and springy and already beautiful painterly markings get covered with drippy paint. The skin holds the paint well. (Field notes, p. 125)

The fieldnote above describes a moment (as one of many different responses), of protection and care emitted by a boy toward a dead fish during a painting and printing activity, expressed through both language

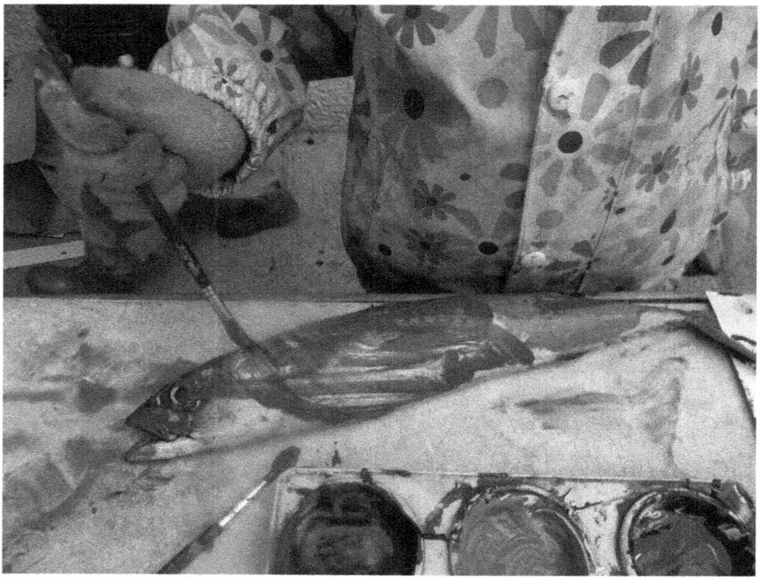

Figure 14: Non-human Agency: Fish

and his body. In this analysis section I focus on 'non-human agency' to follow the affective force generated by the fish.

Gyotaku is a fish printing process that originated in the eighteenth century as a way for fishermen in Japan to record their catch and is still widely used as an artistic process. We used West of Ireland mackerel, which the children each had different previous experience of. Some children had been out in the bay fishing, some had been to an aquarium, some had seen fish in the supermarket, and some had only seen pictures in books or animated representations. During the activity in the outdoor atelier, the fish body is painted, then lifted onto paper and printed, then bathed in a bowl of water and patted dry so that the process can be repeated. Painting on the already beautiful fish skin demands that care is taken, becoming intimate through the process of layering on new colours of paint onto bellies and eyes. Sometimes paint mixes with tiny drops of oozing blood. The children were fascinated by the 'up close' fish bodies, silver tongues, teeth and fan-like fins, while at the same time imagining and discussing fish homes, families and escape strategies, demonstrating children's capacities to envisage agency as always more than human (Puig de la Bellacasa, 2017, p. 122).

In the context of the outdoor atelier the activity facilitated an approach toward the delicate unpacking of human-animal relations that matter to children. Within the frame of posthumanism, the process offered opportunities to consider animals as participants in, and potential generators of, intensely aesthetic events. It provided an opportunity to be bodily confronted by the death of an animal which created what Schulte describes as a 'clotting of attentions' (Schulte, 2019, p. 78) because death of course, is of interest to children. This death was something which occurred with (troubling) intent, and in another context serves the (important) purpose of human sustenance. The question arose of where the fish had come from. I told the children that I had bought them in the supermarket and not caught (killed) them myself. Conversation and ideas about justice and death circulated, with new ideas, concerns, memories, and knowledges being evoked.

On previous occasions of presenting Gyotaku for 2-year-olds I have witnessed children independently swaddle fish in paper towels, then carry them away in the crook of their arms, chatting intently, becoming deeply attached to them like macabre dolls. The fish in these play episodes were whole heartedly accepted by the children as they engaged with them imaginatively and lovingly. On this occasion however, one child in particular insisted on 'investigating' a fish, poking a stick down its mouth which was upsetting and difficult for some and required urgent negotiation amongst the children themselves. The complex argument centred around whether the capacity to feel or not feel, negates maltreatment. The ethical discussions saw children take sides and tease out empathetic 'what ifs' amongst themselves.

While the fish initially appeared helplessly compromised they went on to exert an insistent influence over conversation and sensation (queasy for some adults) for many weeks after they had gone. This could be understood as a form of 'material agency' (Bennett, 2010). Despite my extra efforts at cleaning up afterwards the smell lingered on in unexpected places, silently changing the materiality of everything it clung to and moved with. Weeks later, some mittens and boots still smelled faintly fishy. The reverberations of thinking, imagining, and talking about the fish prompted by the unexpected smell created even more new threads of thinking about entanglements between humans and animals, life and death, and everyday materials.

Experiencing the fish within the new context of an artistic activity and engaging with them in aesthetic ways profoundly altered the relationships (in the moment at least) between both human and non-human. The activity created potential for 'non-human actants' (Latour, 1996) to more than just participate, but to generate the aesthetic aspect of the events. Atkinson explains the unexpected emergence of art as an event, as what he calls 'poietic materialism' which is pedagogical and contributes to the development of new understanding of what bodies can be or do,

> The event of art as an appearing … as poiesis … is not subjective or objective, but intra-active, involving human and non-human actants such as feelings, thoughts, memories, materials such as paint, paper, metal, wood, digital technologies, performances and more. The pedagogical imperative of a poietic materialism is to extend our grasp and potential of what it is to be human, or to put in the words of Spinoza, to extend our compass of what a body can do. (Atkinson, 2018a, p. 167)

Observations: Non-human Agency

This Gyotaku event enabled a consideration of other-than-human bodies as productive of posthuman understandings of agency, and as powerful participants in aesthetic events. Through artistic practice and an ethico-aesthetic lens, other species become more than figurations from which to develop human learning but may be unpredictable, even uncontrollable participants in learning events and experiences. Agency was also increased ideationally and imaginatively through the children's expression of newly shared knowledges and ethical beliefs, which were stimulated by the novelty of the dead fish in school. Prompted by the unexpected but familiar smell of the fish, affective memory also developed new ideas, actions, and feelings. Non-human agency connected and interjected unexpectedly, re-directing human thoughts, activities, and conversations. Further, posthuman perspectives of agency oscillated between both human and non-human and was captured and contained by neither. Artistic, aesthetic contexts can be understood as capable of changing power relationships, here between animals and humans, and also of hierarchies in relation to the consideration of the production of agency.

The concept of non-human agency arose so that other-than-human species (here a dead fish) were seen to contribute to the generation of agency, and to creatively divert human attention, experience, and learning. This redirects and complexifies the consideration of other-than-human species as knowable resources for learning, or as simplified, diminished, objects of affection, as they are frequently made available to children in representational or toy form. Through consideration of non-human participants in the generation of agency, the posthuman ethico-aesthetic perspective unsettles multiple hierarchical and anthropocentric considerations of power in relation to the production of agency. Here, posthuman analysis offers space for the appreciation of the contribution which unknown others might make to more established collective experience, learning and agency.

Agency and (Posthuman) Subjectivity: Paint/Mess

> Some children stay at the table for the hour despite being called to play or join in games, even with the increasing messiness of the table. Some children paint, then leave, then return again. Some choose to paint the table covering rather than the pieces of card. 'Luke' surprises educators by engaging with paint for the first time. He has a strong dislike of getting his hands 'dirty', but here opts to use his fingers tentatively rubbing one at a time into paint then onto paper, until the action slowly becomes more vigorous. He smiles at me and seems pleased. (Fieldnotes, p. 54)

In the field note above, and previously, Luke has consistently expressed a strong dislike of mess, or more precisely, of the sensations that sticky, slippery liquids have to offer his hands, skin, clothing, and body. He is most certainly not alone in this. Many children and adults do not like the various intense sensations of mess, but Luke is the only one amongst his peers at preschool with this particular dislike. The other children like

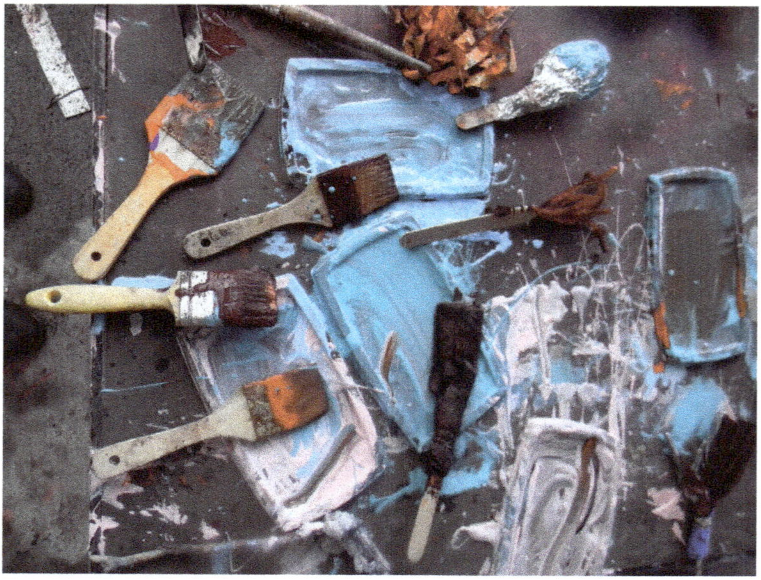

Figure 15: Posthuman Subjectivity: Paint/Mess

to dive in whereas Luke actively avoids paint and other similar materials, quietly but nevertheless resolutely asserting his refusal.

In ECEC, sensory 'mess' and creative activity are frequently conceptually linked and as a result messy play with materials, particularly when proposed for outdoors, is associated with healthy, positive processes of learning (Health Service Executive, 2011; French, 2013). This relatively recent re-evaluation of mess in ECEC also requires tolerant educators who enable children to experience sensory exploration of materials such as water, sand, clay, and paint. A dislike of these forms of play or a need to be clean in these scenarios may be perceived as a lack, or a resistant 'behaviour' (MacLure et al., 2010) that needs to be gently worked on, by educators and by children themselves. Rather than moving with the activity of the rest of the group of children, Luke becomes somewhat isolated through the surfacing of his preference to be clean. This isolating sensation may feasibly generate further feelings of discomfort or potential anxiety for Luke, in addition to the disquiet that arises from the idea of touching the paint. The tensions between these positions are felt by Luke alone in this scenario and appear, through his gentleness and reluctance to create a fuss, to be pushed inward.

Bennett refers to subjectivity as 'the nature of human interiority' (Bennett, 2010, p. 120). Considered to be uniquely human, subjectivity is conceived as the internal world of the (human) individual. In Luke's case, as a child set apart through his difference from the others in this instance, his refusal also appears to be an internalised decision made by him alone, driven by a fixed character which has the effect of either setting him apart or making him unique depending on how positively or negatively the distinction is perceived. Nevertheless, where Luke's difference has emerged from remains entirely speculative. A posthuman understanding of the relational and 'nomadic' view of subjectivity (Braidotti, 2013) is profitable to pursue in relation to envisaging Luke once again as a part of, rather than apart from, his environment. Bennett states that,

> The philosophical project of naming where subjectivity begins and ends is too often bound up with fantasies of a human uniqueness (...), of escape from materiality, or of mastery of nature; and even where it is not, it remains an aporetic or quixotic endeavor. (Bennett, 2010, p. ix)

Posthuman subjectivity considers the complex ecologies of ongoing, immanent relations (Braidotti, 2013). What this means in Luke's case is taking a wider perspective of the entangled material environment which facilitated an uncoerced slippage of Luke's prior refusal, into a transformed acceptance of the messy paint (even if it is momentary). Braidotti (2013) suggests connecting posthuman subjectivity to desire as excess or overflow, rather than desire as lack or need, is a necessary move to dislodge these more negative associations. The excesses and overflowing movement of paint, bodies and their associated sounds spill over and merge with an exciting unpredictability. Luke and the other children and adults are surrounded with a co-motion that is accommodating of transformation in many directions. For Luke, the paint is also transformed as a new, unexpected, and reconfigured 'object of desire',

> To phrase 'the object of desire' as a cluster of promises is to allow us to encounter what is incoherent or enigmatic in our attachments, not as confirmation of our irrationality but as an explanation for our *sense of our endurance in the object,* insofar as proximity to the object means proximity to the cluster of things that the object promises, some of which may be clear to us while others not so much. (Berlant, 2010, p. 93)

Put another way, it can only be speculated as to Luke's reasons for apparently 'changing his mind' about the paint or about what the paint may have emitted to him in terms of a 'cluster of promises'. However, what is clear is that in the material environment surrounding him which he is unavoidably a part of as sounds and sensations pass through his body, the free flow of traffic of children, paint, trees, air etc., are all supportive of change, movement, play, and transformation, and so there is reason to surmise that his previous refusal might also be caught up in these waves towards changes in position.

In her vital materialist account Bennett refers to the Deleuzian concept of 'a pure a-subjective current' (Bennett, 2010, p. 53). This is borrowed from Deleuze 'Immanence – a life' (Deleuze, 1997) which finds through Spinoza, that a life is a transcendental field. Using this Spinozist posthuman view of life beyond fixed notions of subjects and objects, subjectivity is no longer fixed, internalised, or exclusively human. Luke's prior refusal itself then can be understood as a lively force that prevents him from moving in the same direction as his friends. It may also be considered as not attached or fixed to Luke, although it emerged through his voice and under certain material circumstances in which he found himself (when he was required to get messy). As such, the refusal can be read not as stagnation or 'stuck-ness' but rather as a movement in a different direction, away from messy paint rather than towards it with the other children. The reversal of Luke's desire to be clean, also fits the description of an 'a-subjective current' (Bennett, 2010, p. 53) in which he is caught up. The affective 'current' makes itself felt through the tensions which arise between these shifting desires (to touch or not touch), and shifts when an opportunity presents itself, as it did in the outdoor atelier.

The posthuman materialist lens considers the outdoor atelier environment as an active component in an assemblage of movement which here, supports a surprising disordering of things as distinct from those which may be more habitual or even apparently static inside. Paint spilling and overflowing from containers onto table, ground and clothing do not generate immediate effects of adults re-enforcing order by cleaning up as would occur inside. The changes in weather (movements of clouds, wind, temperature), the variable distances from which sounds and weather travel, are joined by new possibilities to accelerate speeds of children's bodies, no longer restrained by the interior frame of the preschool building. The possibility of the sudden arrival of other creatures, often un-noticed, such as birds, snails, and bugs or of projectiles such as sticks and leaves all supports the liveliness of the event, enabling a certain amount of unthreatening chaos. Elizabeth Grosz (2005) writes on the relationship between art and chaos where their co-production is reliant on dynamic self-organising material movement,

> This is not the homeostatic relation of stabilisation, but a fundamentally dynamic, awkward mal-adaptation that enables the production of the frivolous, the unnecessary, the pleasing, the sensory for its own sake. (Grosz, 2005, p. 7)

Posthuman subjectivity, like agency is not tied within an individualised body but emerges through movement and intra-action with the world. This event as the culmination of numerous movements coming together albeit briefly produce transformative thinking and action for Luke in the moment. Nevertheless, given the possibility for movement in multiple directions, and that assemblages also break apart, it is also possible and important to note that Luke's original refusal may also return, flowing back to occupy where it formerly rested. However, what is of significance is that the experience created the potential for movement, newness, and change and that this was acknowledged and felt by Luke, and finally expressed through a smile.

Observations: Posthuman Subjectivity

The concept and question of subjectivity as a process of becoming is fundamental to education theory and practice that is concerned with supporting learners to become aligned with the world around them, as put by Atkinson,

> Where learning is viewed as much more than an accumulation of facts or skills but includes also an expansion of affective processes towards the world and others that include feeling, sensitivity, concern, creativity, perspicacity and adventure. (Atkinson, 2018a, p. 39)

Through Spinozist posthuman theory, subjectivity becomes capable of movement with the material environment and is envisaged as always nomadic and relational, never fixed (Braidotti, 2013). Integral to this movement, Spinozist, posthuman, affirmative ethics reconfigures desire as connected to abundance rather than to more negative notions of lack or need (Braidotti, 2013). This follows Spinoza's claim that 'desire is the very essence of man; that is, the conatus whereby man endeavors to persist in his own being' (Spinoza, 1996, [1677], E4p18dem). In Spinozist posthuman theory this 'promotes a continuing emphasis on the radical ethics of transformation' (Braidotti, 2013, p. 189). It also makes subjectivity an aesthetic concern, as put by Benson, 'art-making is self-extension into the world, thus enabling sharing, and that self-extension is a means of self-creation' (Benson, 2019, p. 15).

This reconsideration of subjectivity formation has implications for understanding behaviours as changeable rather than fixed within human (children's) bodies or minds, as can be seen in the analysis of the messy paint event in the fieldwork. Noticing the small, messy paint moment for Luke became a way of understanding how significant agential moments are produced between children and environments, and as a mode of art, as a fundamental destabilisation.

Refusal in this posthuman analysis becomes envisaged as a lively, changeable, and active movement flowing with and/or against the material environment, and like subjectivity is not fixed, or contained within an internalised human body. In this way the material environment is envisaged as an active component in the event assemblage, but also in the development and understanding of human subjectivity. This also affirms that the material environment can directly impact what developmental pedagogy considers to be uniquely human behaviours or desires. Understanding undesirable behaviours through a posthuman lens releases them from fixed association with particular (human) bodies, which in turn accommodates a more complex reading of subjectivity, and consequently, potentially, of children. Understanding children from a position of complexity is an ethical imperative when understanding that experiences may never be assumed to be fully known in advance, particularly in the context of the Anthropocene, when rapidly changing circumstance bring educators into contact with children whose experience may be far removed from their own. Acceptance of the need to be open to difference and complexity in relation to knowing children, therefore, is an ethical imperative.

Enabling the material environment to do its work in helping us to become, and to produce transformative agential moments, requires a dialling down of meaning, intent and the improving intentions and interventions of adults and curriculum. Sharing the moment for Luke through a smile, was sufficient to acknowledge its potency (and its subsequent insistent re-emergence as a moment for me to think with theory about nomadic processes of becoming). This consideration of the process of becoming with the material environment through desire as affirmative and abundant, facilitates a complex, and therefore decolonising, approach to understanding children in relation to processes of subjectivity formation and agency. Being led by small material moments through theory creates openings for considering children as part of, and complexly in relation with their environments, and reduces potentially confining assumptions of how children become with or extend into the world.

Agency Overflowing: A Cough

> I photograph the small group activity to capture the material impact on the previously clean environment. The traces of the activity feel important and the ways in which the new materials merge with bodies and the fixed materiality of the floor, tables, chairs, and walls. The apparently least material of the small group activities (the letter search) has for me two noticeably material 'events'; The first is when Nathan (child) absent-mindedly presses his cheek into Iris's (educator's) soft woolen cardigan. The second is when a loud cough scatters the fragments of letters across the table leaving a 'u' shaped clear space in the pile of letter pieces. (Field notes, p. 7)

> We cannot help but view the world in terms of solids, as things. But [then] we leave behind something untapped of the fluidity of the world, the movements, vibrations, transformations that occur below the threshold of perception and calculation and outside the relevance of our practical concerns. [Yet] … we have … access to this profusion of vibration that underlies the solidity of things. (Grosz, 2005, p. 136)

This analysis works with some small moments to think about the ways in which voice and agency might rub-up against or overflow into each other. The field note event above occurred during a 'small group' activity. On this morning, the educator led activity is naming letters from cardboard scrabble pieces spread out randomly on the table. There is a physical closeness between the group drawn together by their chairs and purposeful attention to the task. 'Nathan' is sitting directly to the left of 'Iris' the educator. He leans his head against her arm. Iris is wearing a soft woollen jumper that he presses his cheek into, exploring its inviting texture with his cheek while remaining focused on the letter pieces on the table.

I read this moment as one of pre-conscious material intimacy. There is no eye contact or no words, with the only acknowledgement being Iris's small smile while she glances toward Nathan, as though she is never fully habituated to these small gestures, even after working with young children for many years. The moment seems quite routine and yet it is very affecting to observe. It suggests a deep level of ease within the environment as is necessary for these tiny connections to occur. Nathan then climbs onto Iris's knee while still concentrating on the task at hand (finding letters on the table), which seems to have absorbed his attention. Iris could equally be a chair but there must be an understanding, a trust that she won't flip or topple. Then suddenly and unexpectedly, Nathan coughs loudly and openly, without putting his hand over his mouth or into his sleeve as they are taught to. It immediately silences the chatter at the table. As a pre-pandemic event, I think this may not have been because of an awareness of spreading germs, but more because of the striking visual effect the cough has had on the scrabble letters which have been the focus of so much attention and conversation between the children. The letters are moved into a perfect crescent shape by the force of the rapidly ejected coughed air. The shape seems regular and deliberate. Everyone stares at the shape on the table silently for a few seconds before Iris moves things along. The drawing together of everyone's attention into a unified focus on the unintentional material moment is fascinating. The moment is irresistible to everyone. Although it feels intensely significant, enough to stop everyone in their tracks, to command silence and widen eyes, there is no clear explanation or revelation in relation to meaning or understanding,

> What we have so far then is a sense of affect as an intensity, affect as shared, received and transferred, and, although it is often divorced from language or interpretation, or intent, it (is) nonetheless potent. (Vehaba, 2018, p. 132)

There is no picking up on this event through language in the way there can be with other spontaneous observations. Perhaps because Iris doesn't want to draw attention to a misdemeanour of sorts (not covering one's mouth while coughing), or, perhaps because this moment has not been named or framed by language, or perhaps because the event, although emitted through Nathan's body, as a shared event materialised through the scrabble pieces becomes understood as something that the scrabble pieces did in response to the cough, but at a remove from Nathan. It seems that unless an attachment, either verbal or subjective, is assigned then events can slip away. The pandemic context would almost certainly have brought a different response with everybody (children included) having absorbed the persistent flow of verbal warnings relating to the potentially lethal danger of a rogue cough such as this one. However decisions to allow these slippages are communal and yet intensely affective so, 'what the idea of affect ultimately allows us to see is that we are inherently constitutive, that we share certain states of being' (Vehaba, 2018, p. 132). The event in this case is co-constituted by children, educator, table, scrabble pieces, ejected (germ filled) air, soft jumper, chairs, where the cough and perfectly formed crescent shape, magnetises each of these elements into an event assemblage, which then dissipates just as quickly when language diverts activity in other directions. What is interesting is the abundance, frequency, and overflow of these events as uncaptured and unregulated possibilities and as the constant undercurrent to everyday pedagogical practice.

Overflow of a Gallery Visit

Some-time later another similarly surprising material event is called to Iris's attention by Tomas (child), and through prolonged verbal discussion and questioning amongst the children and Iris, is extended as a pedagogical motif for several days after. I did not witness the originating event but was told about it when I commented on some new laminated coloured cellophane artwork displayed in the window. Apparently, while reaching into his schoolbag to tidy away his lunch box and drink bottle, one transparent blue plastic, the other transparent yellow, the sunlight hit both objects at a particular angle which highlighted for Tomas for the first time since owning the objects that placing one on top of the other produced a transparent green colour. Tomas was astonished by his discovery and exuberantly demonstrated it to his friends and Iris through excited conversations. There were many subsequent conversations about colour mixing and transparency, which became extended into small group time activities with paint, and an opportunity to laminate scraps of coloured cellophane, to produce stained glass like artwork. On seeing these, I drew Iris's attention to the visual similarities between the children's artwork and an exhibition of Tom Climent's abstract paintings on in the local gallery, and so we organised to take her 'small group' of children on an outing to the gallery.

At the exhibition, primacy was again given to spoken observations. When asked, Diana (child) said the paintings looked like jewels or crystals. This became a clue for Iris to develop another project on growing crystals in jars on the classroom window as a small group time activity. While this is a perfectly valid, child-centred, exciting, and appropriate activity, it nevertheless overwhelmed a multitude of other complex affective events that occurred both in the gallery space and on the way there. For instance, the children's excitement to walk down the road together in their high-vis jackets, the sensations of holding hands while walking together, of meeting dogs and cats, running sleeves along walls, noticing zebra crossings and doorsteps which afforded possibilities for alternative experimental movement such as jumping, marching, and hopping.

In the gallery, the paintings were hung at adult height and were abstract (without a clear narrative) and did not compete with the novelty of a new space to move in. The children approached the layout of the space (the alcoves, big windows to climb up on and the division of the room which made hiding a possibility) as open to exploration, and experimentation. The artists gallery statement also emphasises the tacit nature of his painting process as one which is a matter of following and experimenting with the possibilities and problems which the materials and spaces within the paintings present,

> The way I work is largely intuitive, painting for me starts a process of discovering unintended connections and relationships, of trying to search for reason and meaning in each work that emerges ... I feel as if I'm in a relationship with the painting, it guides me as much as I control it. (Tom Climent, Custom House Gallery, artist statement, 2017)

While the children did not produce artistic products as the artist did, they each (artist and children) underwent captivating spatial explorations which became a matter of unfolding playful and complex opportunities for engaging with actual and virtual spaces, materially, bodily, and imaginatively. Locating learning within these processes Lenz Taguchi's states that 'a pedagogy that deals with becomings basically means that we move – simultaneously- between what is (the actual) and what might become (the virtual)' (Lenz Taguchi, 2010, p. 176). The virtual spaces in this visit, were present in the ongoing multi-directional experimentation with movement and its imaginative possibilities. In this experimentation, where potential is opened and followed, or not, much of value may be intensely experienced but not accounted for in words. MacRae et al. note,

> A great deal of what we do in everyday life, we do without thinking about it. A great deal of what a child does in a museum, they do without thinking about it, and would struggle to explain it in words. Why did you run up and down that corridor? Why are you so very attached to that small plastic magnifying glass? (…) When research works with conceptual models that can only account for what can be explained in words, other aspects of what takes place are usually disregarded. (MacRae et al., 2017, p. 7)

This observation relates strongly to pedagogy and teaching practices where meaning is prioritised. Massumi suggests that learning from unexpected and unexplainable events, particularly when value, purpose or meaning are unclear, is always full of possibility,

> The way all the elements interrelate is so complex that it isn't necessarily comprehensible in one go. There's always a sort of vagueness surrounding the situation, an uncertainty about where you might be able to go and what you might be able to do once you exit the particular context. This uncertainty can actually be empowering (…) This brings a potential to the situation. (Massumi in Pacini-Ketchabaw et al., 2017, p. 79)

These theorisations help to understand how everyday learning and agency as the ability to act can exceed language. It also suggests that agency and learning are co-produced through experimental movement *with* the world, its flows and overflows, which also locates them firmly within creative practice,

> When children learn; everything becomes movement and experimentation. Letters, light, numbers, colours, everything is thrown up in the air, nothing is wrong and everything is potentiality. Sense and nonsense walk together hand in hand (…) The creative response is not an act of imitation, or a desperate search for a given solution. (…) The creative response lies in the way children vibrate and resonate together with the world. (Olsson, 2009, p. 5)

Observations: Material Intimacy and Visual Voice

This analysis begins by introducing a consideration of pre-conscious material intimacy, where wool draws cheek or skin towards it, and so the temptations of sensation are not only conscious but can also reverberate through pre-conscious activity. Perhaps when conscious activity is diverted into other areas of concentration or directed learning, pre-conscious activity and material intimacy find opportunities to emerge. Crucial to the emergence of intimacy however is the degree of ease and comfort within the environment and that through small, unspoken, 'overflow' acts of material/bodily contact that ease and comfort become visible. If the concept of agency is fixed to conscious control over activity then these pre-conscious moments become shadows of agency and their potential to be read as important markers of movement and growth with/in an environment are potentially lost. A posthuman reading of events does not require an erasure of the human within those events but rather aims to see what focusing on the material environment can make visible, particularly, how we are moved by the material environment. This also exposes how the affective undercurrent of everyday pedagogical practice as something which shifts in and out of view and attention. This is made available through an ethico-aesthetic lens which includes a focus on material intra-activity.

The posthuman lens readjusts the dominance of conscious control as associated with the production of agency and enables focuses on pre-conscious modes of closeness to materials which are experienced in bodily ways (such as, touching soft wool with cheeks). The body appears to lead in these forms of knowing and being, rather than fully conscious attentionality. This presents a movement alongside and with material environments rather than a face to face, fully conscious meeting of things. As such, these small moments of 'intimacy' are part of the constant abundance of experience which lie beyond both conscious and verbal capture.

Attention to material intimacy through an ethico-aesthetic lens creates openings for taking felt, bodily knowledge seriously, with the understanding that all that is unfolding within an experience is neither fully under control, nor fully seen. This has implications for the evaluation and documentation of children's modes of learning and being and how some are resistant to particular forms of capture. A posthuman ethico-aesthetic lens offers possibilities for making these felt moments of experience more visible (although never fully) and for acknowledging their emergence without the requirement to attach meaning to them. Loosening the grip of meaning and conscious control in pedagogy provides openings for other ways of seeing children's engagement with the world as intensely aesthetic.

In the gallery visit event this included those forms of exploration and knowing which connect artist's and children's approaches to the possibilities of space and movement in tacit bodily ways. Creating opportunities for these modes of experience and allowing the confusion they may bring in relation to meaning introduces the idea of an aesthetically tuned evolving pedagogy in the moment, rather than one which projects forward into more intentional forms of practice. Rather, focus and attention were on small felt moments and looking for ways to make them more visible and democratically accessible, that don't rely on attaching singular or certain meaning as stated by Olsson,

> The focus of work with pedagogical documentation must be on the processes of learning, not knowledge or goals to attain. Moreover, learning must be treated as impossible to predict, plan, supervise or evaluate according to predefined standards. This presents a real challenge today, as we have seen (…) how much importance is put on the achievement of predetermined goals. (Olsson, 2009, p. 117)

The dominance of the spoken voice, even of the child's, also brought to the fore in this analysis exposes all that voice pushes to the side-lines. Voice, as related to agency, or the ability to express oneself and be heard, can itself overwhelm other interesting considerations, of which there may not be conscious awareness. The posthuman and materialist focus here brings attention to how experience, movement, art and play always exceed language, that there is always more than can be named. Of interest here also is the consideration of both artist and children's modes of navigating and moving with/in spaces, virtual and actual, in making and breaking problems playfully. This becomes evidence of movement with the material environment as full of creative potential, growth, and learning. This form of learning is an exciting exchange between human bodies, spaces, and materials, and for children and artist, is felt as a challenging, playful way of being in the world. For children however, it often occurs in in-between moments, of what may otherwise be prioritised as valuable learning through discursive pedagogy, or one that is dominated by the verbal. Nevertheless, the material environment constantly 'teaches' by presenting surprising and challenging propositions and temptations, which, when children can participate, become affirmative, agency generating opportunities.

As a concept strongly related to that of agency, through a posthuman ethico-aesthetic lens, 'voice', when understood as exclusively language was seen to potentially mask other forms of knowing and being such as those felt forms of material intimacy discussed above. In my research, documentation was largely produced through photographs, which as well as being a way of looking and coming to know the research site aesthetically, and of thinking with concepts such as 'material agency' and 'material intimacy', were also a way of sharing new, surprising, and sometimes confusing perspectives of the environment with the children and other adults. An approach to documentation that is visual and affective, that doesn't require a return to verbal language to retain affective power, is inclusive of children as producers of their own aesthetic and affective documentation. The children's 'selfies' for example, display children's ways of documenting, which capture event's as experimental, exploratory, aesthetic, and playful. This also introduces the possibility of voice as visual, as an alternative and additional mode of making oneself seen and heard. Visual understandings of voice also present ways for both adults and children, of posing rather than answering questions through experimentation, excitement, and confusion. My own photographic images presented throughout this text are moments when attention was brought to small, overlooked material areas of the ECEC setting environment, as aesthetically and affectively distinct and powerful, and a way to offer the material environment of the setting a 'voice'. They are of course, partial, and inefficient (Knight, 2019, 2021) carriers of information as representational 'documentation' yet they were productive of new ways of looking, seeing, thinking, and feeling. This emphasises the potential of an approach to documentation in ECEC that is grounded by inclusivity (human and non-human) and aesthetic affect as a way of representing the many different 'voices' that may be present and contributing to experience.

Agency and Material Correspondence: The Camera

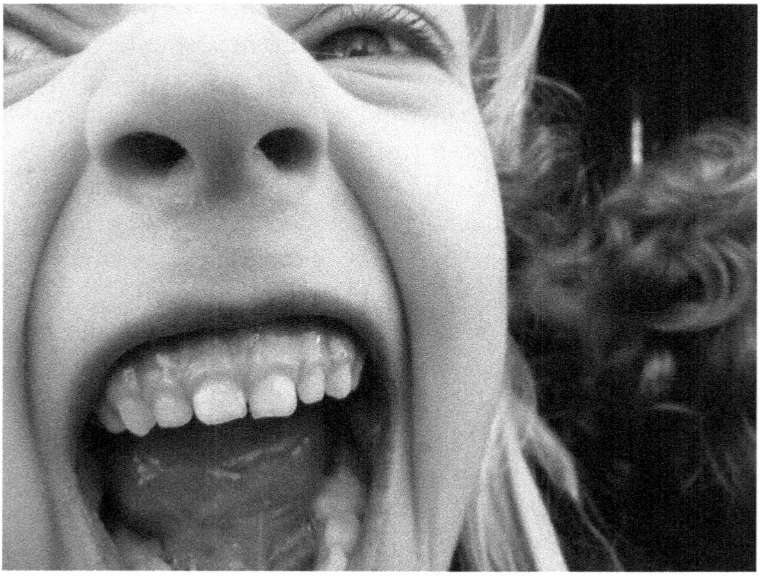

Figure 16: Agency and Material Correspondence: The Camera

> Children also work with the camera, photographing objects, action, and each other. 'Martha' (3) most regularly seeks out the camera and enjoys sharing and talking about the knowledge she is accumulating about the camera, including operating the batteries and memory card. (Fieldnotes, p. 151)

> There was one child who was particularly interested in photography, and she was allowed to have the camera, she had full freedom to take the kind of photographs she wanted to take, and her competence was unbelievable, she became way more capable with the camera than I am. (Educator Interview 'Christine')

Throughout the field work I brought a small white digital camera for the children to use. This came about after the first day when my SLR camera attracted a lot of attention, causing the children to swarm around me hoping they could take a photo. While I facilitated this by allowing them to look through the lens, the camera strap remained around my neck for fear of it getting dropped in the excitement. This was only partially satisfying in that I knew I was restricting the children's opportunities to share in the research process and reducing the potential for them to contribute in a meaningful way to the data gathering. I also felt that it was an issue of equality and fairness that once addressed, could increase the normalisation of photographic activity within the setting, for adults and children. I consulted with the educators and owners who said that while cameras had been used by the children in school before, they rarely lasted very long, were often dropped or else caused arguments amongst children who found them difficult to share, and so were put away. Disposable cameras were suggested as an alternative which I rejected as these do not afford the opportunity to view images taken like a digital camera can. The wind-on mechanism is also difficult to operate, and their disposability makes them feel quite like toys, so I worried that the children may not be as attracted to them as 'proper' cameras. I very much wanted to include the children's images as part of the process and so suggested that I bring a designated children's digital camera of my own. The educators were all happy with this suggestion and with my understanding of the potential breakage risks involved once certain parameters were clarified with the children. The first of these was that we needed to constantly state that if someone did not want to be photographed by either me or the children, it was fine to say no without reason. The educators also decided that the camera would only be used for 'outside time'. On the next day of fieldwork, still at the observation stage, I brought in the children's camera. As the educators had predicted it generated a lot of interest amongst the children leading to a clamouring and dissatisfaction with demands of fairness in the division of time which proved difficult, abstract, and tiresome to monitor. This led to the children's decision to grant each child who wanted to use the camera a condition of taking ten photos before passing it to the next child in line. This clarification eased the facilitation of sharing somewhat but added pressure to take photos, with the counting of shots being called out by the children waiting for their turn. However, after several days interest in the camera waned, leaving a small group of children who were particularly interested and willing to endure the negotiating and the waiting for their turn. It was surprising to me how quickly this relative ease developed given the initial excitement.

The children enjoyed sharing knowledge about the technicalities of the camera such as where the batteries go, how to remove them, what the memory card is and how to access it. They demonstrated several functions on the camera to each other such as the delete and video record buttons. The delete function raised some complex conceptual problems. For example, none of us (adults or children), could adequately explain where deleted images go to, when this question was raised by Luke. Looking for answers, we began by thinking with the blackboard, drawing an image in chalk then rubbing it out, but the materiality of the dust remained as messy evidence of the problem. The images do not just melt or disappear, they must change and go somewhere, but where? Someone suggested the magnetised drawing board as a similar image production mechanism where the magnetised filaments inside the tray become rearranged but unchanged in their material state. This solution created further questions about colours changing and adapting, as did the mention of 'the cloud' which we all quickly retreated from trying to understand or explain. The basic technicalities of digital photography continuously eroded adult confidence and reputations for knowing but enabled us all to try to work out the possibilities, adding to our understanding as the weeks went by through questioning more expert adults and doing google searches for specific questions. This humbling undermining of assumptions of superior knowledge production capabilities elevated our opinions of the camera and its powerful presence in the preschool.

There wasn't any particularly formal demonstrating how the camera worked, rather the information was figured out between the children as they passed the camera onto the next child in line, also drawing on their stated existing knowledges of taking photos with their parent's mobile phones. The children were as free as I was to take photos of what interested them, and to move unrestricted and unmonitored while outside. Due to this level of freedom, I did not follow closely their movements or methods but listened and looked whenever they wished to show me interesting images they had taken, but they did not always want or think to share with me so often I found the images on the camera after the fieldwork had finished for the day.

When taking pictures of friends, the children played with pulling faces to generate photos and reactions to amuse each other. The camera also enabled the children to capture images of adults who also often added performative aspects to their posing in playful ways that would only have been initiated by the presence and directed aim of a camera held by a child. The low positioning of the camera forced adults to stoop to child height for their faces to be captured. The children usually allowed adults to see images of them that they had taken, but not always.

A common theme of taking 'selfies' spread amongst the children over the course of the fieldwork which generated a series of images full of artistic interest. The inability to see the image being composed of oneself in the viewfinder creates a need to trust and play with the camera as an object that is not entirely controllable. In several of the selfies, the children choose to open their mouths and make funny or contorted faces as a novel way of playing with the camera and its potentialities to transform images of themselves, for themselves. Even in images where focus is blurred or obstructed by fingers, there is a striking affirmative quality generated between child and camera. After taking the selfies it seemed almost automatic to look at the image that had been captured, to show friends or to delete it. To mark the end of the fieldwork, we all gathered in the classroom to share a projected slideshow of images we all had taken which was an exciting, noisy, and joyful experience. The children were very pleased to recognise the images they had taken themselves, particularly the selfies.

'Martha' and the Camera

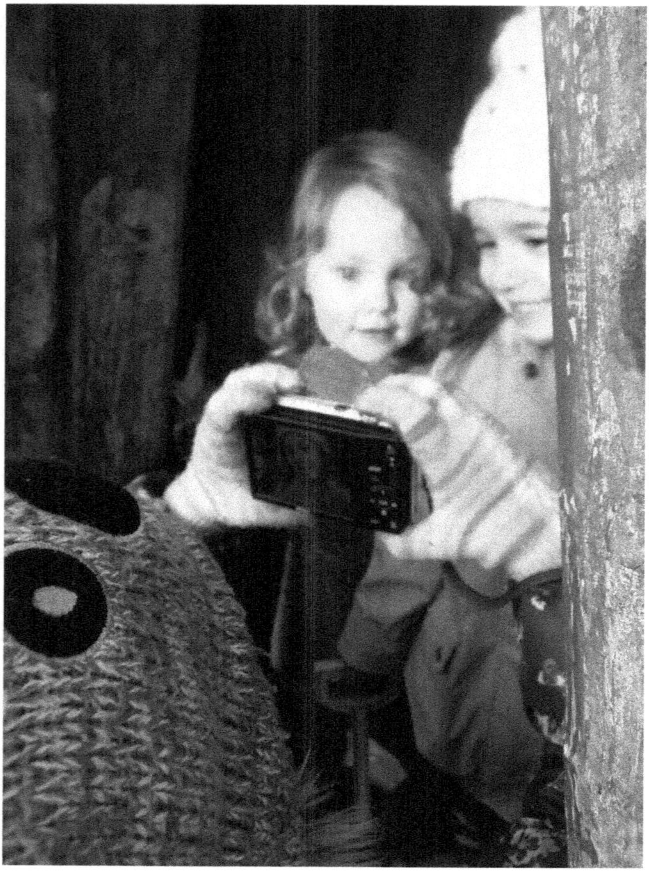

Figure 17: Martha as Photographer

The camera was of particular interest to 'Martha' (age 3). Throughout the fieldwork practice, through her persistence and curiosity she gained a significant reputation as a photographer. Martha developed a series of images of the material environment, of her friends and of snails for example, which were taken with great care compositionally. Martha's photographic competency pleased her greatly and was the subject of conversation amongst children, educators, and parents. The discursive building of her reputation as a photographer developed the idea of 'agency' as a form of expertise or skill building developed through practice. Posthuman and new materialist theorists argue however that the concept of agency should also be attributed to materials and objects, in which case the camera also needs to be considered as an active agent in Martha's skill building process.

In their introduction to 'New Materialisms: Ontology, Agency and Politics' Diana Coole and Samantha Frost (2010) state that new materialism 'sees its task as creating new concepts of nature that affirm matter's immanent vitality' and go on to posit that this can the equated to the concept of 'material agency' (Coole & Frost, 2010, p. 14). While the camera may not be considered as constituting 'natures vitality', being a man-made object rather than 'vibrant matter', Jane Bennett (2010) further proposes the concept of 'thing power', which draws attention to 'the strange ability of ordinary man-made objects to exceed their status as objects and to manifest traces of independence or aliveness' (Bennett, 2010, p. xvi). The intent is not to equate subjects with objects but rather to disrupt anthropocentricism and to work within a space that emphasises how the dichotomy between the two as normally conceived, is problematic. The imperative then is 'to detach materiality from the figures of passive, mechanistic or divinely infused substance' (Bennett, 2010, p. xiii). Bennett exchanges the notion of the 'object' (as static) for the 'thing' (as active) as a way of resisting the taken for granted passivity of matter. Conceiving of objects as vibrant 'things', in this case for example, the camera becomes envisaged as an active entity that is capable of production, not only of photographic images but also of generating confusing abstract thinking, bodily and facial performativity, and affective reputations of competency as discussed above.

Material Correspondence

Anthropologist Tim Ingold takes up the ideas of agency discussed above to confront the substantial theoretical problems associated with assigning agency to materials and objects. The idea of assigning agency to 'cat flaps' and 'speed bumps' (Ingold, 2010, p. 94) and other such objects is of course problematic and potentially undermining. Instead, Ingold radically opposes the notion of agency altogether, for both human and material (Ingold, 2013). Referring to Bennet's uncertainty in both defining and assigning agency (Bennett, 2010, p. 34), Ingold notes how she concludes 'that since we have no idea what agency is or how it works for humans, we have no a priori reason to deny agency to non-humans' (Ingold, 2013, p. 96). To resolve this, Ingold proposes the principle of 'material correspondence' to transform agency as noun into a verb 'agencing' (Ingold, 2016) because,

> the generativity of action is that of animate life itself, and lies in the vitality of materials. We need not a theory of agency but of life, and this theory must be one – as Barad puts it – 'that allows matter its due as an active participant of the worlds becoming'. (Ingold, 2013, p. 97)

Ingold presents the example of kite flying where not only are kite and kite flyer within the frame as encompassing agency, that according to new materialism is equally distributed between both, but consequently, the air as the medium which makes the movement between them possible must also be attributed with agency. Ingold argues that if agency is to be attributed to materials and bodies it must equally be distributed to that which moves or animates the entities involved which would mean ascribing agency, in the example of kite flying that he suggests, to air or the wind which makes the movement. Ingold argues that this is of course impossible because air cannot either contain or be contained by agency, and so he calls for a reconsideration of agency as an action, 'agencing'. Ingold states that,

> As a bundle of potentials in an ever-unfolding field of forces and energies, the body moves and is moved not because it is driven by some internal agency, wrapped up in a package but because as fast as it is gathering or winding itself up, it is forever unravelling or unwinding, alternately breathing in and out. (Ingold, 2013, p. 96)

For Ingold, skill and knowledge building are processes of material correspondence between porous entities where agency is conceived 'as a movement in which partners take it in turns to lead and be led' (Ingold,

2013, p. 100). This also locates learning and skills developed through correspondence as a mode of attention and attunement, where learning occurs by attuning to the material environment through movement with/in it. This speaks to all forms of making where material processes are centralised, or any skill building circumstance where 'makers' become intensely bodily attuned to the particular qualities and movements of the material with which they work. When the notion of 'materials' becomes extended to machines, technologies, languages, histories, ideas, other species, or ecologies perhaps, building skills and learning *with* can be understood to always have both bodily and material implications.

The principle of correspondence fundamentally transforms the consideration of human intent and volition in relation to skill building to a process which requires 'answering' to (Ingold, 2013, 2020; Hackett & Rautio, 2019) and becoming animated by, the world in motion. Ingold explains that the principle of correspondence (Ingold, 2020) is grounded in a biological interpretation of the principle of habit which was first suggested by John Dewey as underpinning what he called 'the principle of continuity of experience' (Dewey, 2015, p. 35). Dewey states that 'the basic characteristic of habit is that every experience enacted and undergone modifies the one who acts and undergoes, while this modification affects, whether we wish it or not, the quality of subsequent experiences' (Dewey, 2015, p. 35). This reading of habit for Ingold shows habit to be 'fundamentally attentional' where 'thinking is not, however, an inside the head cognitive operation but the work of a mind that in its deliberations freely mingles with the body and the world' (Ingold, 2016, p. 16). Ingold goes on to clarify that,

> The principle of habit, ( ) as opposed to the principle of volition ( ) accords ontological priority to attentionality as the fundamental mode of being in the world, whereas intentions are but milestones thrown up along the way, more often than not revealed in hindsight. (Ingold, 2016, p. 19)

Through the principle of correspondence learning can become 'reconciled' to what Hackett and Somerville have called 'children's ways of being in the world' (Hackett & Somerville, 2017) which can emerge 'from the entanglements of bodies, affects, material objects, atmospheres and whatever is to hand, whenever the conditions allow' (Lester, 2020, p. 173). This explains how playful, experimental learning does not function in the singularity of an internalised body but rather 'thought is constructed through encounters and relations' (Olsson, 2009, p. 26). Ingold's important reframing of intent also recalls Deleuze's statement that 'something in the world forces us to think' (Deleuze, 1994, p. 139) which fundamentally includes the material world in consideration of human intent and learning. Such considerations have ethical implications and potential, where experimentation and encounter 'concerns that which is not yet known, it concerns that which comes about, that which is new and that demands more than recognising or representing truth' (Olsson, 2009, p. 26). Ingold clarifies that this is a mode of attention, as relational 'answering to' is innately ethical because for example, 'to care for others, we must allow them into our presence so that we in turn can be present to them' (Ingold, 2016, p. 20).

Ingold's (2013) concept of 'Material Correspondence' between porous entities, has implications for understanding Martha's skill building with the camera. The idea of material porosity which is central to the principle of correspondence describes the perceived boundaries between entities as porous. However, this does not require thinking of entities as becoming subsumed by one another within action. As put by Hackett and Rautio 'in spite of the rhetoric of everything blurring and bleeding, there is always separation and distance, there is always the self and the other – however porous, leaky and intermingling these entities are' (Hackett & Rautio, 2019, p. 1021). Hackett and Rautio further point out that Erin Manning 'warns us against a 'fusional fantasy' and points out that communication requires separation and a respect for alterity (the other)' (Hackett & Rautio, 2019, p. 1021). The idea of porosity does however point to the idea that agency cannot be contained, and therefore cannot be located or claimed, but is produced through action that is driven by 'correspondence' and response-ability .

Martha can be understood to correspond with the camera as an object or 'thing' (Bennett, 2010) which she comes to know through repeated activity with it, both through her body and conscious sharing and seeking of information (related to the memory card for example). She also corresponds with her material environment, moving with it differently, experimentally, noticing and framing it in new ways afforded by the camera lens.

The triangulated actions between Martha, camera and material environment become entwined (such as how to hold the camera, how to frame and select an image) to subsequently and constantly open to new paths to be built (finding new subject matter and seeing it differently for example) through experimental movement and activity between Martha, camera, and material world. Through persistent attraction, a mode of aesthetic attention gradually moves toward becoming habit as envisaged originally by Dewey, in his biological 'principle of continuity of experience' (Dewey, 2015, p. 35) as discussed previously. Ingold explains,

> To start with the principle of habit, rather than that of volition, is to acknowledge that awareness is always awareness with before it is ever awareness of. We can recognise a movement, and respond to it, before we ever fix it in our sights. The operations of the attentional mind in short are not cognitive but ecological. (Ingold, 2016, p. 20)

In this way, neither Martha nor the camera are envisaged as 'agents' but rather participants in an experimental process of nuanced correspondence, or 'agencing' as activity. The idea of 'material correspondence' (Ingold, 2013) still retains and relies upon the unique qualities and differences between each of the elements at play (Martha, camera, and environment). Nevertheless, it requires the sacrifice of the concept of human agency, which has become so central to child-centred education theory, policy, and practice. However, this sacrifice pays dividends by ultimately uniting the understanding of the process of learning, (particularly in the form of promoting the idea of conscious intent rather than the building of habit through attraction), with young children's every-day, experimental, and persistent ways of being in and with the material world (Hackett & Rautio, 2019). Ingold states that,

> If the principle of volition renders a form of attention founded in intentionality, the principle of habit gives us a form of intention founded in attentionality. This is the attentionality of going along with things, opening up to them and doing their bidding. (Ingold, 2016, p. 19)

Observations: Material Porosity and Correspondence

This research story has demonstrated how the technicalities of how things work can be hidden, unknown, and difficult to intuit, so that things can unexpectedly undermine and shift power structures between adults and children. Things can unsettle seemingly solid social structures, hierarchies, and pedagogical norms. Here, the camera framed and directed Martha's activity and her ways of seeing and being, increasing the agency produced through the activity and Martha's sense of participation in it. Coming to know how to move one's body with the camera/thing as a form of skill building or competency for the children was reliant on 'corresponding' with the camera/thing. In this posthuman view, agency (as a concept that is central to rights-based, child-centred ECEC) becomes clarified as an action that is complexly dependent on movement with and in the material environment, and on an availability, or curiosity, which leaves one open to being moved by things.

The concept of 'material porosity' here points to shared animacy produced between bodies. Its shifts away from the notion of human agency, toward a shared correspondence between bodies within their environment. Agency as a verb, 'agencing' as proposed by Ingold (2013), creates an imperative for consideration of the material/affective environment in relation to the production of human thought, action, and opportunities to develop skill, as practising habits, and as an ethical form of attentionality.

Further, Ingold (2013) presents the idea of correspondence as learning and making that requires improvisation through both conscious and preconscious attention to materials, environments, and things. Correspondence requires the learner or maker to inhabit the materiality of the process as being in 'a realm in among () rather than above and beyond () adjusting each in relation to the others, and serving as a kind of go-between in their correspondence' (Ingold, 2013, p. 69). This generates an image of the maker or learner as finely attending (consciously and bodily) to the movement of the material environment and the processes of movement or making that they are experiencing in their bodies, which in time develop as skills or bodily attunements. This also has implications for understanding agency and its dependence on movement, difference, and relationality.

In my research analysis, Martha came to know her environment in new ways facilitated by her interest in the camera and what it could do. Adjusting her own body to the requirements of the camera while also learning to see her everyday environment differently, which produced a sense of agency or empowerment, developed through her close attention to the materiality of the learning process with the camera, as material correspondence. Ingold points out that this mode of attention to materiality is absolutely foundational to experiences of learning and skill building. It requires attunement through the specifics of each learner's unique body and thought as integral to the formation of habit, as a mode of profound attentionality. While every material encounter brings its own specific conditions in order to build knowledge, skilfulness, and habits (as learned bodily ways of being with the material environment), the learner's body and mind attend to the demands of infinite contextual and temporal differences of specific materials in relation to their unique contextualised bodies. Attunement to fine difference is therefore a fundamental mode of learning or coming to know something, both cognitively and bodily. This therefore, is an expansive multiplication process of possible ways of knowing, bringing attention once again to the fundamental ingredient of diversity in the function of attentionality and learning, even in skill building which may otherwise be perceived as relatively confining. I strongly suggest that learning which aspires toward normativity, rather than openness toward infinite difference is a movement against the current of what learning requires.

CHAPTER 7

Storying Small Moments: Affect

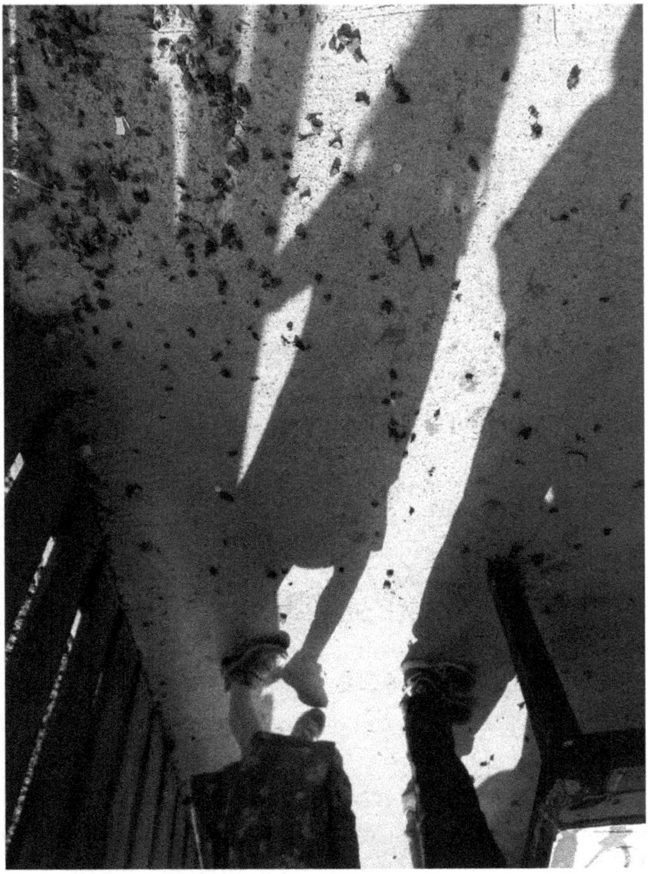

Figure 18: Storying Small Moments: AFFECT

Certain affects are undeniably deeply embedded, and politically inflected in ECEC. As noted by Stuart Lester, 'the concept and production of childhood is affective in that it shapes adult memories, desires and practices about children' (Lester 2020, p. 47). In this section, through another set of analysis narratives, I explore the concept of affect as an experimental conceptual platform for thinking with children's ordinary everyday moments in their ECEC setting. The materials which act as the sparks for the following set of analysis narratives are drawn from both the initial observation phase of the fieldwork where all materials were part of 'ordinary' everyday life of the preschool, as well as from the materials imported by me for the artistic events in the outdoor atelier space. These include cake, bread, ice, and paint. The ideas which these materials support thinking and writing about include 'Mesh-works' (Ingold) 'Affective Resilience' (Loveless, 2018), 'Counter-Aesthetics' (Highmore) and Pleasure and Happiness. These research narratives expose the difficulty of neutralising the affective potential of ordinary things.

Often affects are thought of as being similar to human-centric feelings or emotions, but in the Spinozist sense, affect is the universally available ability to affect and be affected, or, as put by Stuart Lester

> Affects are ways of connecting to other bodies, things, and situations (including imaginary ones) in processes that are larger than the individual. As such, affect is about the forces and flows of encounters. (Lester, 2020, p. 46)

Materials and things which are loaded with powerful affective associations and potential (personal, public, historic, mythic), are both recognised and obscured within education documents and policy. The affective possibilities that everyday objects can generate, demonstrates their potential for spontaneous and enlivening disruption through connection. Thinking about the powerful affects that modest materials/objects might be capable of producing in learning events, is also a way of thinking about and taking seriously, spontaneous events in which children participate without the direction of adults. By following material movements and human/material intra-actions, the aim is to bring to light affects which may be otherwise unaccounted for, but that are unavoidably impactful and connected to processes of knowing and being. Spector and colleagues state that,

> The force of affect with/in the classroom assemblage is constrained and shuttered. Sure, the emergent can and will break loose of its constraints, but it is not invited to. Attending to vitalist conceptions of affect allows us to follow a surge as it passes through students or squats behind and short circuits the objectives of the teacher; it awakens us to the ecology of pedagogical spaces that make some ways of knowing/becoming/doing more possible than others. (Spector, Thiel, & Kuby, 2019, p. 186)

A posthuman ethico-aesthetic lens can bring attention to the affective potential of small ordinary things, which may be unacknowledged or buried in assumptions and fixed functionality. The affective potential of everyday materials may become enlivened through a new artistic context and consideration. I suggest that as a mode through which to 'attend' (think, feel, notice) differently, aesthetic considerations of the ordinary create possibilities for bringing awareness to new, unexpected questions and understanding for children and adults, led by affect as foundational to ECEC.

The analysis or storying process, which enacts a reillumination of the events after the fact, does not set out to find meaning in the specific events, but rather aims to prise them open to possibilities for further connectivity and movement in new directions. This process of bringing things into relation also offers an alternative understanding of ethics. The concept of affective ethics offers another perspective for 'doing' ethics in practice, which provides an additional and alternative approach to morally mandated procedures. Affective, affirmative ethics, as well being moral, consider that everything which is immersed in particular experiences are capable of participating and contributing relationally, collectively, creatively, inventively, unexpectedly, and aesthetically. Finding more ways of understanding, and practising ethics in ECEC, reduces the possibility that the impetus of ethics, its most basic desire for good for children in particular, might become stultified or immobile. The dominance of critique, surveillance, or affective negativity in ethical procedures, renders ethics inaccessible to children as these modes of ethicality necessitate the installation of hierarchies and expertise in which children are unlikely to succeed. Affective affirmative ethics can guide practices with children, that include them in its production, as participants in collective creative experience alongside adults, environments, non-human others, materials, technologies, and things.

Affect and Assemblages: Cake

> The small flames attract everyone's attention while they sing the birthday song and are extinguished with one energetic puff from the birthday child's mouth. Paper plates are handed out and children spin and flap them with their hands against their bodies while they wait for their slice of cake. A small communal chant emerges 'Cake! Cake! Cake!' along with drumming on tables and stamping on the floor in anticipation. Children finish eating at different times with the cake behaving in different ways in different hands, some crumbling into tiny pieces, some staying intact to be pushed into mouths. Some plates are licked to collect the smallest crumbs. (Field notes, p. 19)

The cake is plain, modest, and relatively tasteless. Small, oblong, plastic wrapped, it is an exercise in neutrality, so much so that it could be considered the polar opposite of a celebration cake. I imagine its taste as sweet, monotone, vanilla. Remarkable for its strict uniformity, a single approved recipe producing thousands of identical cakes, it is a perfect machine-made product. The reassurance that this offers, is part of the reason that this cake has been considered as appropriate, where there is awareness of the potentially disruptive volatility that particular foods can generate for children. This cake has no worrying fruit, objectionable cream, or desirable decorations. Its neutrality works to have it slide reassuringly and inclusively into the birthday child's day without the possibility of upset. Its uniformity also rebuts any singling out of children for personalised attention. Everyone knows that this is the form that every child's birthday takes in this preschool as has been outlined in clear communication to parents. All ECEC settings in Ireland are obliged to clarify and communicate their mode of celebration for special occasion events such as birthdays through their policy documents (Department of Health and Children, 2004, p. 39). Policy regarding how birthday parties will be conducted must sit alongside every setting's healthy eating commitments. In addition, where a sessional setting (providing three hours of pre-school only) may not provide meals, children bring their own food from home and so parents are requested to comply with the settings healthy eating policy and birthday celebration policy. Food brought in from home is subject to department of health regulations (Department of Health & Children,

2004) which imposes stringent food storage expectations, heightening awareness of the potential dangers of food, from contaminants through bacterial infection as well as allergic reaction or choking. Nevertheless, food from home may also provide comfort and continuity through personalisation, where love can be expressed in absentia through a familiar aesthetic or intimate parental knowledges (Hackett, 2017), particularly of food preferences or dislikes.

Love, although deeply connected to both food provision as well as the historical foundation of ECEC since its beginnings in Romanticism (Aslanian, 2015) does not feature in policy documents (Page, 2018). Rather, policy documents tend to conflate love in ECEC with a more function fulfilling care-giving. This shift in meaning masks the countless everyday acts of love evident in ECEC, that are not necessarily descriptive as acts of care-giving per se (Page, 2018). Nevertheless, while the complexities of love may be restricted or muddied in policy, Cantillon and Lynch argue that 'love is a political matter because it is vital to creating caring infrastructures for democratic thinking and practice. It is love labour that produces the nurturing capital that enables people to flourish' (Cantillon & Lynch, 2017, p. 178).

Affect is however acknowledged as pivotal to the 'atmosphere' within ECEC settings in all but name in some documents. For example, Barnardo's Handbook for Childcare providers on parental involvement, states that it is vital that 'the settings climate i.e. its social and educational atmosphere, is one that makes families feel welcomed, respected, trusted, heard and needed' (Barnardo's, 2006, p. 9). Attention to affects is understood as worthwhile and important. However, affects are equally complex and mobile, shifting, and illusive, capable of quixotically transforming spaces and relationships.

Affects generated by food for example, zigzag between obligation, compliance, hazard, and love. The tensions, contradictions, and surpluses between ECEC regulation and practice in relation to affect, begin to expose affect itself as a complex undercurrent. Tracing affect as a Spinozist posthuman concern through a birthday cake event for example, what comes into view is what a material/thing/cake does in its tensile relations with other elements rather than what it is as an isolated object in its meagre, singular, relatively chastised state.

Cake Assemblage as Meshwork

Policies have endeavoured to neutralise this cake, which provides neither nutrition nor expressions of love, both of which are essential to human thriving (Brennan, 2004; Cantillon & Lynch, 2017). However, when viewed as part of a meshwork or assemblage, a counterfoil emerges to the affective vacuum which has been created by converging policies. For Deleuze and Guattari 'an assemblage in its multiplicity necessarily acts on semiotic flows, material flows and social flows simultaneously' (Deleuze & Guattari, 1987, p. 2). In the case of the cake event, the concept of an assemblage enables a bringing together of the social (children, educators, researcher, parents, policy makers), the material (cake, table, feet, crumbs, candles, flames, mouths), and the semiotic (policy and regulation documents, gesture, expressions of excitement), that brings to light the assemblage's multiple messy threads.

Ingold thinks of assemblages as being more akin to what he calls a mesh-work than a net-work, because he states that a network connects and disconnects dots or points on a plane, whereas 'the lines of the meshwork, by contrast, are of movement or growth' (Ingold, 2013, p. 132). Ingold goes on to clarify that,

> where the network has nodes, the meshwork (…) has knots. Knots are places where many lines of becoming are drawn tightly together. Yet every line overtakes the knot in which it is tied. Its end is always loose, somewhere beyond the knot, where it is groping towards an entanglement with other lines, in other knots. What is life, indeed, if not a proliferation of loose ends! It can only be carried on in a world that is not fully joined up, not fully articulated. Thus the very continuity of life – its sustainability, in current jargon – depends on the fact that nothing ever quite fits. (Ingold, 2013, p. 132)

Produced by the meshwork of the semiotic, material, and social flows are excitable affects, accelerated by switching off strip lights and lighting small birthday candles. The communal consumption of the birthday cake comes to verge on a joyful riot, producing chanting and synchronised stamping of feet to shouts of 'Cake! Cake! Cake!'. Bodies sway, arms wave, plates flap and hands thump the table in a short-lived excited uproar which dissipates once the cake is eaten. This is tolerated by the adults with good humour, even though they have temporarily been pushed to the 'hinterlands' (Law, 2004, p. 42). A kind of 'monstrous life' (Anastasiou, Holmes & Runswick-Cole, 2018, p. 45) emerges as a surge of feral affects through the chanting and stamping in unison, the different handling of cake, the licking and flapping where 'listening to cacophony and noise tells us that there is a wild beyond to the structures we inhabit and that inhabit us' (Halberstam, in Harney & Moton, 2013, p. 7). The event refuses and exceeds the abstracted diminishing directives of both 'healthy eating' and 'celebration' policy. When this cake is read as part of an affective meshwork assemblage, it brings to light what Osgood describes as the need 'to work with the notion that materiality and affect, space and place, are each equally as significant and agentic as the human subject as they relationally participate in any given assemblage' (Osgood, 2019, p. 117).

Observations: Affects and Mesh-Works

Ordinary objects (such as a birthday cake) can introduce an unexpected, lively swarming of collectively produced affect as a form of unintentional 'feral' resistance to the control of affects in policy. When understood as part of a meshwork of activity between bodies, human and non-human, through a posthuman ethico-aesthetic lens, everyday materials can bring visibility to important relational exchanges and movements between things. Through an ethico-aesthetic lens, affect can be understood as the unpredictable undercurrent to relational experience that is part of children's everyday experience on both micro and macro levels.

Affect and Aesthetics: Bread

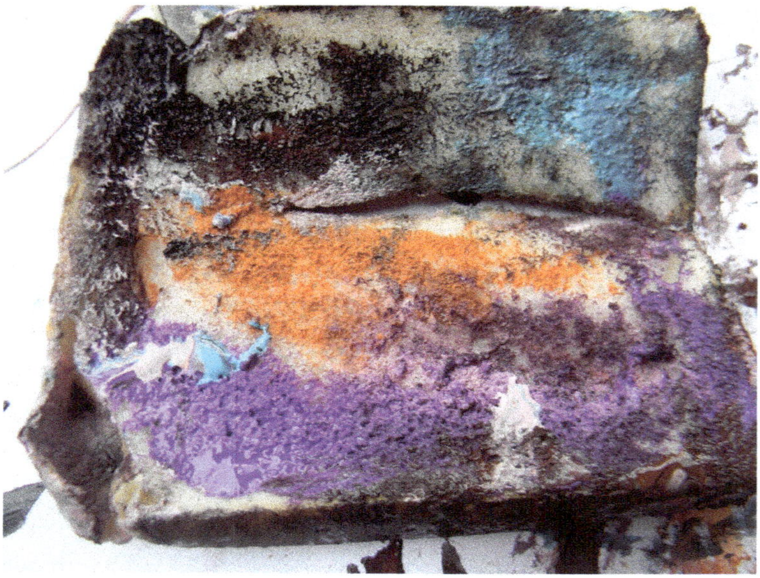

Figure 19: Affect and Aesthetics: Bread

> Before the decision to eat the bread spread amongst the children, there was much hesitation, not due to hygiene I think but due to context. The bread has changed its purpose and stature, the relationship is now complicated by an expectation to participate in a painting activity. Simon is the most tempted by it. He holds the slice of bread with both hands up to his mouth for a long time, making the action of biting without making contact with the bread. He does this, reasoning with others around, whoever will listen, about whether or not to bite the bread. When he finally does, the others follow suit. (Field notes, p. 104)

This section works with a moment described in the fieldnote above, where a slice of bread, which has been proposed as a surface to paint on in the outdoor atelier (along with other sliced foodstuffs such as turnips and cabbages) presents a shift of context. An aesthetic proposal creates a felt dilemma. Art as communicated by material (paint), gave unexpected power to slices of bread.

The prospect of painting on bread to a hungry child created a momentary disorientation. A slice of plain white bread, through its scant association with art developed the power to produce affects of doubt, hesitation, discomfort, and questioning as the essence of inquiry (Loveless, 2019). Simon's question ('will I eat it?') persisted only until overtaken by hunger and the subsidence of worry about etiquettes or permissions. Breads normal service was resumed. Nevertheless, during the inquiry-mode/hesitation moments, there was an unexpected and enforced slowing down. Simon became seized by the bread in a dilemma limbo where 'slowness comes from the work of defamiliarisation and the time it takes to ask questions differently' (Loveless, 2019, p. 107). The affects of the event spread rapidly amongst the other children who joined with Simon's questioning. The importance of such arresting affects in pedagogy and learning, is clarified by Atkinson when he writes,

> It is through the encounter of 'becoming undone' that the pedagogic parameters (…) may be disturbed sufficiently so as to 'make visible' forms of learning and art practice previously not recognised as such. (Atkinson, 2018a, p. 35)

Although the proposition of painting on bread to some children was delightfully silly, the idea unavoidably drew attention not only to breads painterly material compatibility (it fell apart when loaded with too much paint, we discussed toast as a likely better option), but also its capacity to be elevated and reinvented by art.

Questions surrounding the use of food for purposes of play in ECEC circulate widely as morally driven concerns about material waste and cultural disrespect (John, 2011; Schwarz & Luckenbill, 2012; Swim & Freeman, 2004). Providing food as art/plaything for this research felt problematic. However, Aistear, the Irish curriculum framework refers to the use of food as a resource for play (NCCA, 2009, p. 29). Simon's need for permission to eat the bread rather than paint on it, upset learned boundaries surrounding uses of materials and food, but drew attention to the 'what else' that art/materials/things might produce (Osgood, 2019).

The paint in turn was encountered through its potential capabilities rather than its material properties (Pacini-Ketchabaw et al., 2017). Paints' purpose in ECEC is usually for sensory experiencing, for learning about textural properties, for self-expression, or for mastering scientific essentials such as colour mixing. Here it combined with the bread as an idea, to produce an affective dilemma. Inquiry became a form of experimentation, where Simon hovered within the tensions created between purposeful art activity and bodily need (hunger). Manning describes experimentation and invention as a 'body-event',

> To sense is not simply to receive input – it is to invent. Invention springs from open machines of recombination. A body is such a machine, sensing toward infinite recombination. Sense perceptions are not simply 'out there' to be analyzed by a static body. They are body-events. (Manning in Pacini-Ketchabaw et al., 2017, p. 52)

Although the paint in this event remained in its pot and in this moment did not produce either artistic 'products' or 'processes', its implications created powerful affects that shift the 'shabby truism' (Thompson, 2015, p. 554) so intrenched in ECEC, that art is confined to the value binary of either 'process or product' (Thompson, 2015). Through the paint's affective possibilities, art emerged as a form of materially motivated questioning that was both sensed and shared without words. Claire Colebrook writes that,

> Art is not about knowledge, conveying meanings, or providing information. Art is not an ornament or a style used to make data more palatable or consumable. Art may well have meanings or messages, but what makes it art is not its content but its affect, the sensible force or style through which it produces content. (Colebrook, cited in Sakr & Osgood, 2019, p. 115)

Observations: Affect and Aesthetics

In this analysis, art as a proposal was suggested by the materials (paint, bread, etc.) which produced a spontaneous, affective, felt form of inquiry. No prior questions, intentions or directions were offered and not every child responded in the way that Simon did. This particular pause occurred as uniquely related to Simon, his bodily needs, and the way in which the idea of art was transmitted as affects by the materials. Art, through the materials, created an arresting imperative for Simon to pause for thought.

Sensing affect can also be understood as inventing, or as a 'body-event' as suggested by Manning. The power structures pertaining to the need to seek permissions may also have played a part in the generation of the 'pause for thought' nevertheless a new context for the material was introduced by the artistic proposition, and by the paint. The breads affective potential and its contextual repositioning through art, altered its affective value. Context therefore can be understood to alter the affective or sensed value of something, but this is not something fixed or necessarily knowable, but is also relational and 'in the moment', as demonstrated by Simon. As such, emergent change in context can be sensed by the body but is not necessarily easily verbalised. This draws attention to how paying attention to changes in affects, as sensed by the body, can reveal valuable, felt, and difficult to predict insights.

Affect, Touch and Affective Resilience: Ice

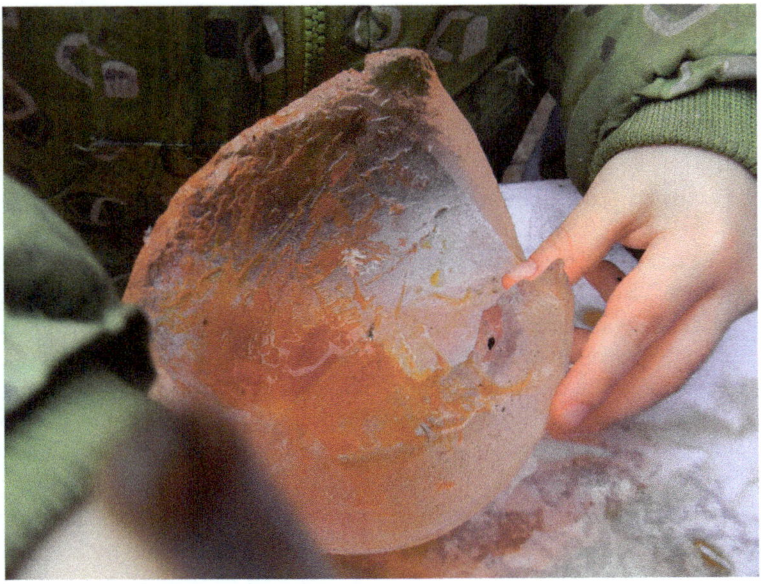

Figure 20: Atelier Ice

> As more children arrived outside, the ice balls generated a lot of scrambling for possession, whining, complaining, grabbing and some general upset. There were 8 balls and 14 children so far, with more children to come. Educators tried to reason and deliver fairness but there was a long period of 'wanting' which seemed to spread through the group. Children wanted their own ice ball, they wanted certain colours, wanted droppers or brushes, wanted space, wanted to work beside certain children. The level of upset was surprising, and yet not. Everyone understood that the balls were made of ice, a material they know and have seen and played with before, but not at this scale. Perhaps there was an awareness of the time limitation, that disappearance of the ice was inevitable. Also, despite the high level of attraction towards them, the intense cold of the ice balls repelled excessive touching, generating low level pain and discomfort. Mittens, coat sleeves, legs and boots were quickly soaked. The tabletops were drenched as pockets of water were released through poking and prodding and cracking thin areas of the ice. (Field Notes, p. 79)

Atelier Ice

For 'Ice Watch London' created in 2018, artist Ólafur Eliasson and geologist Minik Thorleif Rosing created a public artwork from blocks of Arctic ice, hauled to Tate Britain from Greenland by refrigerated fishing boats. The startling beauty and ecological significance of the ice was presented to the public as an invitation to touch and be touched. In an essay written by the artist to accompany the event, Eliasson writes,

> If you take a stroll in central London starting this Tuesday, you may encounter thirty blocks of glacial ice, thousands of years old. Some are transparent, others opaque. Their colours are tones of blue and white. Traces of times long past, in the form of dirt and other natural materials, are encapsulated in the seemingly immobile forms. Put your hand on the ice and feel the cold, smooth surface against your skin. Put your ear to the ice and listen to the crackling noises it produces as it melts. Look – and witness the ecological changes that our world is undergoing. (Eliasson, 2018)

The works important content was created through the arduous process of transforming the materials context, by dragging the ice by boat from Greenland to London. While materials, art and environmental activism have frequently converged to generate public conversation and awareness, here it is the invitation to touch that is of interest. Bodily contact, through touch is inferred as a mechanism for deepening understanding, for being 'in touch'. The material itself is also credited with being capable of more than aesthetic symbolism, it is also relied upon as a mechanism for transmitting affects for political ends, to stir participants into realisation and action. Eliasson states,

> By enabling people to experience and actually touch the blocks of ice in this project, I hope we will connect people to their surroundings in a deeper way and inspire radical change. We must recognise that together we have the power to take individual actions and to push for systemic change. Let's transform climate knowledge into climate action. (Bloomberg Philanthropies, 2018)

The children at the outdoor atelier who were attracted by the ice balls I had brought in a big blue bucket, were caught up in affects of frustration and waves of 'wanting'. While I knew that the ice would be of interest having witnessed the children play with small cubes in the water tray in their classroom, the powerful, shared affects generated by the large ice balls (made by freezing large water filled balloons) was unexpected.

The ice balls engendered an irresistible need to touch and connect, even though the surfaces repelled. The awareness of the inevitable melting processes, anticipating the slow disappearance of the ice seemed to be the root of the anxiety generated. As in Eliassons' glacial Ice Watch artwork, the sense of loss and environmental instability was transmitted by the materiality of the ice and was deeply felt through touch, and the irreversible melting. Through the emphasis on touch, Ice Watch aimed to transmit a sense of 'intensified reality' (Puig de la Bellacasa, 2017) through physical (and visual) contact with the ice. Braidotti writes of the body's relationship to the environment as,

> The minimalist definition of a body-machine is an embodied affective and intelligent entity that captures processes and forces. Being environmentally bound and territorially based, an embodied entity feeds upon, incorporates, and transforms its (natural, social, human, or technological) environment constantly. This high-tech ecological manner entails full immersion in fields of constant flows and transformations. Not all of them are positive. (Braidotti, 2013, p. 140)

In the atelier the children became concerned that the warmth from their hands might be speeding up the 'death' of the ice-balls. Puig de la Bella Casa writes that 'touch and proximity belong to the conceptual nebula of care, but they are not necessarily caring' (2017, p. 106) and further that 'touch is not a harmless affection. Touch receptors, located all over our bodies, are also pain receptors' (2017, p. 106). For the children, these affective tensions of loss, pain, finitude, and care circulated through their contact with the ice, largely through touch. These same affects were also, I suggest, intended for the audience of Ice Watch, where art as affect was centralised.

Reliance on the production of affect by the human/material intra-action, transmittable through touch and the body, also became a means to access a particular vision of reality. The idea that 'truth' is reliant on the connection between humans and touchable, concrete matter is 'supported by a long history in which concrete, factual, material knowledge is opposed to 'bare' belief (…) while faith belongs to trust in untouchable immaterial forces' (Puig de la Bellacasa, 2017, p. 101). In the current environmental emergency, tensions between theoretical belief and empirical/material facts have taken time to align however 'Ice Watch' requires no 'belief' in art to be affectively impacted by the unadulterated ice blocks, which consequently generates the works popular appeal. As with the children in the atelier, the affective magnetism between 'bodies' (both human and melting ice) reinforce the new materialist claim as to the essential vibrancy of matter, where,

> Matter's dynamism is generative not merely in the sense of bringing new things into the world but in the sense of bringing forth new worlds, of engaging in an ongoing reconfiguring of the world. Bodies do not simply take their places in the world. They are not simply situated in, or located in, particular environments. Rather, 'environments' and 'bodies' are intra-actively co-constituted. Bodies ('human', 'environmental', or otherwise) are integral parts of, or dynamic reconfigurings of, what is. (Barad, 2007, p. 70)

This brings attention to Taylors' idea of how bodies and environments are 'ontologically entangled', or utterly inseparable (Taylor, 2018). The hope for Ice Watch is that to touch, also means to be touched, to be in contact with what is being touched, however as Puig de la Bella Casa points out (as the children also sensed through their anxiety that they may be a cause of harm to the ice balls) 'the unavoidable ambivalence of touch is thus of conveying a vital form of relation and a threat of violence and invasion' (Puig de la Bellacasa, 2017, p. 100). This tightrope walk between the anticipation of potentially oppositional outcomes is transmitted and felt through affect. While forms of affect may be expected, choregraphed or even manipulated through art, it is in affects 'excess' that there is always 'more-than' or, that which can spontaneously appear, sink unnoticed, or spread like wildfire.

After some time in the atelier the children gradually, and unpredictably became differently energised as they moved with the melting. Rather than railing against it, they readjusted their needs for the balls not to shrink away. Through the drive to play, they turned their attention to the puddles produced by the melting. The sense of needing to adapt and respond to changing circumstances in order to find a lively, optimistic outcome was felt, and observable, as affects that were transmitted both verbally through excited observations and ideas but were also sensed and shared through differently animated bodily movements and gestures.

While Ice Watch may have produced expected and desired affects on/in its audience, enhanced by the emphasis on touch, its hoped-for effect of radical political environmental change, has yet to materialise. The reliable transference of affect into secured effects, its duration, its direction, scale, and speed cannot be either guaranteed or fixed, not even by art. We had no way of knowing that the dam of the children's upset would be dislodged so quickly by the force of their desire to play and the utter alteration of the ice that they had so clamoured over only minutes before. Movement with lively forces such as play seems to offer optimistic possibilities for confusing and distinctly pessimistic times, nurturing what Loveless describes as 'affective resilience' where 'affective resilience names the practice of nurturing spaces of (…) care, without méconnaissance within our social, political and pedagogical spaces' (Loveless, 2019, p. 106). The children allowed themselves to be carried by the transformed environment, to adapt and find new forms of pleasure and togetherness, that the attendant adults could not have anticipated.

Observations: Affective Resilience

In this analysis, the affective tensions of loss, pain, finitude, and care circulated through contact with the material (ice), largely through touch. The concept of 'affective resilience' (Loveless, 2019) emerges here as important, particularly in relation to forces such as play, as something that develops with/in the material environment, outside of the children, but that the children moved and participated with, demonstrating how bodies and environments are, as put by Taylor 'ontologically entangled' (Taylor, 2018). The concept of affective resilience is also important for understanding how affects and feelings might become dislodged and moved by events in the material environment. Further, while forms of affect may be expected, choregraphed or even manipulated through art (as in the example of 'Ice Watch' presented above), it is in affects 'excess' that there is always a feral 'more', and it is adapting to this unexpectedness, that generates the optimistic possibilities of 'affective resilience' (Loveless, 2019) as one that is important for contemporary ECEC. In the atelier, the melting ice caused high degrees of upset which was overwhelmed by the force of play offered unexpectedly by the material environment, this redirected the children's attention and activity, demonstrating the possibility of affective resilience through the ability to move with the environment. Play that is unexpectedly suggested by the material environment (here, by puddles produced by melting ice) can provide optimistic opportunities to move with the changing material environment and is a capacity of significant importance to children, because the ability to see and to respond to what the material environment presents through collective, aesthetic activity is both cohering and affirming. Movement and play as modes of affective resilience can be understood as more than a developmental concern. Here, play also exceeds its association with potentially pacifying notions of 'well-being' rather, through the idea of affective resilience proposed by Loveless (2019), play becomes the fundamental propellor to essential mechanisms of thriving beyond adversity, and I also suggest, of survival.

Affect and Pleasure: Paint

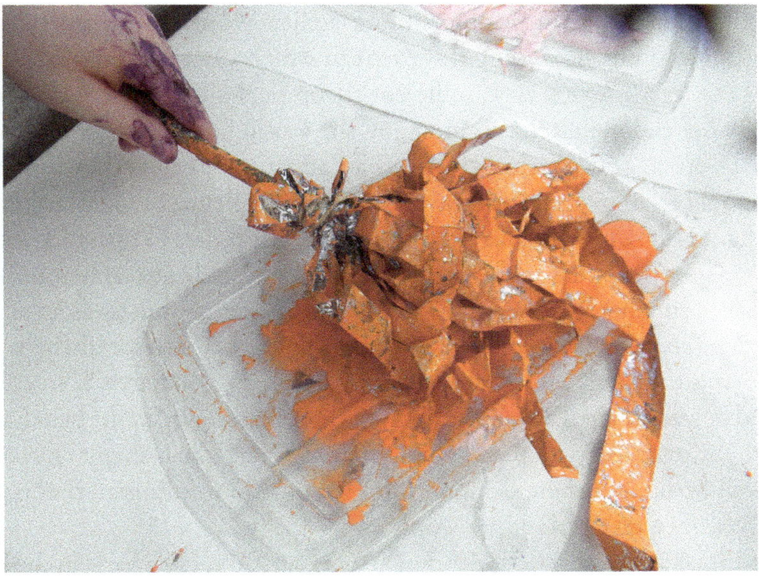

Figure 21: Affect and Pleasure: Paint

> Painting on the 'wall paper' developed quickly. Different approaches were taken from tentative tickles to wild jumping and splashing. As the action moved on attention was also paid to the large paint bottles, searching for more paint to squeeze onto the pallets, the paint squirted and dribbled across surfaces including table, concrete, paper, boots and coats. There was a great deal of pleasure in the activity. Pleasure of unpredictable tools, of large full body scale, of communality, drips, movement back and forth from tables to wall, from horizontality to verticality. In the video recording, Orla declares loudly 'I'm a very good artist!'. (Journal Notes from videos)

Pleasure and Happiness

The atelier materials provided many complex, fleeting, and incomplete affective nuances. Pleasure and happiness spontaneously surfaced regularly (as in the fieldnote above). This eruption of exuberance for Orla for example was instigated by contact with the movement of thick, drippy, brightly coloured paint in the outdoor atelier. What follows is an investigation into understanding this event in which Orla participated, as an aesthetic event which is of sufficient theoretical and artistic value as to justify her claim, that in this moment, she was in fact a very good artist.

Deleuze and Guattari write that 'affects are projectiles just like weapons; feelings are introceptive like tools' (Deleuze & Guattari, 1987, p. 400). Following this analogy, the affect of happiness in the video notes above, shot into the surrounding space and was made available for other atelier occupants to either absorb or deflect. Here, happiness as an affect appeared through the momentum that quickly reached a crescendo between Orla and the paint in her declaration 'I am a very good artist!'. In childhood developmental terms, the focus of this event might be the benefits of aesthetic practices with paint as heightening Orla's involvement and sense of well-being, but there is more to the event, and posthuman theorising enables us to take Orla at her word.

Pleasure as associated with aesthetic experience, has a basis in the history of material engagement as explained by Highmore; 'aesthetics, in its initial impetus, is primarily concerned with material experiences, with the way the sensual world greets the sensate body, and with the affective forces that are generated in such meetings' (Highmore, 2010, p. 121). However, within art theory, conceptualisation of an 'aesthetic experience' has been largely confined to subjects of beauty and the sublime, bypassing all of the complexity and messiness that once saw aesthetics as a much broader field, which, as further suggested by Highmore, begs the question,

> How does a form of inquiry that was once aimed at the entire creaturely world end up as a specialised discourse about fine art? How did an ambitious curiosity about the affects, the body and the senses end up fixated on one tiny area of sensual life – beauty and the sublime? (Highmore, 2010, p. 122)

Participation in aesthetic experience as confined to its consideration as 'the sublime' has exclusionary effects, restricting access to those deemed incapable of experiencing or understanding the sublime, such as animals or children. While happiness and pleasure as optimised experiences are located in the field of aesthetics in that they provide fulfilling, satisfactory and harmonious crescendos of 'completion', Highmore argues for making 'a countertradition of aesthetic thinking' (Highmore, 2010, p. 122) where the incomplete, unruly messiness of everyday affects can challenge the dominant valuing of the harmonious and the exclusionary construction of aesthetics. This calls for a more democratic aesthetics which acknowledges that 'pleasure is not simply human, and any pleasures taken by a human inescapably arise at points of contact between that human and other entities, affects, agencies' (Snaza, 2019, p. 124).

This posthuman perspective connects the concepts of aesthetics with ethics (Harman, 2007) and stretches the availability of aesthetics beyond the confines of the cultured (adult) human. Counter aesthetics becomes inclusive of all entities participating in rich and intense affective experiences and acknowledges the role of the material environment through which the aesthetic event has moved. Children not only fully participate, but also generate and readily expose such everyday aesthetic experience. Rather than being bound to fulfilling the requirement of harmony or completion, the counter-aesthetics as proposed by Highmore, becomes more akin to what Manning describes as the doing of 'artfulness',

> Artfulness does not belong to the artist, nor to art as a discipline. If it need be attached to something, it could be said to be what the most operational process of research-creation seeks to actualize. (…) Artfulness is an immanent directionality, felt when a work runs itself, or when a process activates its most sensitive fold, where it is still rife with intuition. This modality is beyond the human. (Manning, 2016, p. 58)

This description of artfulness aligns with the affirmative sense of joy felt by Orla, which also circulated throughout the atelier, and lead to Orla's declaration, that she was 'a very good artist'. She appeared to have been fully caught up by a form of artfulness just discussed, which Manning explains as ecological as distinct from a more personalised, or internalised explanation of creative 'flow' (Csikszentmihalyi, 1997). The high levels of involvement and well-being displayed by Orla, as key concerns within ECEC (MacRae & Jones, 2020), emerged as a result of her material encounters with paint, large body-scaled paper, and exciting hand-made brushes in the atelier environment.

Orla's sensation of becoming and being an artist, recalls Deleuze and Guattari's writing on becoming and being child, where they write that 'children are Spinozist's' (Deleuze & Guattari, 1987) who 'speak through affectivity' (Hickey-Moody, 2013). Hickey-Moody finds that this state of affective becoming can be understood as much more widely available when envisaged beyond limiting parameters,

> Rather than a chronological bracket or developmental state, becoming-child is a set of affects and capacities to be affected which can be activated at any stage of life. The implications of this for thinking about childhood are that it is not a state that can be plotted on a teleological trajectory. It is an affective capacity or capacity to be affected, both positively and negativity, to grow and connect in new ways (positive affect) and to be eroded by others around oneself (sad affect). (Hickey-Moody, 2013, p. 282)

The joyful counter-aesthetic experience with paint in the atelier suggests that 'becoming artist' and 'becoming child' is a state that is similarly open and available to all, including Orla, enabling her statement at the time that 'I am a very good artist' to make absolute sense.

Observations: Affect, Happiness and Counter Aesthetics

This analysis set helps to reconfigure the restrictions and exclusions that aesthetics and art frequently support, which in turn makes possible the consideration of a child's claim to being or feeling like an artist. In this case, pleasure is understood as potentially emerging through freedom of movement and exciting material encounters.

The concept of 'counter-aesthetics' is useful for understanding how aesthetic experiences as artfulness, might be widely available. Philosophical concepts and approaches to events in ECEC can enable us to take affects seriously, and consequently to take children at their word.

Considerations of affects also helped to interrupt hierarchical boundary lines between child and adult art-making. Affects of pleasure and happiness generated by paint brought attention to the concept of counter-aesthetics, and the proposition that 'becoming child' or 'becoming artist' are widely available affective and temporal possibilities. This disruption of hierarchical positioning of art has important potential for understanding the ways in which affective activity produces intense sensations which are always uniquely felt, by children and adults alike. I suggest that this opens possibilities for collaborative, inventive artistic practices between adults and children, where each bring unique differences, experiences, knowledges, and interests which open to new forms of learning *with* as well as *from*, for children and adults together. Placing consideration of affect at the centre of education practices, is productive, affirmative, ethical, and fundamentally creative. Upholding hierarchical assumptions of art and aesthetics on the other hand, limits their access and diminishes their affective potential.

These explorations of affect through a posthuman ethico-aesthetic lens provide ways not only of seeing everyday events and experiences in which children participate as replete with affective intensity and learning potential, but can also be useful for seeing critically, for example, to expose hierarchical assumptions in new ways, even those which reflect badly on art and aesthetics themselves.

CHAPTER 8

Storying Small Moments: Care

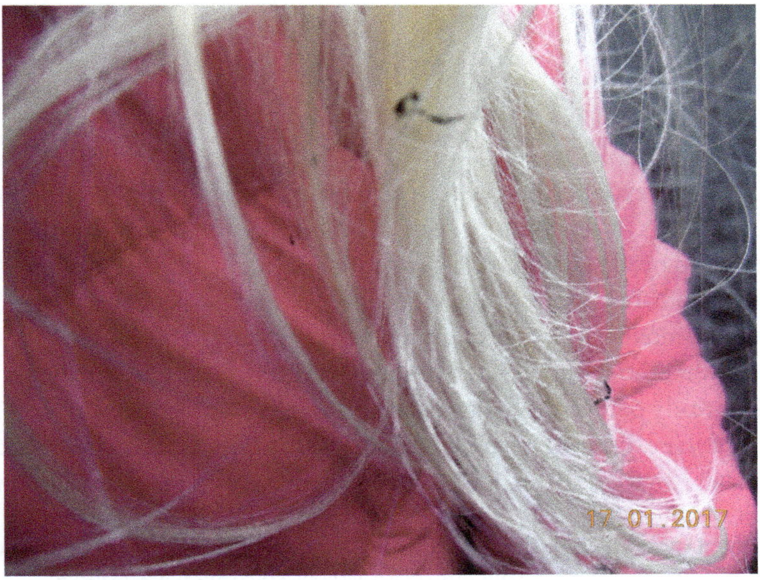

Figure 22: Storying Small Moments: Care

> Care is omnipresent, even through the effects of its absence. Like a longing emanating from the troubles of neglect, it passes within, across and throughout things. It's lack undoes, allows unravelling. To care can feel good; it can also feel awful. It can do good; it can oppress. Its essential character to humans and countless living beings makes it all the most susceptible to convey control. But what is care? Is it an affection? A moral obligation? Work? A burden? A joy? Something we can learn or practice? Something we just do? Care means all these things and different things to different people, in different situations. So while ways of caring can be identified, researched, and understood concretely and empirically, care remains ambivalent in significance and ontology. (Puig de la Bellacasa, 2017, p. 1)

In the following analysis narratives, care in ECEC is explored as an emergent ecology of practices transmitted through the materiality of small moments. Finding care as a 'force' is not to suggest that it is in anyway dispersed or passive, rather it becomes grounded in material and relational activity. As Cantillon and Lynch state, love and care are 'a potentially powerful political force grounded in action, not an abstract sentiment' (Cantillon & Lynch, 2017, p. 181).

Care and Diffraction

To begin to explore the concept of Care in ECEC through an ethico-aesthetic lens, it is useful to begin by clarifying the particular methodology employed to do this and its relationship to the subject, and ethics of Care. In posthuman research, methodologies are understood as specific to the researcher and the research practice context. This means that the research methods and ethics admit and account for the researcher as 'always already part of the apparatus that measures' (Murris, 2017, p. 4). As a result, in posthuman research as in many artistic and emergent practices, methods cannot be prescribed in advance, there is no formula to follow,

> In emergence individual components come together randomly, in an environment that 'participates' as well. All this takes place without a predetermined plan and without a leader (Dalke et al., 2007, 113). There can be no precise recipe either. Because even if you work backwards and trace participating components, you can never reproduce the exact same system. This is why emergent phenomena cannot be fully predicted or pinned down. And furthermore: emergent systems not only allow but require a degree of randomness and autonomy, not control to function. (Rautio, 2019, p. 232)

Posthuman methodologies suggest diffraction as a productive ethical possibility for emergent research and practice. Diffraction is defined by Donna Haraway as (more than) a metaphor for an alternative critical practice to reflection, which is suspected to 'only displace the same elsewhere' (Haraway, 1997, p. 273). Barad finds that diffraction as an analytical methodology through a posthuman lens, can be 'a particularly effective tool for thinking about social natural practices in a performative rather than representationalist mode' (Barad, 2007, p. 88). In theorising about diffraction in relation to the posthuman researcher, Rautio describes how for her 'the intended diffraction turns into distraction more often than not' (Rautio, 2019, p. 229). In searching for an authentic posthuman research practice as might be understood through academic reading and writing, the researcher discovers how interconnected to all facets of her life the author body is 'some encounters force me to think as a mother, others as a scholar, some encounters feed my thinking about horse-riding. They rarely mix, I am many not all' (Rautio, 2019, p. 230). This is of course not a condition unique to posthuman academic researchers but to others including ECEC educators and artists. Ingold points out how distraction can also be viewed positively, as moments of intense attention pulled in different directions at the same time (Ingold, 2016) like multiple forks in a road, or an unravelling thread, revealing openness to possibility and complexity in ethical terms.

Like processes of care, 'diffraction as distraction' can surface and intervene in research, or education or artistic practices, as unavoidable, messy, or un/necessary materialisations, demanding to be dealt with. While these may not appear to be 'emerging' but rather, violently interjecting, forcing action and thought in different directions where 'force arrives from outside to break constraints and open new vistas' (Massumi, 2002, p. xiii), as such they can generate responses that redirect thinking and doing in unexpected ways (or, equally, they can create confusing blind alleys that must be navigated or acknowledged at a minimum). To begin to enact a diffractive analysis here then, I turn to my own fine art interests and training to explore how other artists practices might either shed light or generate new connections for further thinking about fieldwork events, particularly here, in relation to the concept of care. However, the art practices exemplified in the following analysis section are not considered in any way comparatively in relation to each other or to the original field note.

> In my diffractive reading, I am not looking for similarities or differences; I make no comparisons to try to identify themes (…). My reading is not guided by a 'lack' either. The superimposition created by the diffraction is not 'critical' but adds force (…) to do the work of making the reader feel and think differently about pedagogical practice. (Murris, 2017, p. 5)

Although the artists discussed in the following section each work around the same material starting point as is highlighted in the field note extract below, the struggles of their making processes as various enactments of caring, are also pertinent. Each artist's unique approach to the materiality of their work also offers the potential to read the concept of care aesthetically. Further, while the material discussed in the field note overtly links the artists and the field note event, it is a material which may not usually qualify as worthy of consideration in an ECEC context, particularly in relation to artistic or pedagogical practice, however it is nevertheless unavoidably, ubiquitously, and affectively present. To this end, art and artistic practices can offer diffractive perspectives of complex concepts such as care, through attention to materials which may be framed otherwise within a particular cultural context (an ECEC setting for example).

Each of the artist's work is driven by the demands of caring (for bodies, for making, for social justice). For some artists, the making process is exposed as a performative element of the work, for others, complex making process are a form of caring which remains largely hidden within the artistic outcomes. Each artist's practice resonates differently, diffracting/distracting/drawing attention to new and alternative possibilities for extending and thinking about the material choreography of the everyday Care events of the fieldwork context. This exploration affords opportunities to examine how (artful) 'interference patterns can make a difference in how meanings are made and lived' (Haraway, 1997, p. 14) and offer other perspectives on complex concepts and processes such as Care in ECEC.

Care and Art: Urine

> At this point while everyone is moving about busily, a child accidentally urinates on the linoleum floor. There are little shrieks from other children, while the child is carried out to the bathroom smiling, backwards, (and at a slightly peculiar angle to protect the adult's body and clothing). A strong smell of urine quickly moves through the room to loud comments and giggling from children with hands covering mouths. This is accompanied by the educator's swift searches for cleaning equipment as the puddle of urine begins to pool and move across the floor, (more shrieks) while

> educators try to calm the fuss and get it cleaned up. The affective intrusion of this socially unacceptable material is so interesting, creating a bit of commotion and attention on the child involved who needs to be attended to in parallel with the puddle that has been created. (Field note, p. 36 Note #31)

Given the age range of the children attending, the appearance of urine in ECEC settings is not unusual. However, it understandably creates a stir and demands a sequence of actions on the part of the educators that involve adhering to the health and safety commitments of the setting. While sanitary requirements are unambiguous, central also to these events are sensitivities to sustain the dignities of both those who have urinated, as well as those who must clean up. Urine as an ordinary, everyday material, demands regulated and predictable corollaries concerning care, while at the same time has the capacity to generate unpredictable, complex, and nuanced affects.

Affective aspects of urine and human/animal urination, (particularly it's shock value) have been represented for centuries throughout the history of art (Lebensztejn & Nagy, 2017). More recently urine itself as a material has also been used in artistic practice (Ferguson & Brandes, 2012). Transgender activist and artist Cassils for example, used 200 litres of their own urine in an exhibition installation entitled 'Pissed'. The work protests the dangerous and humiliating consequences of the Trump administrations order, denying the most basic rights (of public toilet choice) to people of non-conforming gender (Associated Press, 2019). The use of urine in the artwork was important in highlighting the arduous and demeaning processes of physically managing the material as core to the works message (Cassils & Steinbock, 2018, p. 116). Performance art here becomes a powerful act of care through political and material protest in defence of a marginalised community.

Other artists have also used urine to explore issues of gender and care. Helen Chadwick's twelve bronze sculptures 'Piss Flowers' were made through a labour-intensive and expensive process (Bedell, 1994) that began by urinating outdoors onto pristine snow-covered ground, using a combination of male and female urine flows. Like the processes used by archaeologists in Pompei, where plaster of Paris was poured into the cavities that ancient organic remains had created in the compacted volcanic ash (preserving the material remains of that human disaster), in this case the urine itself also carved hollow spaces into the snow, which were then filled with liquid plaster of Paris by the artist.

The intricacy and delicacy of the forms that Chadwick retrieved from the snow required enormous efforts of commitment and care. In addition, multiple material transformations were also necessary, with each one offering its own specific affordances, in combination with environmental forces, from freezing snow to foundry furnace. Aesthetically beautiful and conceptually dense, the 'Piss Flowers' are presented in gallery contexts where the viewer is drawn in by the tantalising white stalagmite like forms, yet they retain the repellent sensation of their originating material, announced loudly in the title. Even when its materiality is utterly altered through labour-intensive processing which, oddly, both eradicate and preserve it, the urine resolutely retains its coveted shock value. This is achieved through intense processes of attention to material as care in making.

Also exploring affective shock value through art, Marcel Duchamp's audacious proposal that the act of naming something 'Art' is sufficient to make it 'Art', was most famously performed through exhibiting 'Fountain' (1917/1926), a urinal purchased from a plumbing supply shop, as sculpture. This idea of choosing what art can be while at the same time disrupting notions of the elitism of the artist as creator, inspired the feminist artwork of Mierle Laderman Ukeles beginning in the 1960s. After the birth of her first child and experiencing the frustration of the apparent loss of her own artistic (studio based) practice to the relentless and mundane necessities of the daily care of her family, in the spirit of Duchamp, Ukeles defiantly declared 'Maintenance work' to be 'Art'. Ukeles artistic manifesto (Ukeles, 1969) is accompanied by a proposal for an exhibition entitled 'Care' (which was rejected from several art institutions and so never displayed). This exhibition proposed three interconnected ideas of care; first the artist would do 'maintenance' work in the gallery, such as cleaning and washing floors. Second, maintenance workers in the building would be interviewed and asked to categorise their activities as either care or work. Finally, public materials from the city (bags of waste, polluted air, and water) would be processed in the gallery by scientists and artists and returned to the city once cleaned. These activities were to be documented and displayed as art.

Ultimately, Ukeles observed that conceptual art is produced via a system of 'development', whereas care work by contrast is a process of 'maintenance'. Ukeles found these distinctions to be stubbornly hierarchical. Art as a 'development' system, flaunts its required freedom and thus overshadows the drudgery and obligation of everyday care work upon which it nevertheless relies. Development as creative freedom also dominates maintenance in terms of societal value. Ukeles found that where development systems require sufficient space and resources to ignite and enable creativity, maintenance involves highly restricted movement through the enactment of tedious repetitive acts. Ukeles claim was that maintenance as care work is essential to sustain development processes and systems, and as such maintenance can also essentially be understood as foundational to all health and thriving, both personal and systemic. Ukeles framed maintenance care work as artistic practice, through artistic documentation of care in action, particularly of her own domestic circumstances. Ukeles claimed that care of her own family could be considered as a conceptual artform when conceptual artforms frequently repeat the tedious movements of maintenance systems. Rather than idealising 'care' (as in advertising for example), in Ukeles work the tedium and demanding imperatives of caring are brought to light and fully acknowledged as a form of artistic endurance (Ukeles, 1969). This commitment to understanding care work as something necessary to sustain life and vitality, was subsequently escalated by Ukeles through a forty-year unpaid artist residency with the New York City sanitation department (DSNY). A retrospective in 2017 in Queens Museum displays documentation of Ukeles many projects, including 'Touch Sanitation Performance' (1979–1980). For this work Ukeles spent eleven months, following sanitation workers and thanking each of them personally with a documented handshake, for keeping New York 'alive' (Steinhauer, 2017). The etymology of the term maintenance (*main*-hand *tenir*-to take) 'to take in hand', became enacted in this work, however at the time of writing this analysis, during a global pandemic, the symbol of the handshake itself has become utterly upended as a gesture of solidarity and friendship. This pandemic adds further layers of meaning to Ukeles work as an art practice which draws attention to, and so cares for/about, undervalued, unseen systems. Through this radically recalibrated global context, meaning becomes exposed as unstable. It is precisely these shifts in perspective that ultimately locates the power of art, as capable of moving beyond its original context and even the intent of the artist to reframe thinking, here, of how maintenance and care function within the constantly changing context of an unpredictable world where,

> The relationality that art develops with the world is not one to stir connection or familiarity but one that emerges from disjunction, ruptures, disobediences with familiar habits, codes, procedures, in which art engages in the production of the new. Under this perspective, art is neither an object nor a knowledge but a force that moves transversally in a logic of affectual contamination. (Trafí-Prats, 2019, p. 203)

Returning to the Fieldnote Event

The variety of artistic approaches to urine as a material of intense affective impact as outlined above, enables a consideration of the field note event from an aesthetic point of view, while also considering its entanglement with the concept of care. Through each of the artists practices, the parameters for understanding art can be extended beyond 'art as object', or even 'art as a way of knowing', as pointed out by Trafi-Prats above, towards thinking of art as an interference process for exploring and presenting complex concepts such as care. Each artist uniquely brings attention to the idea of care as multiple, situated, localised, difficult, mobile, and never reposing in a state of certainty. While each artist works with matters of the body, of social control and valuing (within art institutional contexts as is required to stake their claim as 'art'), they also explode notions of the aesthetic, and of where and how art as a generative force might emerge.

What was striking about observing the field note moment described above was the choreography of movement through an ordinary everyday ECEC event, that felt replete with multiple layers of care and love. Wrist's twist, and fingers brace to lift a still leaking body, legs dangle, smiles form, odour rises, knees bend, mop mops, bucket stands, disinfectant sprays, urine pools, voices soothe, instructions issue. Tiny movements of thought, bodies, objects, liquids, surfaces, become woven together and through each other, in a sequence of activity that could potentially be read as an 'artful' practice as described by Manning where 'artful practices honour complex forms of knowing and are collective not because they are operated upon by several people but because they make apparent, in the way they come to a problem, that knowledge at its core is collective' (Manning, 2016, p. 13). Tacit care practices of understated understanding of how to move, act, respond as a situation demands, is a way of attending that is always situated and collective. Manning states 'nonconscious thought is everywhere active in experience. It moves at differential speeds. It cuts across. It opens up. It shifts. It is not in the body or in the mind, but across the bodying where world and body co-compose in a welling ecology' (Manning, 2016, p. 115). Care like art then, can be understood also as a 'force' that moves through events, emerging and receding, taking over and becoming undone by the events unfolding where,

> Being in care with children becomes a matter not only of maintenance but of mutual becomings in ecologies of practice. In such ecologies, every practice must be thought anew, with relevant and situated questions that emerge from grappling with the matters that the situation demands. (Trafí-Prats, 2019, p. 192)

An ethico-aesthetic lens also presents an idea of the practice of care, or 'maintenance' as a craft, where both care and craft operate between conscious and tacit ways of knowing, learning, and material ways of being in the world, through 'choreographic thinking', and minor gestures, where 'Choreographing (…) is a call not only for the collective crafting of minor gestures, but for the attunement, in perception, to how minor gestures do their work' (Manning, 2016, p. 130). Therefore, an ethico-aesthetic lens offers different perspectives of care, as well as different routes to understanding how it is materialised.

Observations: Choreographic Thinking

The sudden arrival of urine in the classroom helped me to think about the ways in which difference might interject, sometimes violently, into everyday moments, to produce new collective acts and movements of caring together. Thinking and seeing moments through an ethico-aesthetic lens, which also activates difference, means that these moments can 'begin to have weight they didn't have before' (Loveless, 2019, p. 20). To give small things weight through theory is not about assigning load bearing meaning, but rather it is about giving them new life to move in new directions. In this case, bringing 'weight' as more, and as movement, involved tuning into movement as choreography, which Manning thinks of as the 'more than' that movement carries where,

> the choreography of collective movement is made possible by the interrelation between the intervals the movement creates and the collective capacity to cue and align to them, in the moving. Cueing is an important activity in the relational field. It is not directly tied to volition or intentionality. It happens in the moving. (Manning, 2016, p. 121)

For Manning, thinking and movement are simultaneous collective activity that involve anticipating both consciously and non-consciously, the movement of other bodies. This places thinking right in the middle of movement. In the same way, in my research caring was considered as existing right in the middle of education practice, as integral to it as thinking is to movement. My analysis therefore understands education and care as inseparable and 'sympoietic' (Haraway, 2016) practices of being alongside, *with* and *together*. This consideration of an ordinary small moment in ECEC, has implications for questioning on a larger scale how and why education and care could have been perceived a separatable pursuits and destinations in ECEC.

Art was presented here, as a mode of caring in itself, through materialised practices, as productive of diverse affects of caring. As such, art can became a lens for valuing and extending everyday moments of care or 'maintenance', and as a way of seeing these moments differently. Through an exploration of art which is concerned with diverse perspectives, hierarchies within both art and care become exposed. 'Maintenance' here becomes elevated as a practice which derives from a distinct form of attention to/movement with an event, viewed as a form of tacit and collective 'choreographic thinking'. The concept of 'choreographic thinking' through 'minor gestures' of both care and art can also be seen as collectively produced.

Through art, care may also be seen as a form of crafting, that is both bodily sensed and consciously developed in community with others.

Exposing and reframing assumptions and hierarchies within care and art has the effect of questioning the ways in which such value systems are supported. An aesthetic lens creates possibilities for valuing mundane and collective acts of caring differently. Where ECEC settings are sites of caring in complex, multiple and collective ways which impact children, finding new ways to both see and value the diversity of caring practices is useful, because caring practices need to be made visible from many perspectives in order to be valued more fully.

Care and Nature: Plants and Charcoal

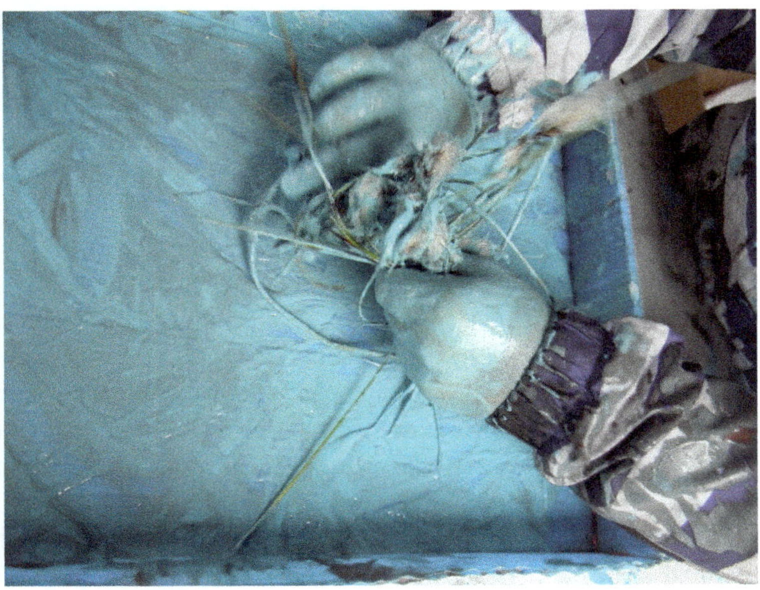

Figure 23: Care and Nature: Plants and Charcoal

> I had (brought in) things like heather and bog cotton, and different kind of grasses and wild flowers and I was looking for things with different textures maybe, like the bog cotton, I thought the kids would love the softness of it, maybe even they'd be just kind of putting it up to their face, you know, the interesting thing was with the bog cotton was that one of the kids just picked up the whole lot and fired it into the paint and squished it around (laughs) and that was the end of that! ('Sasha' Educator Interview Transcript)

Plants

The timing and arrangement for the educator's atelier sessions had been working well until Sasha's turn arrived. Having prepared so carefully, she was unexpectedly distracted. The previous afternoon her deep interest in and knowledge of plants drew her to foraging in the countryside near her home for a wide range of grasses and plants for her small group of children to explore at the outdoor atelier. However, on that morning, one of the children in her small group was feeling unwell, and so Sasha needed to communicate with the child's parents. Her concern for the child who was intermittently distressed, and the practical arrangements with the parents took time and attention away from her atelier activity.

She had laid out the materials on the table, adding large trays of blue paint alongside the carefully curated plants, but then had to leave the table regularly during the session. My role was to continue as an observant participant as before, but to allow the educators take the lead. Sasha spoke to me while setting up about the time and pleasure that had formed part of her foraging outing the previous day with her own children. Bog cotton, delicate heathers, drifty grasses, wild mint, and many other plants were laid carefully in the centre of the table. She was excited to begin and was looking forward to the children's responses. Sasha's expectations were tempered by her desire to share her personal interest and love of these natural materials with the children, however as an experienced educator, she understood to have very open expectations of what might unfold. Nevertheless, her investment of time, attention, love, and careful planning seemed completely overlooked and overwhelmed by Michael, who scrunched up of all the plants together and mashed them into the blue paint tray. It felt shocking to watch.

Caring for the sick child had subsumed Sasha's intended care for the atelier experience. Further, her training strongly encourages the facilitation of children's sensory or messy play, which is what Michael's engagement with plants and paints appeared to be. Justification for Michael's immersion in the plant/paint mashing process is provided by child-centred pedagogy and the valuing of 'messy play'. However, this worked against Sasha's idea of touch as reciprocal between nature and child, which as pointed out by Puig de la Bellacasa,

> Thinking touch through care and as sensory values, invites us to distribute and transfer ethicality through multilateral asymmetrical agencies that don't follow unidirectional patterns of individual intentionality. (Puig de la Bellacasa, 2017, p. 122)

Despite the care and attention in gathering, curating, and displaying, the plants did not transmit Sasha's individual intent or any apparent indication of requirements for specific modes of touch or expressions of care to Michael. The expectation that the natural materials might elicit particularly caring responses from the children such as holding the plants up to their cheeks, was disrupted by the presence of the paint. Art, as represented by paint, once again becomes a disruptive force.

Rousell and colleagues (2018) suggest that rather than presenting artistic modes of approaching 'Nature' through pedagogy, nature itself could be considered as the mode through which both learning and caring occur. If we consider nature, not as passively represented by the plants in this case, but as actively present in the movement of materials and events, in the children and adult's responses, where everything, in Spinozist terms, may be considered as part of nature. Rousell and colleagues (2018) found in their artistic research that the environment also,

> became active and agentic elements of an environmental arts pedagogy – with or without the intentionality of the artist, researcher or teacher as masterful human identities. This makes the environment itself the medium and milieu through which artful learning processes occur, rather than being the background, object, or container for learning that is primarily determined by human design and interpretation. (Rousell et al., 2018, p. 26)

Learning in this plant/paint event was powerful for the adults, particularly when framed by prior expectations of care for nature. Issues surrounding of the economies of care (Lynch, Lyons & Cantillon, 2007), what it requires and demands, how it becomes distributed, generates uncomfortable problems which circulate on both micro and macro scales. In this case, the affective environment which included excitement, expectation, anticipation, distraction, anxiety, shock, as well as the materiality of paint and beautiful plants, converged to present the adults (educator and researcher) with an opportunity for thinking about the limiting ways in which we may conceive of nature and care as somehow separated from everyday movement with the world. In the next section we follow Sasha's next opportunity to bring her own interests once again into pedagogical practice with the children, with very different forms of learning, caring, and experience produced.

Charcoal

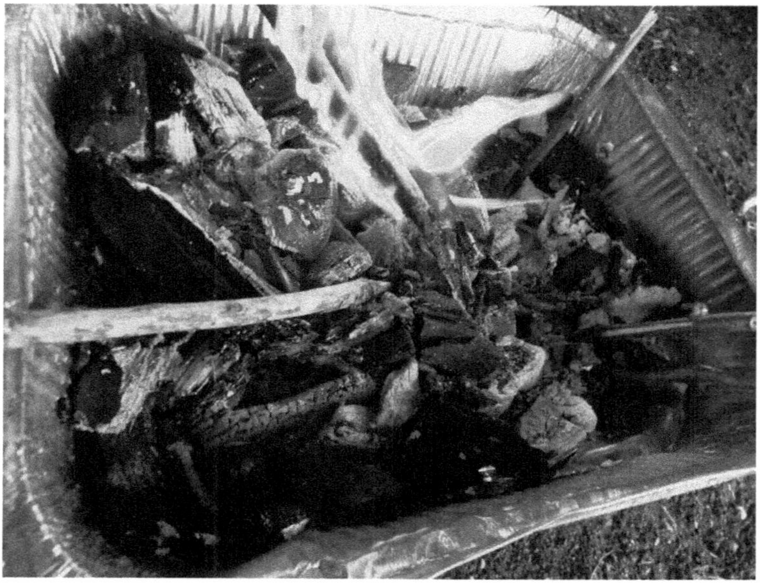

Figure 24: Charcoal

> The fire was very exciting through its heat, flame, smoke, interaction, danger, and a bit like the ice session, the children seemed to sense it had a finite time limit. Talking about fire, being with it and feeling it through skin, nose and mouth generated a lot of energy and enthusiasm to relay dramatic fire related stories, imaginary and real. Using the charcoal to draw with was surprising and satisfying, each burnt stick created different weights of blackness and widths of line. The short bursts of sunshine acted like an outdoor projector affording opportunities to engage with the plant shadows, to notice the fine details of the silhouettes. The ability to smudge the drawn lines invited the charcoal to stick to skin, highlighting lines in hands and hairs on arms. Its crumbs were mashed into the table, and as dust, was free to spread and move by air, skin, and water. (Field notes, p. 174)

The idea for making willow charcoal to draw with outside, grew out of Sasha's previous experience of presenting the plants and paint. Making pretend campfires from sticks and pieces of turf had been a strong emerging interest for the children during their outdoor play time and so we decided to use Sasha's extensive experience of wilderness skills education to build a small campfire with the children to make some willow charcoal. This time, working in teams of two educators, made the process more collaborative and convivial for the adults, while also alleviating situations such as had arisen previously for Sasha. In this instance, Christine (a co-owner of the setting) encouraged and fully supported the use of Sasha's skills and interest. Christine had recently returned from a trip to ECEC settings in Norway where children frequently engaged in risky play such as climbing tall trees and using knives and so she was excited to explore the possibilities presented by Sasha's extensive experience and confidence in setting campfires safely.

Our objective of burning willow sticks to make charcoal we could draw with became a way of extending the activity into the atelier, while the fire setting occurred on an earthy slope in the garden, away from the main building. The fire itself required and generated a substantial amount of talk between everyone, including instruction, discussion, and storying. The children listened and watched intently as Sasha spoke about the need to take care, of both the fire and of each other while close to it. The children seemed to sense the seriousness of what we were doing as an unusual but nevertheless exciting and much desired event. Sasha's expertise and confidence were reassuring for everyone. As we gathered around the fire, many stories emerged, including both factual memories as well as remembered fictions, all provoked by the fire. Ominous tales of warning, as well as imaginative flurries became shared and inflated between the children.

We selected small willow sticks to poke into the fire and designated an area where they would cool after. Although technically, simply burning the sticks is not the correct way to make charcoal (it should be enclosed in an airtight tin for several hours) it was quicker and just as effective to use the charred ends of the twigs for drawing with. Afterwards, together we put out the fire with water to satisfying hissing sounds and then carried the cooled charred sticks to the atelier table. The sunlight intermittently created strong shadows of the leaves and plants we wanted to draw, allowing the children to observe the detail of the plants and to see them in new ways. The charcoal produced exciting and difficult to control blacks and greys, smudging onto hands, faces and paper. Pacini-Ketchabaw et al. (2017) poetically describe a similar experience with charcoal,

> Charcoal is intensely hospitable to encounters with others. It marks, spreads, covers, envelopes, draws in. As it does this, it announces its presence and compels a response. It is difficult to remain neutral to charcoal and unaffected by it. Charcoals rich blackness, its infinite tiny particles, its chalky softness compels, repels, affronts. Such hospitality is imbued with the act of listening. (Pacini-Ketchabaw et al., 2017, p. 36)

Listening, learning, caring, researching, storying and being together with the fire, for both adults and children, offered a potential view of pedagogy as a materialised 'sympoiesis' as explained by Haraway,

> Sympoesis is a simple word; it means 'making-with'. Nothing makes itself; nothing is really autopoietic or self-organising. (…) Sympoiesis is a word proper to complex, dynamic, responsive, situated, historical systems. It is a word for worlding-with, in company. (Haraway, 2016, p. 58)

Adults, children, materials, and environmental elements including fire, sunlight, shadow, smoke, and water were thus all active participants in the production of a multi directional, wholly encompassing and care-full artistic experience, where essential elements of destruction and production both moved through the creative event.

Observations: Care and Nature.

This research story evoked a range of disruptions to assumptions surrounding nature and care. Nature, both destructive and constructive, becomes more than passively represented by materials such as plants. Rather it is endlessly lively, unpredictable, and visible through diverse intra-acting bodies. Perceiving 'natural' materials as resolutely both good and stable, is a limitation of their potential. It is also a restriction of the understanding of nature which is inherent to far more than that which usually represents it. This idea aligns with Spinoza's conceptualisation of Nature as Substance, or as that through which everything exists. This involves a flattening of the hierarchical expectation and anxiety which notions of Nature inspire. Diss-assembling the assumptions of purity associated with Nature as a category which ECEC frequently installs, is important because it makes possible an openness to the idea that everything, not just prioritised categories, require collective practices of care.

Care and Diffraction

'Life goes on through a process of diffraction – disturbances and agitations that keep life moving' (Lester, 2020, p. 219). Diffraction in this work is envisaged as strongly connected to the concept of the ethics of care, where attentionality can be pulled in many directions at once, but not as a negatively inflected malfunction in the powers of concentration. Rather, as the way the material world draws attention unexpectedly, creatively, and at different speeds and times. Manning notes how,

> Most of our education systems are based in stillness. We learn in chairs. We associate concentration with being quiet. We discourage the movement of thought we call daydreaming, particularly in the context of 'learning'. We consider the immanent movements of doodling to be a distraction. We are told not to fidget. Reason is aligned with keeping the body still. What if instead we invested in movement-moving, asking children not to stop moving but to become increasingly aware of

> the share of creativity in the incipient directions of the movements that move them? (Manning, 2016, p. 122)

This is of course, not a new plea for movement and play in education contexts. The arguments for play and activity have been pioneered through ECEC over centuries, nevertheless they remain under threat, particularly from the pressures of measurement (Urban, 2018). While the forms that playful activity might take in education settings are constantly restricted by multiple factors, the material environment presents openings and opportunities as diffractive playful possibilities, and 'children are able to navigate and negotiate through adult control of time and space to find such possibilities' (Lester, 2020, p. 218). The cultivation of the capacity to take up and be taken by diffractive moments as they present themselves is an optimistic practice of following openings as a way of bringing more to life and living. The concept of diffraction then, provides another way of understanding how children, in collusion with their material environments find ways of doing this, despite all that is set against them, making these diffractive micro-movements political,

> For these moments, life is temporarily enlivened, sites of adult production and consumption are transformed by children's desire to unsettle and stake a claim, as children. (Lester, 2020, p. 168)

Diffractions underscore how knowing and not knowing are in relation with one another through both difficulty and understanding as ongoing, trouble-making activities. Diffraction presents spaces or gaps through which finding 'in the moment' ways of being, caring, and knowing together with others becomes possible.

Final Thoughts: Everyday Artfulness

> Theoretical work can be as much grounded in the materials and forces of the inhabited world as the conduct of any other craft. To practice theory as a mode of habitation is to mix and mingle, in one's thinking, with the textures of the world. (Ingold, 2020, p. 14)

As has been explored throughout this book, a posthuman theoretical lens can bring to light how education and care emerge from small moments of affective attentionality that constantly make themselves available to response. This requires following, responding, corresponding, and improvising with the environment as a site of diversity, spontaneity, complexity, movement, and relationality. It means finding value in the ordinary and can generate important disturbances of assumptions which impact children and education practice more widely. It reveals the absolute inclusivity of the material environment in making aesthetic experience available.

In this art education research practice, I did not set out to educate children, nor did I aim to criticise or disrupt practices of teaching, learning, or ways of being in an ECEC setting. I have also avoided following up or making new claims for art in education, particularly for young children, as activity that benefits other areas of developmental and curriculum concerns. These arguments and positions for art in education have not been pursued because through an ethico-aesthetic lens such rationales and aims are seen to erode the potential and force of art in education. Rather, I have worked toward finding other ways of seeing and thinking about children and about their education setting.

Here, the setting was found to be enlivened by the diverse movements of children, adults, materials, and things which young children both create and inhabit differently. Noticing deeply relational movement between humans and non-humans generated openings for possible ways of paying attention to complex affects. The ethico-aesthetic lens activated my attunement to a multitude of small moments as they emerged as aesthetic, affective sensations, disruptions, and questions for thinking and being with, and as modes of art, care, and education in themselves. But those moments don't necessarily end with sensing, noticing, or thinking. Doing again, in new ways, in new spaces, with new relationships to explore can also play a part in keeping these moments active and valued.

When Spinozist ethics and aesthetics join forces, they resist agendas which exert multifaceted pressures on education. Affirmative ethics and aesthetics reorient and counterbalance each other's potentially negative tendencies. Aesthetics' predilections for purity, beauty, and exclusivity are held in check by an affirmative ethics that is fundamentally democratic, particularly through its diverse openness and availability. In turn, aesthetics dilutes ethics desires to survey, police, regulate or master, and instead offers, through its capacity to trouble-make, create interruptions and disturbances as part of its enlivening purpose, a route to taking and spending time along-side others, care-fully, modestly, generously, artfully. A posthuman ethico-aesthetic lens provides ways of paying attention and including children's 'voice' as whole bodily movement with, and response to, materials, environments, affects, and things. This in turn generates a radically unifying perspective of children's unique, experimental modes of exploration and expression in the world with diverse others as everyday artfulness.

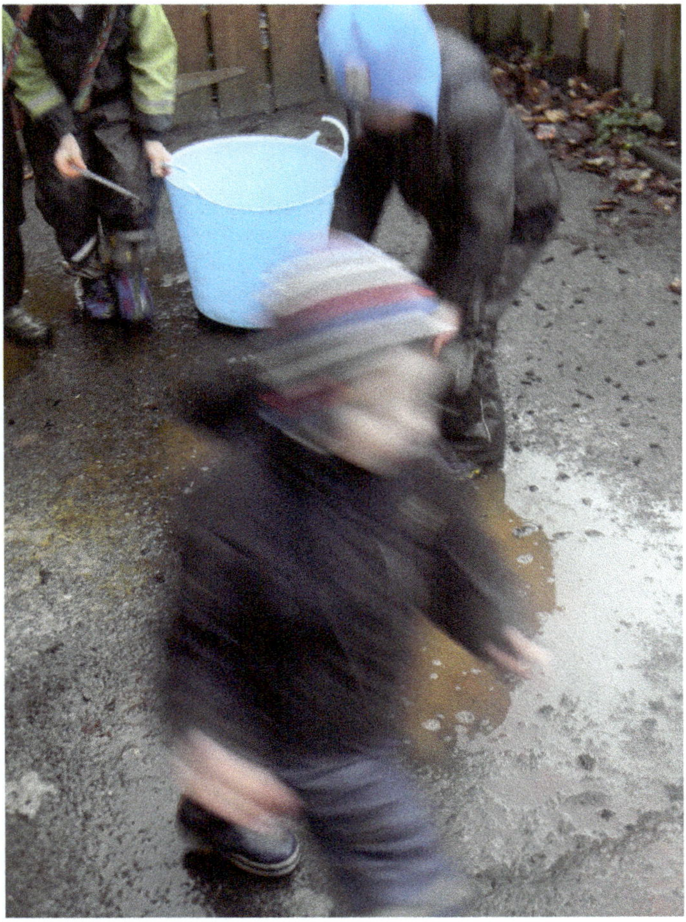

Figure 25: Everyday Artfulness

Bibliography

Akomolafe, B. (2019) 'What Climate Collapse Asks of Us', *Bayo Akomolafe*. Available at: <https://www.bayoakomolafe.net/post/what-climate-collapse-asks-of-us>.

Alliance for Children (2004) *Tech Tonic: Towards a New Literacy of Technology*. Baltimore: College Park.

Anastasiou, T., Holmes, R. and Runswick-Cole, K. (2018) 'Becoming Monsterous: On the Limits of the Body of a Child', in Riddle, S., Bright, D. and Honan, E. (eds) *Writing with Deleuze in the Academy*. Singapore: Springer Nature, pp. 45–60.

Aslanian, T. K. (2015) 'Getting Behind Discourses of Love, Care and Maternalism in Early Childhood Education', *Contemporary Issues in Early Childhood*, 16(2), pp. 153–165.

Aslanian, T. K. (2018) 'Recycling Piaget: Posthumanism and Making Children's Knowledge Matter', *Educational Philosophy and Theory*, 50(4), pp. 417–427.

Associated Press (2019) 'Gavin Grimm: Victory for Trans Student as US Judge Rules Bathroom Bill Violated Rights', *The Guardian*, 10 August.

Athey, C. (1990) *Extending Thought in Young Children*. London: Paul Chapman Pub.

Atkinson, D. (2018a) *Art, Disobedience, and Ethics: The Adventure of Pedagogy*. 1st edn. New York, NY: Nature America Ltd.

Atkinson, D. (2018b) 'Art, Pedagogies and Becoming: The Force of Art and the Individuation of New Worlds', in Knight, L. and Lasczik Cutcher, A. (eds) *Arts-Research-Education*. Cham: Springer International Publishing (Studies in Arts-Based Educational Research), pp. 3–16.

Badmington, N. (ed.) (2000) *Posthumanism*. Houndmills: Palgrave.

Barad, K. (2003) 'Posthumanist Performativity: Toward an Understanding of How Matter Comes to Matter', *Signs: Journal of Women in Culture and Society*, 28(3), pp. 801–831.

Barad, K. (2007) *Meeting the Universe Halfway: Quantum Physics and the Entanglement of Matter and Meaning*. Durham: Duke University Press.

Barad, K. (2014) 'Diffracting Diffraction: Cutting Together-Apart', *Parallax*, 20(3), pp. 168–187.

Barnardo's (2006) *Parental Involvement: A Handbook for Childcare Providers*. Dublin: National Children's Resource Centre, Barnardos.

Bateson, G. (1972) *Steps to an Ecology of Mind: Collected Essays in Anthropology, Psychiatry, Evolution, and Epistemology*. New York: Chandler Publishing Company.

Bateson, G. (1978) *Steps to an Ecology of Mind: A Revolutionary Approach to Man's Understanding of Himself.* 7. printing. New York: Ballantine Books.
Bateson, G. (1985) *Mind and Nature: A Necessary Unity*. London: Fontana.
Bedell, G. (1994) *Show People: Blood and Chocolate: Helen Chadwick, The Independent.* Available at: <http://www.independent.co.uk/arts-entertainment/show-people-blood-and-chocolate-helen-chadwick-1384945.html>.
Bennett, J. (2001) *The Enchantment of Modern Life: Attachments, Crossings, and Ethics*. Princeton, NJ: Princeton University Press.
Bennett, J. (2010) *Vibrant Matter: A Political Ecology of Things*. Durham: Duke University Press.
Benson, C. (1979) *The Place of the Arts in Irish Education*. Dublin: The Arts Council.
Benson, C. (2019) 'Time, Vocabulary, & Art's Thoughtful Uses of Feeling?', in *Fortieth Anniversary Lecture the Place of the Arts in Irish Education.* Dublin: Dublin City University.
Berardi, F. (2009) *The Soul at Work: From Alienation to Autonomy*. Los Angeles, CA: Semiotext(e) (Semiotext(e) Foreign Agents Series).
Berger (2017) 'The Potential of Pedagogical Documentation for Leadership Enactment', in Fleet, A., Patterson, C. and Robertson, J. (eds) *Pedagogical Documentation in Early Years Practice: Seeing through Multiple Perspectives*. 1st edn. Thousand Oaks, CA: SAGE.
Berlant, L. (2010) 'Cruel Optimism', in Gregg, M. and Seigworth, G. J. (eds) *The Affect Theory Reader*. Durham: Duke University Press.
Bhalla, N., Chandran, R. and Nagarai, A. (2016) 'Blood Mica: Key Findings of Investigation into Child Deaths in India's Illegal Mica Mines', *Reuters*, 3 August Available at: <https://www.reuters.com/article/idUSKCN10D2NG/>.
Biesta, G. (2021) *World-Centred Education: A View for the Present*. New York, NY: Routledge.
Bignall, S., Hemming, S. and Rigney, D. (2016) 'Three Ecosophies for the Anthropocene: Environmental Governance, Continental Posthumanism and Indigenous Expressivism', *Deleuze Studies*, 10(4), pp. 455–478.
Bird Rose, D. (2013) 'Anthropocene Noir', in James, P. et al. (eds) *People and the Planet: Transforming the Future.* Melbourne: RMIT University.
Blenkinsop, S. et al. (2018) 'Wild Pedagogies: Six Touchstones for Childhoodnature Theory and Practice', in Latiner Raby, R. and Valeau, E. J. (eds) *Handbook of Comparative Studies on Community Colleges and Global Counterparts.* Cham: Springer International Publishing (Springer International Handbooks of Education), pp. 1–18.
Bloomberg Philanthropies (2018) *Olafur Eliasson Brings Major Public Art Installation Ice Watch to London to Inspire Action Against Climate Change*. Press and Media. bloomberg.org/press/releases/olafur-eliasson.

Boetzkes, A. (2015) 'Ecologicity, Vision and the Neurological System', in *Art in the Anthropocene Encounters among Aesthetics, Environments and Espistemologies*. London: Open Humanities Press, pp. 271–282.

Bohlmann, M. P. J. and Hickey-Moody, A. (2019) *Deleuze and Children*. Edinburgh: Edinburgh University Press.

Bone, J. (2019) 'Ghosts of the Material World in Early Childhood Education: Furniture Matters', *Contemporary Issues in Early Childhood*, 20(2), pp. 133–145.

Boscacci, L. (2019) 'Ecologising Affect and Atmosphere in the Anthropocene: dear Rachel', in Meco Network (ed.) *100 Atmospheres: Studies in Scale and Wonder. London: Open Humanities Press*, pp. 193–215.

Braidotti, R. (2006) 'Affirmation versus Vulnerability: On Contemporary Ethical Debates', *Symposium: Canadian Journal of Continental Philosophy*, 10(1), pp. 235–254.

Braidotti, R. (2013) *The Posthuman*. Cambridge, UK: Polity Press.

Braidotti, R. (2019) 'A Theoretical Framework for the Critical Posthumanities', *Theory, Culture & Society*, 36(6), pp. 31–61.

Braidotti, R. and Hlavjova, M. (2018) *The Posthuman Glossary*. London: Bloomsbury Academic.

Brennan, C. (2015) 'Artistic Enquiry in Early Childhood Education.' *Arts in Education Portal*. Available at: <http://artsineducation.ie/wp-content/uploads/Artistic-Enquiry-in-Early-Childhood-Education.pdf>.

Brennan, T. (2004) *The Transmission of Affect*. Ithaca: Cornell University Press.

Cantillon, S. and Lynch, K. (2017) 'Affective Equality: Love Matters', *Hyopatia*, 32(1), pp. 169–186.

Cassils and Steinbock, E. A. (2018) 'On Propagating Collective Resilience in Times of War: A Conversation with Cassils', *Performance Matters*, 4(3), pp. 108–127.

CECDE. (2006) *Siolta, the National Quality Framework for Early Childhood Education*. Dublin: Centre for Early Childhood Development & Education.

Ceder, S. (2015) *Cutting through Water: Towards a Posthuman Theory of Educational Relationality*. Division for Education, Department of Sociology. Lund, Sweden: Lund University.

Ceppi, G. and Zini, M. (1998) *Children, Spaces, Relations: Metaproject for an Environment for Young Children*. Italy: Reggio Children.

Childrens Rights Alliance. (2012) *Briefing Note to the Children's Referendum*. Dublin: Childrens Rights Alliance.

Colebrook, C. (2012) 'The Multiple, The Letter, and The Theorist', in *Mapping Multiple Literacies an Introduction to Deleuzian Literacy Studies*. London: Continuum Books, pp. vii–xii.

Colletti, L. (1972) *From Rousseau to Lenin: Studies in Ideology and Society*. London: Monthly Review Press.

Coolahan, J. (2015) 'A Portal to the Future of the Arts in Education', *The Irish Times*. Available at: <https://www.irishtimes.com/news/education/a-portal-to-the-future-of-the-arts-in-education-1.2212746>

Coolahan, J. (2017) *Towards the Era of Lifelong Learning: A History of Irish Education, 1800–2016*. Dublin, Ireland: Institute of Public Administration.

Coole, D. and Frost, S. (2010) *New Materialisms: Ontology, Agency, and Politics*. Durham & London: Duke University Press.

Creswell, J. W. (1998) *Qualitative Inquiry and Research Design: Choosing among Five Traditions*. Thousand Oaks, CA: SAGE.

Creswell, J. W. (2003) *Research Design: Qualitative, Quantitative, and Mixed Method Approaches*. 2nd edn. Thousand Oaks, CA: SAGE.

Crutzen, P. J. (2006) 'The Anthropocene – The Current Human Dominated Geological Era', *Paths of Discovery, Pontifical Academy of Sciences* (Acta 18), pp. 199–211.

Crutzen, P. J. and Stoermer, E. F. (2000) 'The "Anthropocene"', *Global Change Newsletter*, 41, pp. 17–18.

Csikszentmihalyi, M. (1997) *Creativity: Flow and the Psychology of Discovery and Invention*. New York: Harper Collins Publishers.

Dahlberg, G. (2016) 'An Ethico-aesthetic Paradigm as an Alternative Discourse to the Quality Assurance Discourse', *Contemporary Issues in Early Childhood*, 17(1), pp. 124–133.

Dahlberg, G. and Moss, P. (eds) (2014) 'Series Editors' Foreword', in *Listening to Children: Being and Becoming*. London: Routledge, Taylor & Francis Group (Contesting Early Childhood).

Dahlberg, G., Moss, P. and Pence, A. R. (2007) *Beyond Quality in Early Childhood Education and Care: Languages of Evaluation*. 2nd edn, repr. New York, NY: Routledge.

Dalke, A., Cassidy, K., Grobstein, P. and Blank, D. (2007) 'Emergent Pedagogy: Learning to Enjoy the Uncontrollable – and Make It Productive', *Journal of Educational Change*, 8(2), pp. 111–130.

Davies, B. (2014a) *Listening to Children: Being and Becoming*. London: Routledge, Taylor & Francis Group (Contesting Early Childhood).

Davies, B. (2014b) 'The Affective Flows of Art-Making', *Ocassional Paper Series*, 2014(31), p. 17.

Davies, B. (2018) 'Ethics and the New Materialism: A Brief Genealogy of the "Post" Philosophies in the Social Sciences', *Discourse: Studies in the Cultural Politics of Education*, 39(1), pp. 113–127.

Davis, H. and Turpin, E. (2015) *Art in the Anthropocene: Encounters among Aesthetics, Politics, Environments and Epistemologies*. London: Open Humanities Press.

Deleuze, G. (1988) *Spinoza, Practical Philosophy*. Translated by Robert Hurley. San Francisco: City Lights Books.

Deleuze, G. (1997) 'Immanence: A Life', *Theory, Culture & Society*, 14(2), pp. 3–7.

Deleuze, G. (2004) *The Logic of Sense*. London: The Athlone Press.

Deleuze, G. and Guattari, F. (1987) *A Thousand Plateaus: Capitalism and Schizophrenia*. Translated by B. Massumi. London: Continuum.

Department of Health and Children. (2004a) *Food and Nutrition Guidelines for Pre-school Services*. Dublin: Health Promotion Unit Govt of Ireland.

Dewey, J. (2005) *Art as Experience*. New York: Berkley Pub. Group.

Dewey, J. (2015) *Experience and Education*. New York: Free Press.

Dickens, C. (2003) *Hard Times for These Times*. Translated by K. Flint. London: Penguin (Penguin Classics).

Dissanayake, E. (2000) *Art and Intimacy: How the Arts Began*. Seattle, WA: University of Washington Press.

Dolphijn, R. (2018) 'Ecosophy', in Braidotti, R. and Hlavjova, M. (eds) *The Posthuman Glossery*. London: Bloomsbury Academic.

Dolphijn, R. and Van der Tuin, I. (2012) *New Materialism: Interviews & Cartographies*. London: Open Humanities Press.

Dowling-Long, Siobhán (2015) 'The Arts In and Out of School: Educational Policy, Provision and Practice in Ireland Today', *International Electronic Journal of Elementary Education*, 8(2), pp. 267–286.

Ehret, C. and D'Amico, D. (2019) 'Why a More Human Literacy Studies must Be Posthuman', in Leander, K. M. and Ehret, C. (eds) *Affect in Literacy Teaching and Learning Pedagogies, Politics, and Coming to Know*. New York: Routledge (Expanding Literacies in Education).

Eisner, E. W. (2002) *The Arts and the Creation of Mind*. New Haven: Yale University Press.

Eliasson, O. (2018) *Climate Action: Challenge Your Status Quo Bias!* Politiken, Denmark: Studio Olafur Eliasson.

Elkins, J. (1999) *What Painting Is: How to Think About Oil Painting, Using the Language of Alchemy*. London and New York: Routledge.

Fahey, T. (1992) 'State, Family and Compulsory Schooling in Ireland', *The Economic and Social Review*, 24(4), July, 1992, pp. 369–395.

Fairchild, N. (2016) 'Plugging into the Umbra: Creative Experimentation (in)(on) the Boundaries of Knowledge Production in ECEC Research', *Reconceptualizing Educational Research Methodology*, 7(1), pp. 16–30.

Fay, R. and McCabe, C. (2015) *30 Years of Pavee Point*. Dublin: Pavee Point Publications.

Ferguson, G. and Brandes, S. (2012) 'Piss Flowers, Piss Christ, and Piss Paintings – The Use of Urine in Art', *The Journal of Urology*, 184(4S), pp. 426–427.

Ferrando, F. (2013) 'Posthumanism, Transhumanism, Antihumanism, Metahumanism, and New Materialisms Differences and Relations', *Existenz an International Journal in Philosophy, Religion Politics and the Arts*, 8(2), pp. 26–32.

Ferrando, F. (2014) 'The Posthuman – Rosi Braidotti', *Science Fiction Studies*, 41(1), p. 238.

Ferrando, F. (2016) 'A Feminist Genealogy of Posthuman Aesthetics in the Visual Arts', *Palgrave Communications*, 2(1), pp 1–12.

Filippini, T. and Vecchi, V. (eds) (1996) *The Hundred Languages of Children: Narrative of the Possible*. Reggio Emilia, Italy: Reggio Children.

Flannery Quinn, S. (2013) *Froebel's Gifts*. London: Froebel College.

Fleet, A., Patterson, C. and Robertson, J. (eds) (2017) *Pedagogical Documentation in Early Years Practice: Seeing through Multiple Perspectives*. 1st edn. Thousand Oaks, CA: SAGE.

Fredriksen, B. C. (2012) 'Providing Materials and Spaces for the Negotiation of Meaning in Explorative Play: Teachers' Responsibilities', *Education Inquiry*, 3(3), pp. 335–352.

Freire, P. (2005) *Education for Critical Consciousness*. London: Continuum (Continuum Impacts).

de Freitas, E., Sellar, S. and Bang Jensen, L. (2018) 'Thinking with Spinoza about Education', *Educational Philosophy and Theory*, 50(9), pp. 805–808.

French, G. (2007) *Children's Early Learning and Development – A Research Paper*. Dublin: NCCA.

French, G. (2013) *The Place of the Arts in Early Childhood Learning and Development*. Ireland: Commissioned Paper from The Arts Council.

Froebel, F. (1974) *The Education of Man*. Clifton, NJ: A. M. Kelley.

Frost, S. (2010) 'Fear and the Illusion of Autonomy', in Coole, D. and Frost, S. (eds) *New Materialisms: Ontology, Agency, and Politics*. Durham: Duke University Press, pp. 158–177.

Fuji, L. A. (2015) 'Five Stories of Accidental Ethnography: Turning Unplanned Moments in the Field into Data', *Qualitative Research*, 15(4), pp. 525–539.

Fuller, M. (2008) 'Art Methodologies in Media Ecology', in O'Sullivan, S. and Zepke, S. (eds) *Deleuze, Guattari, and the Production of the New*. London: Continuum.

Gandini, L. (ed.) (2005) *In the Spirit of the Studio: Learning from the Atelier of Reggio Emilia*. New York: Teachers College Press (Early Childhood Education Series).

Geerts, E. and Van der Tuin, I. (2016) 'Literacy & Agential Literacy', *New Materialism Almanac* (2016) [Preprint].

Glover, W. J. (2005) 'Objects, Models, and Exemplary Works: Educating Sentiment in Colonial India', *The Journal of Asian Studies*, 64(3), pp. 539–566.

Gopnik, A. (2009) *The Philosophical Baby: What Children's Minds Tell Us about Truth, Love and the Meaning of Life*. London: Bodley Head.

Gopnik, A., Meltzoff, A. N. and Kuhl, P. K. (1999) *The Scientist in the Crib: Minds, Brains, and How Children Learn*. 1st edn. New York: William Morrow & Co.

Gray, J. (2002) *Straw Dogs Thoughts on Humans and Other Animals*. London: Granta Books.

Grazzini, C. (2013) 'Maria Montessori's Cosmic Vision, Cosmic Plan, and Cosmic Education', *The NAMTA Journal*, 38(1), pp. 107–116.

Gregg, M. and Seigworth, G. J. (eds) (2010) *The Affect Theory Reader*. Durham, NC: Duke University Press.

Grosz, E. (2005) 'Chaos, Territory, Art, and the Framing of the Earth', *IDEA Journal*, 6(1), pp. 15–29.

Guattari, F. (2000) *The Three Ecologies*. London: The Athlone Press.

Hackett, A. (2017) 'Parents as Researchers: Collaborative Ethnography with Parents', *Qualitative Research*, 17(5), pp. 481–497.

Hackett, A. (2018) 'Inchoate Literacies; Leaking, Entwining, Messyways of Parents and Children Being in the World', in *Mattering, Knowing, Ethics and Care; Post-human Approaches to Parenting in Neo-liberal Times: RECE Reconceptualising Early Childhood Education Conference*. Copenhagen, Denmark.

Hackett, A., MacLure, M. and Pahl, K. (2020) 'Literacy and Language as Material Practices: Re-thinking Social Inequality in Young Children's Literacies', *Journal of Early Childhood Literacy*, 20(1), pp. 3–12.

Hackett, A., Pahl, K. and Pool, S. (2017) 'In Amongst the Glitter and the Squashed Blueberries: Crafting a Collaborative Lens for Children's Literacy Pedagogy in a Community Setting', *Pedagogies: An International Journal*, 12(1), pp. 58–73.

Hackett, A. and Rautio, P. (2019) 'Answering the World: Young Children's Running and Rolling as More-than-Human Multimodal Meaning Making', *International Journal of Qualitative Studies in Education*, 32(8), pp. 1019–1031.

Hackett, A. and Somerville, M. (2017) 'Posthuman Literacies: Young Children Moving in Time, Place and More-than-Human Worlds', *Journal of Early Childhood Literacy*, 17(3), pp. 374–391.

Halberstam, J. (2013) 'The Wild Beyond: With and for the Undercommons', in Harney, S. and Moten, F. (eds) *The Undercommons: Fugitive Planning & Black Study*. Wivenhoe: Minor Compositions.

Haraway, D. J. (1992) 'The Promises of Monsters: A Regenerative Politics for Inappropriate/d Others', in Grossberg, L., Nelson, C. and Treichler, P. A. (eds) *Cultural Studies*. New York: Routledge, pp. 295–337.

Haraway, D. J. (1997) *Modest_Witness@Second_Millennium.FemaleMan_Meets_OncoMouse: Feminism and Technoscience*. New York: Routledge.

Haraway, D. J. (2015) 'Anthropocene, Capitalocene, Plantationocene, Chthulucene: Making Kin', *Environmental Humanities*, 6(1), pp. 159–165.

Haraway, D. J. (2016) *Staying with the Trouble: Making Kin in the Chthulucene.* Durham: Duke University Press (Experimental Futures: Technological Lives, Scientific Arts, Anthropological Voices).

Harman, G. (2007) 'Aesthetics as First Philosophy: Levinas and the Non-human', *Naked Punch*, 9, pp. 21–30.

Harper, H. (1997) 'Disturbing Identity and Desire Adolescent Girls and Wild Words', in Todd, S. (ed.) *Learning Desire: Perspectives on Pedagogy, Culture, and the Unsaid.* New York: Routledge, pp. 141–161.

Hayles, N. K. (1999) *How We Became Posthuman: Virtual Bodies in Cybernetics, Literature, and Informatics.* London: University of Chicago Press.

Hayles, N. K. (2017) 'Inside Out, Outside In: Recursive Dynamics in Posthumanism and in Nam June Paik's Artwork', in International Symposium Publication, presented by Nam June Paik Art Centre *Coevolution: Cybernetics to Posthuman.* Gyeonggi-do, Korea: Nam June Paik Art Center (Nam June Paik Reader #7).

Health Service Executive. (2011) *The Child, Health, Welfare & Development Assessment Guide.* Dubin: Health Service Executive.

Hickey-Moody, A. (2016) 'A Femifesta for Posthuman Art Education: Visions and Becomings', in Taylor, C. A. and Hughes, C. (eds) *Posthuman Research Practices in Education.* New York, NY: Palgrave Macmillan.

Hickey-Moody, A. and Page, Tara (eds) (2015) *Arts, Pedagogy and Cultural Resistance: New Materialisms.* London: Rowman & Littlefield International.

Hicky-Moody, A. (2016) 'A Femifesta for Posthuman Art Education: Visions and Becomings', in Taylor, C. A. and Hughes, C. (eds) *Posthuman Research Practices in Education.* Basingstoke: Palgrave Macmillan, pp. 258–266.

Hickey-Moody, A. C. (2013) 'Deleuze's Children', *Educational Philosophy and Theory*, 45(3), pp. 272–286.

Higgins, M. (2017) 'Post-qualitative Mo(ve)ments: Concluding Remarks on Methodological Response-Abilities and Being Wounded by Thought', *Reconceptualizing Educational Research Methodology*, 8(3), pp. 89–101.

Highmore, B. (2010) 'Bitter After Taste: Affect, Food and Social Aesthetics', in Gregg, M. and Seigworth, G. J. (eds) *The Affect Theory Reader.* Durham: Duke University Press, pp. 118–137.

Hill, L. and Lyons, A. (2020) 'Strawing: Perpetual Line', in Trafí-Prats, L. and Schulte, C. M. (eds) *Language, Sense and the Event of Drawing in Childhood.* Switzerland: Springer.

Hill, L. and O'Gorman, A. (2020) 'For the Love of Small Stuff: Materialising Theory in an Early Years Artist Residency', in Hackett, A., Holmes, R. and MacRae, C.

(eds) *Working with Young Children in Museums: Weaving Theory and Practice*. London: Routledge/Taylor & Francis Group, pp. 62–70.

Hodgins, B. D. (2019) 'Caring: Method as Affect, Obligation and Action', in Hodgins, B. D. (ed) *Feminist Research for 21st-Century Childhoods Common Worlds Methods*. London: Bloomsbury Academic.

Hohti, R. and Osgood, J. (2020) 'Pets That Have "Something Inside": The Material Politics of in/Animacy and Queer Kin within the Childhood Menagerie', *Genealogy*, 4(2), p. 38.

Holmes, R. and Jones, L. (2016) 'Flickering, Spilling and Diffusing Body/Knowledge in the Posthuman Early Years', in Taylor, C. .A. and Hughes, C. (eds) Posthuman Research Practices in Education. London: Palgrave Macmillan. Available at: <https://doi.org/10.1057/9781137453082_8>.

Honan, E. and Bright, D. (2016) 'Writing a Thesis Differently', *International Journal of Qualitative Studies in Education*, 29(5), pp. 731–743.

Huizinga, J. (1949) *Homo Ludens a Study of the Play-Element in Culture*. London: Routledge & Kegan Paul.

Hultman, K. and Lenz Taguchi, H. (2010) 'Challenging Anthropocentric Analysis of Visual Data: A Relational Materialist Methodological Approach to Educational Research', *International Journal of Qualitative Studies in Education*, 23(5), pp. 525–542.

Independent Editors. (2018) *Sexual Abuse, Exploitation of Women and Paedophile Priests: The Scandals That Have Rocked the Catholic Church, Independent Newsdesk*. Irish Independent Newspaper Newsdesk, 26 Aug 2018.

INFORM. (2020) 'Act Now: Re-imagining Early Childhood Education and Care in Ireland a Discussion Paper'. Submission for consideration for the Program for Government.

Ingold, T. (2010) 'The Textility of Making', *Cambridge Journal of Economics*, 34(1), pp. 91–102.

Ingold, T. (2013) *Making: Anthropology, Archaeology, Art and Architecture*. London: Routledge.

Ingold, T. (2016) 'On Human Correspondence', *Journal of the Royal Anthropological Institute (NS)*, (23), pp. 9–27.

Ingold, T. (2020) *Correspondences*. Cambridge, UK: Polity.

Irwin, R. L. (2013) 'Becoming a/r/tography', *Studies in Art Education*, 54(3), pp. 198–215.

Irwin, R. L. and De Cosson, A. (2004) *A/r/tography Rendering Self through Arts-based Living Inquiry*. Vancouver: Pacific Educational Press.

Jackson, A. Y. (2013) 'Posthumanist Data Analysis of Mangling Practices', *International Journal of Qualitative Studies in Education*, 26(6), pp. 741–748.

Jackson, A. Y. and Mazzei, L. A. (2012) *Thinking with Theory in Qualitative Research: Viewing Data Across Multiple Perspectives*. 1st edn. Abingdon, Oxon: Routledge.

Johansson, L. (2016) 'Post-qualitative Line of Flight and the Confabulative Conversation: A Methodological Ethnography', *International Journal of Qualitative Studies in Education*, 29(4), pp. 445–466. doi: 10.1080/09518398.2015.1053157.

John, P. (2011) 'Collage: Playing with Food?', *Teaching Young Children*, 4(3), p. 5.

Jones, L, MacLure, M, Holmes, R. and Macrae, C (2012) 'Children and Objects: Affection and Infection', *Early Years*, 32(1), pp. 49–60. doi: 10.1080/09575146.2011.593029.

Jordan, D. (2015) *The Dual Identity of the Artist-Teacher: What Does Teaching Do to the Artist-Teacher in a Contemporary Educational Context?* Dublin: Dublin City University.

Juffé, M. (2007) 'Lévinas as (Mis)reader of Spinoza', in Bugni, B. (trans) *Levinas Studies*, 2, pp. 153–173.

Kellog, R. (1959) *What Children Scribble and Why*. California: NP Publishers.

Kennedy, D. (2006) *Changing Conceptions of the Child from the Renaissance to Post-modernity: A Philosophy of Childhood*. Palo Alto: Edwin Mellen.

Kind, S. (2014) 'Material Encounters', *International Journal of Child, Youth and Family Studies*, 5(4.2), pp. 865–877.

Kind, S. (2018) 'Collective Improvisations: The Emergence of the Early Childhood Studio as an Event-Full Place', in Schulte, C. M. and Thompson Marme, C. M. (eds) *Communities of Practice: Art, Play, and Aesthetics in Early Childhood*. New York, NY: Springer.

Kind, S. and Argent, A. (2017) *Pedagogical Documentation in Early Years Practice: Seeing through Multiple Perspectives*. Edited by Fleet, A., Patterson, C. and Robertson, J., 1st edn. Thousand Oaks, CA: SAGE.

Kind, S. and Argent, A. (2019) 'Fabricating: Fabric Fluidities and Studio Encounters', in Hodgins, B. D. (ed.) *Feminist Research for 21st-Century Childhoods: Common Worlds Methods*. London: Bloomsbury Academic, pp. 35–42.

Kindler, A. M. (2010) 'Art and Art in Early Childhood: What Can Young Children Learn from Art Activities?', *International Art in Early Childhood Research Journal*, 2(1), pp. 1–14.

Knight, L. (2009) 'Desire and Rhizome: Affective Literacies in Early Childhood Education', in Masny, D. and Cole, D. R. (eds) *Multiple Literacies Theory: A Deleuzian Perspective*. Rotterdam: Sense Publishers, p. 12.

Knight, L. (2013) 'Not as It Seems: Using Deleuzian Concepts of the Imaginary to Rethink Children's Drawings', *Global Studies of Childhood*, 3(3), pp. 254–264.

Knight, L. (2018) 'Digital Aesthetics and Multidimensional Play in Early Childhood', in Schulte, C. M. and Thompson, C. M. (eds) *Communities of Practice: Art, Play, and Aesthetics in Early Childhood*. Cham: Springer International Publishing (Landscapes: The Arts, Aesthetics, and Education), pp. 133–151.

Knight, L. (2019) 'Playing: Inefficiently Mapping Human and Inhuman Play in Urban Commonplaces', in Hodgins, B. D. (ed.) *Feminist Research for 21st-Century Childhoods : Common Worlds Methods*. London: Bloomsbury Academic, pp. 139–145.

Knight, L. (2021) *Inefficient Mapping: A Protocol for Attuning to Phenomena*. Santa Barbara CA: Punctum Books.

Koro-Ljungberg, M., MacLure, M. and Ulmer, J. (2018) 'D… a…t…a…, Data++, Data, and Some Problematics', in Denzin, N. K. and Lincoln, Y. S. (eds) *The Sage Handbook of Qualitative Research*. 5th edn. Los Angeles: SAGE, p. 23.

Kuby, C. R. and Rowsell, J. (2017) 'Early Literacy and the Posthuman: Pedagogies and Methodologies', *Journal of Early Childhood Literacy*, 17(3), pp. 285–296.

Kucirkova, N. and Sakr, M. (2015) 'Child–Father Creative Text-Making at Home with Crayons, iPad Collage & PC', *Thinking Skills and Creativity*, 17, pp. 59–73.

Kummen, K. (2019) 'Crowing: Co-evolving Relationships', in Hodgins, B. D. (ed.) *Feminist Research for 21st-Century* Childhoods: Common Worlds Methods. London: Bloomsbury Academic.

Lather, P. (2013) 'Methodology-21: What Do We Do in the Afterward?', *International Journal of Qualitative Studies in Education*, 26(6), pp. 634–645.

Lather, P. and Pierre, E. A. S. (2013) 'Post-qualitative research', *International Journal of Qualitative Studies in Education*, 26(6), pp. 629–633.

Latour, B. (1996) 'On Actor-Network Theory: A Few Clarifications Plus More Than a Few Complications', *Soziale Welt*, 47, pp. 369–381.

Law, J. (2004) *After Method: Mess in Social Science Research*. London: Routledge.

Lebensztejn, J.-C. and Nagy, J. (2017) *Pissing Figures 1280–2014*. New York: David Zwirner Books (Ekphrasis).

Lenz Taguchi, H. (2010) *Going Beyond the Theory/Practice Divide in Early Childhood Education: Introducing an Intra-active Pedagogy*. London: Routledge (Contesting Early Childhood).

Lenz Taguchi, H. (2011) 'Investigating Learning, Participation and Becoming in Early Childhood Practices with a Relational Materialist Approach', *Global Studies of Childhood*, 1(1), pp. 36–50. doi: 10.2304/gsch.2011.1.1.36.

Lenz Taguchi, H. (2012) 'A Diffractive and Deleuzian Approach to Analysing Interview Data', *Feminist Theory*, 13(3), pp. 265–281.

Lenz Taguchi, H. (2016) 'Deleuzo-Guattarian Rhizomatics: Mapping the Desiring Forces and Connections between Educational Practices and the Neurosciences', in Taylor, C. A. and Hughes, C. (eds) *Posthuman Research Practices in Education*. Basingstoke: Palgrave Macmillan, pp. 37–57.

Lenz Taguchi, H. and St Pierre, E. A. (2017) 'Using Concept as Method in Educational and Social Science Inquiry', *Qualitative Inquiry*, 23(9), Sage Journals. doi: org/10.1177/1077800417732634.

Lester, S. (2020) *Everyday Playfulness: A New Approach to Children's Play and Adult Responses to It*. London: Jessica Kingsley Publishers.

Lewis, S. L. and Maslin, M. A. (2015) 'Defining the Anthropocene', *Nature*, 519(7542), pp. 171–180.

Lloyd, G. (1994) *Part of Nature: Self-knowledge in Spinoza's Ethics*. Ithaca: Cornell University Press.

Lodge, A. and Lynch, K. (2004) *Diversity at School*. Dublin: Institute of Public Administration for the Equality Authority.

Lord, B. (2010) *Spinoza's Ethics: An Edinburgh Philosophical Guide*. Edinburgh: Edinburgh University Press (Edinburgh Philosophical Guides Series).

Louv, R. (2005) *Last Child in the Woods: Saving Our Children from Nature-Deficit Disorder*. 1st edn. Chapel Hill, NC: Algonquin Books of Chapel Hill.

Loveless, N. (2019) *How to Make Art at the End of the World: A Manifesto for Research-Creation*. Durham: Duke University Press.

Lucero-Montaño, A. (2012) 'Spinoza's Ethics: Freedom and Determinism', *SSRN Electronic Journal* [Preprint]. doi: 10.2139/ssrn.2010571.

Lucretius and Ferguson-Smith. (1969) *Lucretius on the Nature of Things*. London: Sphere Books.

Lynch, K., Lyons, M. and Cantillon, S. (2007) 'Breaking Silence: Educating Citizens for Love, Care and Solidarity', *International Studies in Sociology of Education*, 17(1–2), pp. 1–19.

Lyons, A. (2020) *Oona*. Dublin: Liliput Press.

MacCormack, P. (2012) *Posthuman Ethics: Embodiment and Cultural Theory* (1st edn.). Routledge. Available at: <https://doi.org/10.4324/9781315601670>.

MacCormack, P. (2018) 'Posthuman Ethics', in Braidotti, R. and Hlavjova, M. (eds) *The Posthuman Glossery*. London: Bloomsbury Academic.

MacFarlane, R. (2016) 'Generation Anthropocene: How Humans Have Altered the Planet Forever', *The Guardian*, 1 April. Available at: <http://www.theguardian.com.books/2016/apr/01/generation-anthropocene-altered-planet-for-ever>.

MacLure, M., Holmes, R., Jones, L. and MacRae, C. (2010) 'Silence as Resistance to Analysis: Or, on Not Opening One's Mouth Properly', *Qualitative Inquiry*, 16(6), pp. 492–500.

MacLure, M. (2013a) 'Classification or Wonder: Coding as an Analytic Practice in Qualitative Research', in Coleman, R. and Ringrose, J. (eds) *Deleuze and Research Methodologies*. Edinburgh: Edinburgh University Press.

MacLure, M. (2013b) 'Researching without Representation? Language and Materiality in Post-qualitative Methodology', *International Journal of Qualitative Studies in Education*, 26(6), pp. 658–667.

MacRae, C. (2008) 'Representing Space: Katie's Horse and the Recalcitrant Object', *Contemporary Issues in Early Childhood*, 9(4), pp. 275–286.

MacRae, C. (2011) 'Making Payton's Rocket: Heterotopia and Lines of Flight', *International Journal of Art & Design Education*, 30(1), pp. 102–112.

MacRae, C. (2012) 'Encounters with a Life(Less) Baby Doll: Rethinking Relations of Agency through a Collectively Lived Moment', *Contemporary Issues in Early Childhood*, 13(2), pp. 120–131.

Macrae, C., Hackett, A., Holmes, R. and Jones, L. (2017) 'Vibrancy, Repetition and Movement: Posthuman Theories for Reconceptualising Young Children in Museums', *Children's Geographies*, 16(1), pp. 1–13.

MacRae, C. (2019) 'The Red Blanket: A Dance of Animacy', *Global Studies of Childhood*, 12(4), pp. 1–11.

MacRae, C. (2020) 'Tactful Hands and Vibrant Mattering in the Sand Tray', *Journal of Early Childhood Literacy*, 20(1), pp. 90–110.

MacRae, C. and Jones, L. (2020) 'A Philosophical Reflection on the "Leuven Scale" and Young Children's Expressions of Involvement', *International Journal of Qualitative Studies in Education*, 36(4), 36(4), pp. 1–13.

Malafouris, L. (2013) *How Things Shape the Mind: A Theory of Material Engagement*. Cambridge, MA: MIT Press.

Malaguzzi, L. (1993) 'For an Education Based on Relationships', *Young Children*, 49(1), pp. 9–12.

Malaguzzi, L. (1994) 'A Bill of Three Rights', *Innovations in Early Education: The International Reggio Exchange*, 2(1). Available at: <https://www.reggioalliance.org/downloads/v2.n1.rights.pdf>.

Malaguzzi, L. (1997) 'The Hundred Languages of Children', in Filippini, T. and Vecchi, V. (eds) *The Hundred Languages of Children*. Reggio Emilia, Italy: Reggio Children.

Malaguzzi, L. (2000) *The One Hundred Languages of Children*. Reggio Emilia: Reggio Children.

Malone, K. (2018) 'Reconfiguring the Child in the Anthropocene', in Malone, K. (ed.) *Children in the Anthropocene*. London: Palgrave Macmillan UK, pp. 247–257.

Malone, K. (2019) 'Re-turning Childhoodnature: A Diffractive Account of the Past Tracings of Childhoodnature as a Series of Theoretical Turns', in Latiner Raby,

R. and Valeau, E. J. (eds) *Handbook of Comparative Studies on Community Colleges and Global Counterparts*. Cham: Springer International Publishing (Springer International Handbooks of Education), pp. 1–30.

Manning, E. (2016) *The Minor Gesture*. Durham: Duke University Press (Thought in the Act).

Marmé Thompson, C. (2019) '"So You Will Remember Me as an Artist": Art-Making as a Way of Being in Early Childhood', in Sakr, M. and Osgood, J. (eds) *Postdevelopmental Approaches to Childhood Art*. London: Bloomsbury Academic, pp. 137–152.

Masny, D. (2018) 'Becoming Childhoodnature: Experimenting a Research Assemblage', in Cutter-Mackenzie, A., Malone, K. and Barratt Hacking, E. (eds) *Research Handbook on Childhoodnature*. Cham: Springer International Publishing, pp. 1–18.

Masny, D. and Cole, D. R. (2009) *Multiple Literacies Theory: A Deleuzian Perspective*. Rotterdam: Sense Publishers.

Massumi, B. (2002) *Parables for the Virtual: Movement, Affect, Sensation*. Durham, NC: Duke University Press.

Mayo, E. (1832) *Lessons on Objects as Given to Children between the Ages of Five and Eight, in a Pestalozzian School, at Cheam, Surrey*. 3rd edn. London: R. B. Seeley and W. Burnside.

Mazzei, L. A. (2013) 'A Voice without Organs: Interviewing in Posthumanist Research', *International Journal of Qualitative Studies in Education*, 26(6), pp. 732–740.

McCarthy, S. (2016) *Cost of Child Abuse Inquiry and Redress*. Comptroller and Auditor General, Special Report 96. Dublin, Ireland.

McClure, M. (2011) 'Child as Totem: Redressing the Myth of Inherent Creativity in Early Childhood', *Studies in Art Education*, 52(2), pp. 127–141.

McGinnity, F., Murray, A. and McNally, S. (2013) *Growing Up in Ireland – National Longitudinal Study of Children: Mothers' Return to Work and Childcare Choices for Infants in Ireland*. Dublin: Stationery Office.

McMillan, M. (1927) *The Life of Rachel McMillan*. London: J. M. Dent.

Mitchelmore, S. and Fleet, A. (2017) 'The Worlds of the Very Young: Seeing the Everyday in Small Pieces', in Fleet, A., Patterson, C. and Robertson, J. (eds) *Pedagogical Documentation in Early Years Practice: Seeing through Multiple Perspectives*. 1st edn. Thousand Oaks, CA: SAGE, pp. 61–72.

Montessori, M. (2014) *The Montessori Method*. New Brunswick, USA: Transaction Publishers.

Murris, K. (2016) *The Posthuman Child: Educational Transformation through Philosophy with Picture Books*. London: Routledge, Taylor & Francis Group.

Murris, K. (2017) 'Reading Two Rhizomatic Pedagogies Diffractively Through One Another: A Reggio Inspired Philosophy with Children for the Postdevelopmental Child', *Pedagogy, Culture & Society*, 25(4), pp. 1–20.

Myers, C. Y., Smith, K. A. and Tesar, M. (2017) 'Diffracting Mandates for Reflective Practices in Teacher Education and Development: Multiple Readings from Australia, New Zealand, and the United States', *Journal of Early Childhood Teacher Education*, 38(4), pp. 279–292.

Nancy, J.-L. (2015) *After Fukushima: The Equivalence of Catastrophes*. Translated by C. Mandell. New York: Fordham University Press.

NCCA. (2009) *Aistear: The Early Childhood Curriculum Framework*. Dublin: National Council for Curriculum and Assessment. Available at: <https://www.ncca.ie/media/1112/how-aistear-was-developed-research-papers.pdf>

NCCA. (2012) *Literacy in Early Childhood and Primary Education*. Dublin: National Council for Curriculum and Assessment.

NESF. (2005) *Early Childhood Care and Education*. Dublin: National Council for Curriculum and Assessment.

Nutbrown, C. (1994) *Threads of Thinking: Young Childrens Learning and the Role of Early Education*. London: Paul Chapman Pub.

Nutbrown, C., Clough, P. and Selbie, P. (2008) *Early Childhood Education: History, Philosophy, Experience*. Los Angeles: SAGE.

Odegard, N. (2012) 'When Matter Comes to Matter: Working Pedagogically with Junk Materials', *Education Inquiry*, 3(3), pp. 387–400.

Odegard, N. and Rossholt, N. (2016) 'In-betweens Spaces: Tales from a Remida', in Reinert, A. B. (ed.) *Becoming Earth: A Posthuman Turn in Educational Discourse Collapsing Nature/Culture Divides*. Rotterdam: Sense Publishers, pp. 53–63.

O'Donnell, A. (2015) 'Experimental Philosophy and Experimental Pedagogy: A Single Vision', in Hickey-Moody, A. and Page, Tara (eds) *Arts, Pedagogy and Cultural Resistance New Materialisms*. London: Littlefield International.

O'Donnell, A. (2016) 'For the Scavengers and the Gleaners: An Anti-heroic Vision of Education', *Other Education: The Journal of Educational Alternatives*, 5(2), pp. 17–38.

O'Donnell, A. (2017) 'Spinoza, Experimentation and Education: How Things Teach Us', *Educational Philosophy and Theory*, 50(9), pp. 819–829.

OECD. (2012) PISA 2009 Technical Report, PISA, OECD Publishing. Available at: <http://dx.doi.org/10.1787/9789264167872-en>.

Olsson, L. M. (2009) *Movement and Experimentation in Young Children's Learning: Deleuze and Guattari in Early Childhood Education*. London: Routledge (Contesting Early Childhood).

O'Neill-Butler, L. (2016) *Donna J. Haraway Speaks about Her Latest Book, Artforum.* Available at: <https://www.artforum.com/interviews/donna-j-haraway-speaks-about-her-latest-book-63147>

Osgood, J. (2019) '"You Can't Separate It from Anything": Glitter's Doings as Materialized Figurations of Childhood (and) Art', in *Postdevelopmental Approaches to Childhood Art*, . London: Bloomsbury Academic, pp. 111–136.

Osgood J. (2022) 'New Images of Thought in the Study of Childhood Drawing', in Trafí-Prats, L. and Schulte, C. M. (eds.) *Children: Global Posthumanist Perspectives and Materialist Theories.* Springer Nature: Switzerland, p. 176. Available at: <https://doi.org/10.1007/978-3-031-07143-0>.

O'Sullivan, S. (2006) *Art Encounters Deleuze and Guattari: Thoughts Beyond Representation.* London: Palgrave.

Pacini-Ketchabaw, V., Clark, V. and Hodgins, B. D. (2014) 'Thinking with Paint: Troubling Settler Colonialisms through Early Childhood Art Pedagogies', *International Journal of Child, Youth and Family Studies*, 5(4.2), pp. 751–781.

Pacini-Ketchabaw, V., Kind, S. and Kocher, L. L. M. (2017) *Encounters with Materials in Early Childhood Education.* New York: Routledge.

Pacini-Ketchabaw, V., Taylor, A. and Blaise, M. (2016) 'Decentring the Human in Multispecies Ethnographies', in C. A. and Hughes, C. (eds) *Posthuman Research Practices in Education.* Basingstoke: Palgrave Macmillan, pp. 149–167.

Page, J. (2018) 'Love, Care and Intimacy in Early Childhood Education and Care', *International Journal of Early Years Education*, 26(2), pp. 123–124. doi: 10.1080/09669760.2018.1459509.

Page, T. (2018) 'Teaching and Learning with Matter', *Arts*, 7(4), p. 82.

Papatheodorou, T. and Moyles, J. (2009) *Learning Together in the Early Years Exploring Relational Pedagogy.* London: Routledge.

Parikka, J. (2015) *The Anthrobscene.* Minneapolis: University of Minnesota Press.

Pedersen, H. and Pini, B. (2017) 'Educational Epistemologies and Methods in a More-than-Human World', *Educational Philosophy and Theory*, 49(11), pp. 1051–1054.

Pestalozzi, J. H. (2008) *How Gertrude Teaches Her Children.* Edited by Holland, L. E. and Turner, F. C. Translated by Cooke, E. Whitefish, MT: Kessinger Publishing.

Petersen, E. B. (2018) '"Data found us": A Critique of Some New Materialist Tropes in Educational Research', *Research in Education*, 101(1), pp. 5–16.

Piaget, J. (1952) *The Origin of Intelligence in Children.* Translated by Cook, M. New York: International Universities Press.

Piaget, J. (1971) *Mental Imagery in the Child: A Study of the Development of Imaginal Representation.* London: Routledge & Kegan Paul.

Pine, L. (1996) 'The Dissemination of Nazi Ideology and Family Values through School Textbooks', *History of Education*, 25(1), pp. 91–109.

Pope Edwards, C. (2002) 'Three Approaches from Europe: Waldorf, Montessori, and Reggio Emilia.', *Early Childhood Research & Practice*, 4(1), pp. 1–24.

Pope Edwards, C. (2003) '"Fine Designs" from Italy: Montessori Education and the Reggio Approach', *Faculty Publications, Department of Child, Youth, and Family Studies*, 20, p. 7.

Provenzo, E. F. (2009) 'Friedrich Froebel's Gifts: Connecting the Spiritual and Aesthetic to the Real World of Play and Learning', *American Journal of Play*, Summer, 2(1), pp. 85–99.

Puig de la Bellacasa, M. (2017) *Matters of Care: Speculative Ethics in More than Human Worlds*. Minneapolis: University of Minnesota Press (Posthumanities, 41).

Rautio, P. (2013) 'Children Who Carry Stones in Their Pockets: On Autotelic Material Practices in Everyday Life', *Children's Geographies*, 11(4), pp. 394–408.

Rautio, P. (2019) 'Theory That Cats Have about Swift Louseflies: A Diffractive Response', in Kuby, C. R., Spector, K. and Thiel, J. (eds) *Posthumanism and Literacy Education: Knowing/Becoming/Doing Literacies*. New York: Routledge (Expanding Literacies in Education Series).

Rautio, P. and Jokinen, P. (2015) 'Children's Relations to the More-Than-Human World Beyond Developmental Views', in Evans, B., Horton, J. and Skelton, T. (eds) *Play, Recreation, Health and Well Being*. Singapore: Springer, pp. 1–15.

Reggio Children. (2005) 'Remida: The Creative Recycling Centre in Reggio Emilia: An Interview with Elena Giacopini, Graziella Brighenti, Arturo Bertoldi and Alba Ferrari', *Innovations in Early Education*, 12(3), pp. 1–13.

Rekret, P. (2016) 'A Critique of New Materialism: Ethics and Ontology', *Subjectivity*, 9(3), pp. 225–245.

Richards, J. M. (1976) *Provision for the Arts: Report of an Enquiry Carried Out During 1974–75 Throughout the Twenty-Six Counties of the Republic of Ireland*. The Arts Council (Ireland) and the Gulbenkian Foundation.

de Rijke, V. (2019) '"It Might Get Messy, or Not Be Right": Scribble as Postdevelopmental Art', in Sakr, M. and Osgood, J. (eds) *Postdevelopmental Approaches to Childhood Art*. London: Bloomsbury.

Rinaldi, C. (2006) *In Dialogue with Reggio Emilia: Listening, Researching and Learning*. London: Routledge.

Rogers, Y., French, G. and EarlyArts UK (2013) *Early Childhood Arts Three Perspectives*. Dublin: The Arts Council.

Rooney, T. (2019) 'Sticking: Children and the Lively Matter of Sticks', in Hodgins, B. D. (ed.) *Feminist Research for 21st Century Childhoods*. London: Bloomsbury Academic, pp. 43–51.

Rotas, A. (2015) 'Ecologies of Practice: Teaching and Learning against the Obvious', in Snaza, N. and Weaver, J. A. (eds) *Posthumanism and Educational Research*. New York: Routledge, pp. 91–104.

Rotas, N. (2019) 'Mashing: A Practice that Makes Vision Felt', in Hodgins, B. D. (ed.) *Feminist Research for 21st-Century Childhoods: Common Worlds Methods*. London: Bloomsbury Academic.

Rousell, D. et al. (2018) 'Propositions for an Environmental Arts Pedagogy: A/r/tographic Experimentations with Movement and Materiality', in Latiner Raby, R. and Valeau, E. J. (eds) *Handbook of Comparative Studies on Community Colleges and Global Counterparts*. Cham: Springer International.

Sakr, M. and Osgood, J. (eds) (2019) *Postdevelopmental Approaches to Childhood Art*. London: Bloomsbury.

Sandvik, N. (2010) 'The Art of/in Educational Research: Assemblages at Work', *Reconceptualizing Educational Research Methodology*, 1(1), pp. 29–40.

Schulte, C. M. (2019) 'The Untimely Death of a Bird: A Posthuman Tale', in Kuby, C. R., Spector, K. and Thiel, J. (eds) *Posthumanism and Literacy Education*. New York: Routledge.

Schwarz, T. and Luckenbill, J. (2012) 'Let's Get Messy! Exploring Sensory and Art Activities with Infants and Toddlers', *Young Children*, 67(4), pp. 26–34.

Sehgal, M. (2014) 'Diffractive Propositions: Reading Alfred North Whitehead with Donna Haraway and Karen Barad', *Parallax*, 20(3), pp. 188–201.

Seigworth, G. J. and Gregg, M. (2010) 'An Inventory of Shimmers', in Gregg, M. & Seigworth, M. (eds) *The Affect Theory Reader*. Durham: Duke University Press.

Sellers, M. (2015) '… Working with (a) Rhizoanalysis … and Working (with) a Rhizoanalysis', *Complicity: An International Journal of Complexity and Education*, 12(1), pp. 6–31.

Sellers, M. A. (2009) 'Re(con)ceiving Children in Curriculum: Mapping (a) Milieu(s) of Becoming'. Available at: <https://espace.library.uq.edu.au/view/UQ:180106>

Sengupta, P. (2003) 'An Object Lesson in Colonial Pedagogy', *Comparative Studies in Society and History*, 45(1), pp. 96–121.

Sheldrake, M. (2020) *Entangled Life: How Fungi Make Our Worlds, Change Our Minds, and Shape Our Futures*. London: The Bodley Head.

Shields, R. (2015) 'Ludic Ontology Play's Relationship to Language, Cultural Forms, and Transformative Politics', *American Journal of Play*, 7(3), pp. 298–321.

Shotter, J. (2015) 'On Being Dialogical: An Ethics of "Attunement"', *Context*, 137, p. 4.

Sinner, A. (2017) 'Cultivating Researchful Dispositions: A Review of A/r/tographic Scholarship', *Journal of Visual Art Practice*, 16(1), pp. 1–22.

Snaza, N. (2013) 'Bewildering Education', *Journal of Curriculum and Pedagogy*, 10(1), pp. 38–54.

Snaza, N., Appelbaum, P., Bayne, S., Morris, M., Rotas, N., Sandlin, J., Wallin, J., Carlson, D. and Weaver, J. (2014) 'Toward a Posthumanist Education', *Journal of Curriculum Theorizing*, 30(2), p. 17.

Snaza, N. (2019) *Animate Literacies: Literature, Affect, and the Politics of Humanism*. Durham: Duke University Press (Thought in the Act).

Snaza, N. and Weaver, J. A. (2016) *Posthumanism and Educational Research*. New York: Routledge.

Soëtard, M. (1994) 'Johann Heinrich Pestalozzi', *Prospects: The Quarterly Review of Comparative Education (UNESCO: International Bureau of Education)*, XXIV(1/2), pp. 297–310.

Somerville, M. (2016) 'The Post-human I: Encountering "data" in New Materialism', *International Journal of Qualitative Studies in Education*, 29(9), pp. 1161–1172.

Somerville, M. (2018) 'Posthuman Theory and Practice in Early Years Learning', in Cutter-Mackenzie, A., Malone, K. and Barratt Hacking, E. (eds) *Research Handbook on Childhoodnature*. Cham: Springer (Springer International Handbooks of Education), pp. 1–25.

Sorensen, E. (2009) *The Materiality of Learning: Technology and Knowledge in Educational Practice*. New York: Cambridge University Press.

Spector, K., Thiel, J. and Kuby, C. R. (2019) 'Affect', in Kuby, C. R. (ed.) *Posthumanism and Literacy Education: Knowing/Becoming/Doing Literacies*. New York: Routledge (Expanding Literacies in Education Series).

Spinoza, B. (1996) *The Ethics*. Translated by Curley, E. London: Penguin.

Springay, S. (2016) '"Approximate-Rigorous Abstractions" Propositions of Activation for Posthumanist Research in Education', in Snaza, N. and Weaver, J. A. (eds) *Posthumanism and Educational Research*. New York, NY: Routledge, pp. 76–88.

Springay, S., Irwin, R. L. and Kind, S. (2008) 'A/R/Tographers and Living Inquiry', in Knowles, J. G. & Cole, A. L. (eds) *Handbook of the Arts in Qualitative Research: Perspectives, Methodologies, Examples, and Issues*. Los Angeles: SAGE, p. chap. 7.

St Pierre, E. A. (2011) 'Post Qualitative Research: The Critique and the Coming After', in Denzin, N. K. and Lincoln, Y. S. (eds) *Sage Handbook of Qualitative Inquiry*. 4th edn.Los Angeles: SAGE, pp. 611–635.

St Pierre, E. A. (2013) 'The Posts Continue: Becoming', *International Journal of Qualitative Studies in Education*, 26(6), pp. 646–657.

St Pierre, E. A. (2014) 'A Brief and Personal History of Post Qualitative Research: Toward "post inquiry"', *Journal of Curriculum Theorizing*, 30(2), pp. 2–19.

St Pierre, E. A. (2017) 'Deleuze and Guattari's Language for New Empirical Inquiry', *Educational Philosophy and Theory*, 49(11), pp. 1080–1089.

Steinhauer. (2017) *How Mierle Laderman Ukeles Turned Maintenance Work into Art, Hyperallergic*. Available at: <https://hyperallergic.com/355255/how-mierle-laderman-ukeles-turned-maintenance-work-into-art/>

Stengers, I. (2005) 'An Ecology of Practices', *Cultural Studies Review*, 11(1), pp. 183–196.

Stewart, K. (2007) *Ordinary Affects*. Durham, NC: Duke University Press.

Strom, K. J. (2020) *Learning from a 'Lost Year': An Autotheoretical Journey through Anxiety and Panic, Capacious Journal for Emerging Affect Inquiry*. Edited by Seigworth, G. J. and Arthur, M., 1(2), pp. 127–148. Available at: <http://capaciousjournal.com/article/learningfromalostyear/>

Sutton-Smith, B. (2006) 'Play and Ambiguity', in Salen, K. and Zimmerman, E. (eds) *The Game Design Reader a Rules of Play Anthology*. Cambridge, MA: The MIT Press, pp. 296–313.

Swim, T. J. and Freeman, R. (2004) 'Viewpoint. Time to Reflect: Using Food in Early Childhood Classrooms', *Young Children*, 59(6), pp. 18–22.

Syvitski, J. (2012) *Anthropocene: An Epoch of Our Making – IGBP, Global Change IGBP*. Available at: <http://www.igbp.net/news/features/features/anthropoceneanepochofourmaking.5.1081640c135c7c04eb480001082.html>.

Tarr, P. (1990) 'More than Movement: Scribbling Reassessed', *Visual Arts Research*, 16(1), pp. 83–89.

Tarr, P. (2001) 'Aesthetic Codes in Early Childhood Classrooms: What Art Educators Can Learn from Reggio Emilia', *Art Education*, 54(3), p. 33. doi: 10.2307/3193922.

Taylor, A. (2013) *Reconfiguring the Natures of Childhood*. London: Routledge.

Taylor, A. and Pacini-Ketchabaw, V. (2019) *The Common Worlds of Children and Animals: Relational Ethics for Entangled Lives*. London: Routledge.

Taylor, C. A. (2016) 'Edu-crafting a Cacophonous Ecology: Posthuman Research Practices for Education', in Taylor, C. A. and Hughes, C. (eds) *Posthuman Research Practices in Education*. Basingstoke: Palgrave Macmillan, pp. 5–24.

Taylor, C. A. (2018) 'What Can Bodies Do? En/gendering Body-Space Choreographies of Stillness, Movement and Flow in Post-16 Pedagogic Encounters', *International Journal of Educational Research*, 88, pp. 156–165.

Taylor, C. A. and Hughes, C. (eds) (2016) *Posthuman Research Practices in Education*. Basingstoke: Palgrave Macmillan.

Thiel, J., Kuby, C. R. and Spector, K. (2019) 'Agency', in Kuby, C. R., Spector, K. and Thiel, J. (eds) *Affect in Literacy Learning and Teaching*. New York: Routledge.

Thompson, C. M. (2015) 'Prosthetic Imaginings and Pedagogies of Early Childhood Art', *Qualitative Inquiry*, 21(6), pp. 554–561.

Thorp, A. (2020) 'On What Grounds', in Hackett, A., Holmes, R. and MacRae, C. (eds) *Working with Young Children in Museums: Weaving Theory and Practice*. London: Routledge/Taylor & Francis Group, pp. 187–194.

Todd, S. (2001) '"Bringing More Than I Contain": Ethics, Curriculum and the Pedagogical Demand for Altered Egos', *Journal of Curriculum Studies*, 33(4), pp. 431–450.

Todd, S. (2016) 'New Ethical Challenges within Environmental and Sustainability Education: A Response', *Environmental Education Research*, 22(6), pp. 842–844.

Todd, S., Jones, R. and O'Donnell, A. (2016) 'Shifting Education's Philosophical Imaginaries: Relations, Affects, Bodies, Materialities', *Gender and Education*, 28(2), pp. 187–194.

Todd, Z. (2015) 'Indigenizing the Anthropocene', in *Art in the Anthropocene: Encounters among Aesthetics, Politics, Environments and Epistemologies*. London: Open Humanities Press, pp. 241–255.

Tooze, A. (2020) 'We Are Living through the First Economic Crisis of the Anthropocene', *The Guardian*. Available at: <https://amp.theguardian.com/books/2020/may/07/we-are-living-through-the-first-economic-crisis-of-the-anthropocene>

Trafí-Prats, L. (2017) 'Learning with Children, Trees, and Art: For a Compositionist Visual Art-Based Research', *Studies in Art Education*, 58(4), pp. 325–334.

Trafí-Prats, L. (2019) 'Thinking Childhood Art with Care in an Ecology of Practices', in Osgood, J. and Sakr, M. (eds) *Postdevelopmental Approaches to Childhood Art*. London: Bloomsbury Academic, pp. 191–209.

Trafí-Prats, L. and Caton, L. (2020) 'Towards an Ethico-Aesthetic of Parenting: Sensing Ritornellos of Play with GoPro Data', *Genealogy*, 4(2), p. 34.

Tsing, A. L. (2015) *The Mushroom at the End of the World: On the Possibility of Life in Capitalist Ruins*. Princeton, NJ: Princeton University Press.

Ulmer, J. B. (2017) 'Posthumanism as Research Methodology: Inquiry in the Anthropocene', *International Journal of Qualitative Studies in Education*, 30(9), pp. 832–848.

UNESCO. (2006) *World Conference on Arts Education: Building Creative Capacities for the 21st Century*. Lisbon: Division of Arts and Cultural Enterprise of Sector for Culture.

Urban, M. (2016) 'At Sea: What Direction for Critical Early Childhood Research?', *Journal of Pedagogy*, 7(1), pp. 107–121.

Urban, M. (2018) '(D)Evaluation of Early Childhood Education and Care? A Critique of the OECD's International Early Learning Study', in Matthes, M. et al. (eds) *Improving the Quality of Childhood in Europe*. Brussels: Alliance for Children European Network Foundation, pp. 91–99.

Van Dooren, T. (2016) *Flight Ways: Life and Loss at the Edge of Extinction*. Paperback edition. New York: Columbia University Press (Critical Perspectives on Animals Theory, Culture, Science, and Law).

Vecchi, V., Chieli, F. and Reggio Children Srl (eds) (2008) *Children, Art, Artists: The Expressive Languages of Children, the Artistic Language of Alberto Burri ; [catalogue]*. 3. print. Reggio Emilia: Reggio Children.

Vehaba, A. (2018) 'Traversing Sites of Affective Immersion', *Capacious Journal for Emerging Affect Inquiry*. Edited by Seigworth, G. J. and Arthur, M., 1(2), pp. 127–148.

Vice News. (2017) *This Trans Artist Collected 200 Gallons of Urine to Protest Trump* [You tube short]. Vice News. Available at: <https://www.youtube.com/watch?v=p-TT7GoJ2iw&t=11s>.

Vygotsky, L. S. (1978a) 'Interaction between learning and development.' From: *Mind and Society* (pp. 79–91) Cambridge, M.A. Harvard University Press.

Vygotsky, L. S. (1978b) *Mind in Society: The Development of Higher Psychological Processes*. Translated by Cole, M. Cambridge: Harvard University Press.

Vygotsky, L. S. (1990) 'Imagination and Creativity in Childhood', *Journal of Russian and East European Psychology*, 28(1), pp. 84–96. doi: 10.2753/RPO1061-0405280184.

Weaver, J. A. and Snaza, N. (2017) 'Against Methodocentrism in Educational Research', *Educational Philosophy and Theory*, 49(11), pp. 1055–1065. doi: 10.1080/00131857.2016.1140015.

Wilson, B. (2003) 'Three Sites for Visual Cultural Pedagogy: Honoring Students Interests and Imagery', in *The International Journal of Arts Education*, 3(1).

Wilson, B. (2007) 'Art, Visual Culture, and Child/Adult Collaborative Images: Recognizing the Other-than.', *Visual Arts Research*, 33(65), pp. 6–20.

Wilson, F. R. (1999) *The Hand: How Its Use Shapes the Brain, Language, and Human Culture*. New York: Vintage Books.

Winner, E., Goldstein, T. R. and Vincent-Lancrin, S. (2013) *Art for Art's Sake?: The Impact of Arts Education*. Paris: OECD (Educational Research and Innovation).

Wolfe, C. (2010) *What Is Posthumanism?* London: University of Minnesota Press (Posthumanities; 8). Available at: <http://capitadiscovery.co.uk/ncad/items/63808>

Yunkaporta, T. (2019) *Sand Talk: How Indigenous Thinking Can Save the World*. Melbourne, VIC: Text Publishing.

Zuckerman, O. (2006) *Historical Overview and Classification of Traditional and Digital Learning Objects*. MIT Media Lab.

Index

New Disciplinary Perspectives on Education

Series Editors

Stephen Cowden is a Social Work educator and researcher with an interest in the relationships between pegagogy, social justice and equality.

Jones Irwin, Associate Professor in Philosophy and Education, Dublin City University

Published Volumes

Vol 1 Stephen Cowden and David Ridley (eds): The Practice of Equality: Jacques Rancière and Critical Pedagogy. 2019. 206 pages.
ISBN 978-1-78874-029-6

Vol 2 David Ridley: The Method of Democracy: John Dewey's Theory of Collective Intelligence. 2021. 230 pages.
ISBN 978-1-78997-337-2

Vol 3 Marina Avelar: Disrupting Education Policy: How New Philanthropy Works to Change Education. 2020. 222 pages.
ISBN 978-1-78707-688-4

Vol 4 Jones Irwin and Letterio Todaro (eds): Paulo Freire's Philosophy of Education in Contemporary Context: From Italy to the World. 2022. 216 pages.
ISBN 978-1-80079-689-8

Vol 5 Gordon Asher, Stephen Cowden, Shirin Housee and Alpesh Maisuria (eds): Critical Pedagogy and Emancipation: A Festschrift in Memory of Joyce Canaan. 2022. 400 pages.
ISBN 978-1-80079-692-8

Vol 6 Susan Bailey: The Levinasian Teacher. 2023. 188 pages.
ISBN 978-1-80079-781-9

Vol 7 Lucy Hill: Everyday Artfulness: A posthuman perspective on young children's play with materials. 2024. 262 pages.
ISBN 978-1-80079-784-0

www.ingramcontent.com/pod-product-compliance
Ingram Content Group UK Ltd.
Pitfield, Milton Keynes, MK11 3LW, UK
UKHW020712071026
15590UKWH00010B/327

9 781800 797840